Street Smart Franchising

Second Edition

Joe Mathews
Don Debolt
Deb Percival

Entrepreneur®
Press

Publisher: Jere Calmes
Cover Design: Andrew Welyczko, CWL Publishing Enterprises, Inc.
Editorial and Production Services: CWL Publishing Enterprises, Inc.,
Madison, Wisconsin, www.cwlpub.com

This publication is designed to provide accurate and authoritative information in regard to the subject matter covered. It is sold with the understanding that the publisher is not engaged in rendering legal, accounting,
or other professional services. If legal advice or other expert assistance is
required, the services of a competent professional person should be
sought.

> —From a Declaration of Principles jointly adopted by a
> Committee of the American Bar Association and
> a Committee of Publishers and Associations

ISBN 13: 978-1-59918-411-1
      10: 1-59918-411-7

Every effort has been made to ensure that the information in this book
is accurate and current at the time of publication. However, laws, regulations, policies, contact information, and so on may be changed without notice. This book is not a substitute for individual advice rendered
by a professional who is able to work with you one-on-one.

Street Smart Franchising

Contents

Introduction   ix

**Part One. What You Need to Know Before
You Start Looking**   **1**

1. What Is Franchising   **3**
Franchising as a Distribution Model   3
A Better Definition: Franchising as a Relationship   4
Franchising as a Strategy to Achieve an Objective   5
Franchising as a Calling   5
The Best Definition: Franchising as One Body   5
The Bottom Line   7
How Many Franchisees Define Winning   7
Why Do Companies Franchise Their Businesses?   8
Spotting a High-Road Franchisor   12
Win–Lose Franchising   15
Developing Peak-Performing Franchisees   19
Building a Strong Franchisee Community   22

2. Why Should I Invest in a Franchise?   **25**
The Path of the 99%   26
The Path of the 1%   27

Contents

The Voice of the Inner Critic 29

The "Right" Business 30

The "Right Time" to Start a Business 30

The Bottom Line 33

The Differences Between the 1% and 99% 33

How to Join the 1% 34

Creating Your Desired Future 35

3. Understanding Your Behavior Style 39

Behavior Styles 39

How Does DISC Work? 44

You Are an Action Hero If ... 45

You Are a Comedian If . . . 50

You Are a Faithful Sidekick If . . . 54

You Are a Private Eye If . . . 58

What Character Do You Play? 62

How Can I Predict Others' Styles? 64

4. What Does Winning Look Like? 62

Goal Setting and Benchmarks 63

Goals Schmoals! Why Should I Care About Goals 71

Making Your Desired Future S.M.A.R.T 73

How Do You Eat an Elephant? 75

The Seven Truths About Real Time 77

5. What Does It to Take to Win as a Franchisee? 93

The KASH Model of Success 98

The Costs of Poor Performance 102

The KASH Deficit Analysis 104

What Is Your Starting KASH Balance? 108

**6. The Learning Curve of a Franchisee:
From the Launch to the Zone 111**

Three Modes of Franchisor KASH Distribution 114

The Launch 121

Strategies for a Successful Launch 125

The Grind 126

Strategies to Successfully Navigate The Grind 138

How Franchisors Can Help You 140

Winning 141

Contents

Strategies for Successfully Navigating from
    Winning to Peak Performance   146
How Franchisors Can Help You   147
The Zone   147
How the Franchisor Can Help You   150
The Goodbye   151
How the Franchisor Can Help You   156

**7. The Evolution of the Franchisee–
Franchisor Relationship**   **157**
The Glee Stage   159
The Fee Stage   161
The Me Stage   163
The Free Stage   165
The See Stage   167
The We stage   169

Part Two. Investigating Franchises   **175**

8. Locating Franchise Opportunities   **177**
Franchise Opportunity Websites   178
Franchise Brokers   179
Magazines   180
Franchise Expos   180
Google and Other Search Engines   181

**9. Following a Six-Step Franchise
Investigation Process**   ~~185~~ 181
Overview of the Six-Step Franchise
    Investigation Process   188
Step 1: The Initial Interview   191
Step 2: Qualification   198
Step 3: Reviewing the FDD and
    Franchise Agreements   204
Step 4: Franchisee Validation, Data Gathering,
    and Analysis   223
Step 5: Attending a Discovery Day or
    Visiting the Home Office   235
The Four Franchisor Corporate Cultures   238
The Bureaucracy   239

Contents

Benevolent Dictatorship   241
Command and Control   244
Achievement   248
Decision–Making Checklist   252
Step 6: Making an Investment Decision   255
Final Decision Worksheet   258
Conclusion   258

Index   **261**

Introduction

Your Purpose—Our Purpose

If you are reading this you are probably looking for some way to create a happy, normal, and productive life for yourself and your family in the face of economic turmoil and uncertainty. Perhaps since the great economic collapse of 2008 you are in catch-up mode, trying to claw your way back to where you once were. And if you're a normal functioning human being, you may be scared, thinking, "I have far fewer resources than I once did. I can't afford to make a mistake." Some people standing where you are standing become frustrated and discouraged, missing their past. Others become pumped up, excited about the prospect of taking action and making positive changes. They think, "I needed a kick in the pants and I got one!" Others are simply paralyzed with fear while mourning the past and thinking, "I never thought I would be in this position at my age and I don't know my next move." Regardless of where you are, what you are experiencing, or how you got here, *you are exactly where you need to be.* This book was written to

Introduction

meet you where you are and propel you forward, regardless of what "forward" looks like for you and your family.

The purpose *of Street Smart Franchising* is to prep you about what it takes to succeed in franchising, walk you to the starting line of owning a franchise, show you the finish line of peak productivity and personal success (however you measure success), and give you a proven strategy on how to win the race.

In tough economic times, franchising has created a safe harbor for hundreds of thousands of corporate refugees. According to Volume 2 of *The Economic Impact of Franchised Businesses*, a recent study commissioned by The International Franchise Association and conducted by PriceWaterhouseCoopers, there were over 900,000 franchisor and franchisee-owned outlets representing more than 80 industries in the United States alone. According to the same study, U.S. franchises generated nearly 11 percent of the entire U.S. private-sector economy.

Simply put, franchising works and people just like you are winning, even in tough times.

But three words of caution.

1. Self-employment simply is not for everyone. Starting a business is a lonely and emotionally taxing undertaking, and isn't for the weak at heart.
2. Not every franchise represents a good opportunity. Franchising is like any other business, encompassing everything from genius to conventionality to incompetence.
3. Not every franchise is right for every person. Just like some people aren't wired to be accountants or salespeople, not everyone is wired for every franchise concept.

But by reading this book and studying its contents, you will walk away with three positive outcomes or more:

1. You will know ifself-employment is right for you.
2. You will learn the telltale signs of what genius, conventionality, and incompetence look like in franchising so you know the best place to put your money if you decide to move forward.

3. You will follow a proven process to help you look beyond possible fears and self-limitation to determine which companies and opportunities deliver the life and rewards you want for yourself and your family.

For the first-time businessperson, starting any business can be an emotional rollercoaster. Right now, you are in the first rollercoaster car, slowly clicking your way up to the top of the first steep incline. You can see the top, but you can't see past it. The anticipation of what happens next makes the ride both frightening and exciting. At the end of the wild ride, as you contemplate the wind in your hair and the speed and twists of the track, chances are you will be happy you bought the ticket.

It's estimated that more than 1 million people per year (mostly employees) investigate starting a franchise. Conversely, relatively few existing franchise owners leave self-employment to look for jobs. Be careful, once you take on the mantle of "entrepreneur," you may never want to take it off again. While the personal transformation from employee to entrepreneur may be uncomfortable at first, it's also liberating. Few seek to reverse the process. Pick your metaphor: "Once a pickle, never a cucumber again," or "Once the genie is out of the bottle, you can't get him back in."

If you're a normal-functioning human, you'll be both thrilled by the possibilities—and petrified of (or, perhaps, intrigued by) the unknown. "I don't understand franchising. It's intimidating. How will I pick the right one? What will happen to me and my family if I fail?"

That's where we come in. We've bought franchises, sold franchises, trained franchisees (people like you who have invested in a franchise), coached franchisors (companies who license their business systems to franchisees), supplied franchisors and franchisees, and held leadership roles in franchising's premier organizations. We've experienced three recessions and understand the impact on franchising.

We have seen every side of franchising in every economic condition.

Introduction

We have reached out to highly talented franchise executives and asked what information they would want you to have. What do you need to know to win?

No other franchising book that we know of covers the depth of material we will give you here. You are holding the insider's guide to franchising.

We wrote this book to guide you through the process of investigating a franchise and being a useful handbook for years to come. We will give you the tools to create a customized launch pad *and* a personal plan for success. If you already have a plan for success, this book will help you develop a better, more informed plan.

You've already heard that franchising is not for everyone. As a matter of fact, franchisors report that out of 100 people who request information about starting a business, *only 1 percent* actually join the franchise.

You may ask yourself, "If franchising is so successful [and it is] and the vast majority of franchisees succeed [and they do], why do only 1 percent of the people invest in a franchise?"

That's a very good question. However, consider that logic has little to do with it. Most people don't make logical decisions, they make emotional decisions ... and the emotional decision as to whether to start a franchise is almost always "no." Furthermore, most of the 99 percent who investigate starting a franchise start with "no" and then find reasons to be right. Regardless of the franchise, you can always find a reason to say "no."

For instance, how would you like to own a business that has high employee turnover, high overhead, high lease costs, high equipment costs, low margins, and high advertising costs? The average customer only spends a few dollars, so you're forced to do hundreds of transactions a day just to keep the lights on. You have to move customers through your business with such feverish energy, you can't provide much in the way of customer service. As a matter of fact, extended customer interactions make the business model break down. You have got to keep your cus-

Introduction

tomers moving in and out, in and out. Speed is the key. Furthermore, your business is completely dependent on 80 or more minimum wage workers. Because employee turnover is so high, you're always on the lookout for minimum wage workers. Sometimes you'll keep more people on the payroll than you really need because you know some people are going to quit. Other times, you're left understaffed and have to hire the first breathing human being who walks through the door. Would you ever want own a business like that?

If you would be a "no" to owning this business, you just rejected McDonald's.

Now, let's rephrase the question. Assuming you had the necessary capital, met their stringent qualifications, and the opportunity existed for you, how would you like to own a McDonald's? Did your answer change?

Every business has its own share of problems. When you invest in a franchise, you're investing in proven solutions to these daily challenges of business. For instance, McDonald's has processes and systems that make high employee turnover manageable.

With a healthy dose of self-awareness, the proper preparation, the ability to pick not only a good franchise but the right franchise for you, and knowledge of how to be an effective franchise owner, your chances of success increase exponentially. And that's an increase over the already-tremendous success ratio that franchising enjoys.

Whether your dream is to make more money, have multiple streams of income, have more control, spend time with your family, travel, retire early, or leave a legacy for your family, franchising can help you get there.

Before you flip to the last page, the contents in this book will:

▶ Help you decide if franchising is for you;
▶ Tell you what you will see, feel, and experience before you invest;
▶ Help you manage your emotions and perceptions throughout your investigation process;

Introduction

- ► Help you determine what type of franchise—with your specific skills, talents, and shortcomings—you can have the greatest success in;
- ► Show you how to accelerate your learning curve to achieve peak performance; and
- ► Give you real-world tactics and strategies to develop your own comprehensive plan for success.

Perhaps most important you will have a road map to help you act from a place of logic rather than fear.

Street Smart Franchising is divided into two parts. Part 1, consisting of the first seven chapters, is designed to give you an insider's look at what it takes to win in franchising. While most books on franchising discuss franchising from an independent, academic perspective, we show you how franchising *really works from down in the trenches.* Among other things:

- ► We show you exactly what competent and incompetent franchisors look like, and detail for you the telltale signs and indicators.
- ► We tell you exactly what franchising is and isn't, addressing common misperceptions.
- ► You identify the style by which you naturally produce results, learning what will and won't work running your own business.
- ► You will discover the obstacles and barriers you may put in your own way, limiting your success and stealing your dreams.
- ► You will understand exactly what you can and can't count on a franchisor for, and what a franchisor will count on you for.

When you complete Part 1, you will be clear as to what to look for in a franchise and what to avoid, what works and what doesn't.

In Part 2, we take you through an intelligent, six-step investigation process to help you identify whether a particular franchise you're investigating fits who you are, delivers what you're

Introduction

looking to achieve with a high degree of probability, is run by a competent franchisor, and is buit to last. When you turn the last page you'll be ready to make a yes-or-no decision. This isn't a book that will leave you thinking, "Maybe someday my ship will come in."

Do you want this book to do these things for you? If so, you need to go through this book from beginning to end, start to finish, chapter by chapter. Don't skip around or the work will lose its impact. In franchising it's critical to be able to follow a proven process from start to finish, a process that was designed by someone else for your benefit. If you find yourself jumping around this book after we already informed you the value of this work is diminished, use this as your first indicator as to whether franchising is right for you.

After reading *Street Smart Franchising,* your plans may take you in a direction toward or away from franchising and entrepreneurship, but you will have done so from a place of knowledge and real-world experience, rather than driven by fear, false hopes, bad data, or misperceptions. This book is designed to give you freedom and acceptance with either the next career path you choose or the career path you're already on.

Whatever you decide, it's your decision. It's our commitment to you that your decision brings you and your loved ones freedom and peace in these turbulent and uncertain times.

1

What Is a Franchise?

Franchise/fran chiz/

According to Merriam-Webster's dictionary, a franchise is "the right or license granted to an individual or group to market a company's goods or services in a particular territory." The company offering the license is called "the franchisor," the person investing in the license is called "the franchisee," and the license is called "the franchise." The dictionary defines franchising in terms of a legal business relationship. This is an important aspect of franchising, but it doesn't tell the whole story.

Franchising as a Distribution Model

A popular book on franchising defines a franchise as "a system for expanding and distributing goods and services—and an opportunity to operate a business under a recognized brand name." Here franchising is described as both a distribution model for getting products and services to market and as a business opportunity. Franchisors rely on franchisees, who are independent businesspeople, to get the franchisor's products and services to market.

These are important aspects of franchising, but they don't capture the essence of what franchising really is or can be.

A Better Definition: Franchising as a Relationship

The relationship between franchisees (the independent businesspeople who license the franchisor's name and operating systems) and skilled franchisors (the parent company) transcends the boundaries of any legal and business relationship that exists. Theirs are highly personal relationships. The franchisees and the franchisor, in their successful dealings with each other, form a tight-knit community. Franchising melts down into a business relationship only when these personal relationships either break down or were never properly cemented in the first place. Franchising further degenerates into a legal relationship when business relationships are harmed. If franchisees and franchisors only define their relationship in terms of legal and business relationships, they aren't thinking large enough. Trust, respect, and open communication define good relationships.

The franchise relationship is grounded in a sacred trust and mutual respect between franchisees and franchisors. Each has a mission-critical job to do something that greatly impacts the other. Like combat soldiers in a platoon, franchisees and franchisors completely depend on each other to execute their jobs well to ensure mutual survival.

The franchisees' job is to serve their customers to the best of their ability consistent with the original intent of the franchisor. The franchisor's job is to maintain the integrity of the brand and create processes, systems, structures, products, marketing, and other resources that produce results far superior to any that one or two franchisees could produce for themselves.

Franchising as a Strategy to Achieve an Objective

Zig Ziglar once said, "People don't buy drill bits; they buy holes." Consider the people who invest in franchises, they really invest in some plan to achieve a desired future consisting of both the financial and quality-of-life rewards associated with owning a business.

Franchising as a Calling

To franchisees, the franchisor is their chosen vehicle to get them from where they are now to where they want to be in the future. They experience being called forward to risk their dreams and resources to the care and talents of the franchisor to assist the franchisees in creating their desired life.

To the franchisor, the franchisee is the chosen vehicle to take the franchisor from where they are now to where they want to be in the future. The franchisor risks their proprietary systems, products, and business secrets to the care of the franchisees.

Each is called forward into the service of the other.

As the founder and CEO of a youth sports franchisor once said, "This franchise has ceased being a business to me. I am called to be a force in youth sports ... it's bigger than me. I am blessed by surrounding myself with franchisees who experience the same calling.

The Best Definition: Franchising as One Body

Oddly enough, perhaps the best definition of franchising was written 2,000 years ago. As you read this definition on the next page, think of a franchise as one body consisting of several members: the franchisor (the parent company), franchisees (business owners), suppliers and customers.

While many franchisors may embrace this definition, not all do. The founder and CEO of a successful national franchise recently spoke at a national convention for franchise executives.

Street Smart
Franchising

> The body does not consist of one member but of many. If the foot would say, "Because I am not a hand, I do not belong to the body," that would not make it any less a part of the body. And if the ear would say, "Because I am not an eye, I do not belong to the body," that would not make it any less a part of the body. If the whole body were an eye, where would the hearing be? If the whole body were hearing, where would the sense of smell be? … If all were a single member, where would the body be? As it is, there are many members, yet one body. The eye cannot say to the hand, "I have no need of you," nor again the head to the feet, "I have no need of you." On the contrary, the members of the body that seem to be weaker are indispensable … But God has so arranged the body, giving the greater honor to the inferior member, that there may be no dissension within the body, but the members may have the same care for one another. If one member suffers, all suffer together with it; if one member is honored, all rejoice together with it.
>
> *(1 Corinthians, The Bible)*

During his presentation a member of the audience asked, "How do you resolve conflicts with your franchisees?"

He proudly threw his shoulders back and chest out and proclaimed, "When push comes to shove, the franchisees know *this is my company!*"

Keep in mind, this company is currently highly successful. However, his approach to franchising causes the pushing and shoving he spoke of. In these tough economic times, franchisees and franchisors need to fight the competition for market share, not each other for power and control. This "way too common" leadership philosophy of the franchisor is like the head of one's body saying to the feet, "When push comes to shove, *this is my body!*" And perhaps according to terms of the franchise agreement it is. But someday, the head will want to walk someplace when the feet are sore and tired. That's when the head will have rude awakening.

What Is a Franchise?

While franchising is fraught with franchisors that value the head more than the hands and feet, you will also find franchisors whose leadership sees franchising as one body. If in your search you find a franchisor who thinks it's their body—where they are the head and the lowly franchisees are at the feet—temporarily agree with them. Seize your opportunity to be the feet ... and run away as fast as you can!

The Bottom Line

A franchise agreement doesn't define franchising any more than a marriage certificate defines marriage. When a franchisor or franchisee feels compelled to pull out their franchise agreement, trust has broken down. Franchising only works when both franchisee and franchisor share a deep concern about the other's interests. Franchising is as much about committed interpersonal relationships as it is about processes and systems, when each party accepts responsibility to help the other win.

How Many Franchisees Define Winning

Remember, "People don't buy drills; they buy holes." The franchise is a drill. The most common reasons people report looking into franchising as a career option are:

- **Stability and security in tough economic times.**
- **More flexibility in their day.** Franchisees look for greater say-so in their day-to-day activities.
- **More control.** Franchisees want the authority and responsibility to make the decisions that impact their businesses and careers. They look to create a more performance-based and less political-based work life.
- **More work–life balance.** Many franchisees found that their past careers were consuming them, jeopardizing their closest personal relationships. Many start franchises as a way to spend more time with family, which may also include working with family members.
- **Greater personal challenge.** Many franchisees had either

reached the pinnacle of the professional careers or were competent to the point of no longer being challenged. They were in some version of a career rut and desperately needed a change.

▶ **Giving back to the community or making a difference in the lives of others.** Many franchisees have achieved financial stability or a measure of success in their past careers. They felt it was time to give something back.

▶ **Financial gain.** Many franchisees have a track record of success, creating wealth for shareholders or owners of other companies. It became time to create more equity and greater wealth for themselves and their families.

▶ **Create multiple streams of income.** At retirement, many franchisees don't expect the government to have the money to fund their medical and other retirement expenses. And they don't want to be a burden to their children when they grow older. They want to make today's time and money resources pay out in the future.

Why Do Companies Franchise Their Businesses?

There are two prevailing reasons why companies choose to franchise. The first we call "the high road" and the second we call "the low road."

The High Road to Franchising

Franchisors who take the high road possessed multiple options to expand their business. They had a proven business model that produced great results, including replicating their success in other markets. Possible expansion strategies included bringing in investors, raising capital, and expanding through the chain method (where the parent company would own all the individual distribution points) or restructuring their companies and expanding through franchising.

They chose franchising because franchising could provide them advantages that the chain method couldn't.

The first competitive advantage franchising can offer companies is stronger tactical execution of their business model by having highly skilled and motivated entrepreneurs run point on the implementation rather than perhaps less skilled company managers. An entrepreneur with their dreams and money at stake usually try harder and therefore produce greater results than an employee with a bonus and job security at stake.

Second, franchising is a financing vehicle. Rather than having to raise millions of dollars to expand their business, franchisors leverage the franchisees' ability to raise capital through the SBA, home equity, family, and other sources.

Third, a franchise is typically better positioned to grow more quickly than a company that chooses the chain method of expansion. It has been said, "Timing is everything." Good businesspeople know when a market opportunity presents itself, it must be seized.

Fourth, franchising can be lower risk. Franchisors earn fees (royalties) that are paid by the franchisees typically from gross sales, not cash flow. The start-up capital of the new business is the franchisees' risk, not the franchisor's. Although the franchisees assume much of the financial risk, the franchisor is dependent on the continuing royalty stream paid in by franchisees. Additionally franchisors won't grow if the franchisees aren't making money and achieving great results. Therefore franchisors have a vested interest in helping the franchisees become profitable, but don't take the hit if they fail.

Fifth, they want to share their successes and make a difference in the lives of others. Most franchisors are deeply committed people who love to see their teammates win.

Lastly, franchisees have a collective genius that's hard to replicate in a chain method. For instance, a McDonald's franchisee thought of the Big Mac. A Subway franchisee thought of Five-Dollar Subs. Most of the breakthrough "million-dollar ideas" in a franchise organization are thought of by franchisees, not by employees of the franchisor.

The Low Road to Franchising

Many franchisors get into franchising because some consultant or attorney in a blue pin-striped suit and a snappy red power tie told them they could get rich using other people's money. And for only $150,000 they'll show them how!

You can spot a "low road" franchisor by the following indicators:

► They are undercapitalized. The financial survival of their company is completely dependent on the short-term revenue from selling franchises instead of long-term revenue from collecting royalties. There appears to be no other source of expansion capital available. They have to sell you a franchise to survive.

► They haven't been in business more than five years or they lack a proven business model. They expect you to invest your money for the privilege of proving their business model for them.

► They've never expanded in multiple units and therefore have not proven they can replicate their success. They're expecting you to jump at the opportunity to let them experiment with your money while their cash sits in their bank ... assuming they have cash at all.

► Their unit economics don't provide them a healthy enough return to expand by investing their own money. Yet somehow they believe it's good enough for you.

► They don't interview you for the franchise to determine the fit as they would if they were making a key management hire. They sell franchises as if they were selling a car or vinyl siding.

Not all "low road" franchisors are low-integrity people.

The founder of a fitness franchisor was looking for assistance in recruiting franchisees. When the consultant reviewed the franchisor's financial statement, it showed the franchisor had a corporate worth of $25 ... no kidding, twenty-five bucks. Some people have lost more money behind their sofa cushions than the franchisor had in his whole company. He was asked, "Does this financial statement accurately reflect your financial position or do you franchise under a shell corporation?" Keep in mind, many franchisors are private companies, and as such, their attorneys and accountants advise them not to keep large assets in their corporations. That's why many franchisors are actually stronger financially than they appear on paper.

However, this man responded, "That is all I have." Sadly, this good man was rejected as a client because he was not in a financial position to be able to support franchisees and grow his company.

This franchisor only had twenty-five bucks because some consultant clipped him for all he had to set him up as a franchisor. The founder had the noble intention of curbing the out-of-control obesity rate in America and promote active and healthy lifestyles. This did not happen. The road to hell is paved with good intentions.

Most franchise consultants and attorneys are respectable people and good at what they do. Just as there are a small number of franchisors that prey on the dreams and best intentions of gullible prospective franchisees, there are a small number of consultants and attorneys who prey on the dreams and best intentions of prospective franchisors. Both predators are a stain on franchising.

The good news is that franchise candidates can learn as much about a franchisor and its leadership through their online reputation as they can by having conversations with the franchisor. Through social technology, disgruntled franchisees have more opportunity to state their dissatisfaction than ever before. It's important to remember that many anti-franchisor claims made on social media sites are done so anonymously by the poster. In addition, many sites don't fact check or require evidence for even the most egregious claims of fraud and deceit against the franchisor. On the flip side, we were once contacted by a dubious franchisor whose failing franchisees had taken to voicing their concerns on franchising blogs and websites. They wanted us to write and post phony positive articles to drown out the voice of the franchisees and make it harder to find negative articles on the search engines. So take both positive and negative anonymous feedback as a data point, *but not necessarily the truth*.

Most franchisors are high-road franchisors with great reputations and some are low-road who fly above or below the radar screen of the Internet. Most low-road franchisors, such as the fitness franchisor in the previous example, are simply weak companies whose franchisees aren't going to make it during these tough economic times. As you read on, you'll learn how to distinguish which is which.

Spotting a High-Road Franchisor
What Business Are They In?

While every franchisor distributes its own brand of products and services, the franchise business model is a business unto itself.

For example, Subway restaurants are in the business of selling sandwiches. Thousands of restaurants, diners, and delis across the United States have made sandwiches a staple item on their menus. Any of these could have been "Subway." The difference was that Subway founder Fred Deluca looked at a sandwich and saw opportunity, where others simply saw meat between two slices of bread.

Deluca knew, like McDonald's mastermind Ray Kroc before him knew, that it wasn't enough just to be brilliant at making sandwiches. Fred Deluca knew he not only had to be a brilliant restaurateur, but also he had to become a brilliant franchisor. Deluca saw franchising was a business unto itself. As you investigate franchises, you'll find that brilliant business models are a dime a dozen. However, brilliant franchisors are few. It takes a brilliant franchisor to build a strong regional or national brand.

If you were to ask CEOs of franchise companies, "What business are you in?" you'll probably hear about the products and services they distribute, such as, "I am in the auto repair business" or "I am in the home furnishings business." You will seldom hear, "I am in the franchising business."

Before investing your savings in a franchise, you may want to make sure you're doing business with a franchisor who knows they are in the franchising business and are committed to being brilliant at it. While most people investigating franchises examine the franchisor's effectiveness in distributing their products and services, few people look to determine whether the franchisor is skilled in the business of franchising.

How you identify a brilliant franchisor is to first identify how a franchisor makes money. Forgetting about any cash flow generated by company store operations, a typical franchisor makes money in two or three ways.

1. **Franchise fee revenue.** The franchisor charges franchisees upfront fees typically ranging from $20,000 to $40,000. This is not a big moneymaker to most franchisors. For the majority of franchisors this fee doesn't cover, or barely covers, the cost of running their internal franchise sales departments. In other words, awarding you a franchise is typically a break-even proposition at best. By the time you write the franchisor a check for your franchise fee, chances are they've already spent that money in advertising and departmental costs trying to find you. The most successful franchisors make most of their cash flow from royalties. This means they can only make it if you make it. Be wary of franchisors that take big upfront fees (over $50,000) but don't produce the results to cost-justify this investment.

2. **Royalties.** Franchisees pay franchisors a percentage of their gross revenue typically ranging from 5–10 percent. Fees could be higher, but higher fees should reflect more services. Express Personnel, for instance, charges higher fees; however, they manage the entire backroom payroll operation for their franchisees. So a portion of these royalties could be considered labor cost. On the other hand, some franchisors

charge little or no royalties. They depend more on proprietary product sales to their franchisees. Companies like
Merle Norman Cosmetics, Rita's Water Ice, and Chem-Dry fall
into this category. Continuing fees, such as royalties or product purchases, are the life-blood of a franchisor's business.
Brilliant franchisors are in the business of maximizing continuing fees while maximizing franchisee results. To maximize revenue from continuing fees, they must be first brilliant at developing peak-performing franchisees. This means
they win big when you win big.

3. **Products.** As we touched on above, some franchisors are
also vendors, selling proprietary products and services to
their franchisees at a profit. Companies like Ben and Jerry's
have exclusive vendor relationships with their franchisees.
Franchisors that make money selling products are generally
in the minority. Having a franchisor that is also an exclusive
vendor is not necessarily a bad thing, although it can be
very limiting. If the franchisor's prices are competitive, their
products are unique, don't run the risk of being obsolete,
and they have strong national distribution network (meaning they can effectively get your products to your front door
in a cost-effective manner), this can even be a competitive
advantage.

Out of these revenue streams, royalties and (for those franchisors who are also vendors) product sales should be most
important to the franchisor. Again, be wary of franchisors whose
financial statements show they need the upfront franchise fee
revenue to survive. They'll be tempted and probably will suc-
cumb to the financial pressure of awarding franchises to marginal candidates who have a higher probability of failure.
Franchisors whose franchisees fail will probably not survive as
franchisors. A franchisee failure is a black mark against the brand
for customers, suppliers, and other surviving franchisees.

If you find a franchisor in the business of maximizing revenue
from continuing fees while at the same time producing healthy

returns for franchisees, you have found a franchisor that gets the business they are in.

Who Butters Their Bread?

If a franchisor is truly in the business of maximizing royalty revenue (and possibly driving product sales to their franchisees), how will they accomplish this? On whom are they counting? Don't peak-performing franchisees sell the most products and services to their customers, and therefore pay the highest royalties and purchase the most products from the franchisor? Don't peak-performing franchisees do a better job at making money for themselves, creating job satisfaction for themselves and their employees, and taking care of their customer needs? For these franchisors to be successful, doesn't it mean they are committed to taking you along for the ride? Can you see the potential for a win–win?

However, don't assume because franchising works best as win–win, that franchisor executives in authority are always operating from there.

Win–Lose Franchising

Once, a bunch of veteran franchisee recruiters were together at a conference huddled around a table discussing franchisee recruitment strategies. A vice president of franchise sales from a large national automotive franchisor shared his views on franchisee recruitment. "It is not my job to qualify franchise candidates," he stated. "I will give anyone their God-given right to fail." This person thought it was his responsibility to take money from anyone with the financial capital and interest in opening a business, regardless of their background, skills, and aptitudes. He absolved himself of all personal responsibility for how well the franchisees he recruited performed; instead he let God sort it out. This is a violation of the sacred trust that is franchising.

You may be surprised to learn how many franchisors award franchises to franchise candidates whom they wouldn't hire to manage the same business. And in these tough economic times, sometimes franchisors need the money from the upfront franchise fee to sustain their operations, make payroll, and deal later with what they call "operational problems." Keep in mind "operational problems" is a franchisor-speak for failing or underperforming franchisees.

Many of these near-sighted franchisors simply aren't going to survive. Others will limp along and mature before the brand establishes any real value or means anything to the public. Of these, most won't produce acceptable value for themselves, their customers, their franchisees, or suppliers as a whole.

Prior to the economic collapse, the free market propped up many mediocre business models. In the new economy, where consumers are more cautious and spending less, many of these companies are going to be swallowed up or bypassed by peak-performing franchisors and franchisees who understand what it takes to win. Ultimately, this means greater financial rewards for those franchise candidates who align themselves with the right franchisors, and greater risk for those who choose wrong.

Ultimately, if your investment as a franchisee is going to pay out, you must successfully find two things.

1. The right franchise for you that unleashes the full force of your potential and inspires you into action daily
2. A successful franchisor who possesses the capital, vision, commitment, culture, and talent to build a meaningful, sustainable brand

Often, you won't know whether the franchisor possesses all of what it takes to win until you are franchisee of the system. So the trick is to look for the telltale signs, the simple snapshots that give you access to the full story.

Your first snapshot will be the franchisor's online reputation as a company and as a franchise opportunity. What are people saying?

Your second snapshot will be how the franchisor representatives handle your request for more franchise information.

What Is a
Franchise?

Here are six qualities that most franchisors with meaningful and sustainable values have in common.

1. They're dedicated to helping you determine whether your personal objectives can be met using their business model. *If your objectives can't be met with a high degree of probability, they'll walk away from the deal.* Their franchise opportunity website equips you with balanced information you can trust. Their people appear credible and informed. They're dedicated to helping you make the right decision for yourself and your family and don't appear to be overselling or manipulating.

2. They have a clear understanding of the individual traits, background, and capital necessary to produce success within their business model. In other words, they know who wins and who loses. They educate you online or by conversation about what it takes to win.

3. They evaluate you to determine whether you match their profile of a successful franchisee. They don't ask questions to simply ask questions, to "schmooze," or to win your trust. They ask questions to determine whether you fit their success profile. They are only interested in doing business with those who will win and they say "no" to everyone else. This means you must have the experience of being effectively interviewed and screened, just as if you were applying for a key management position within the organization.

4. They have a candidate-friendly process. *They discard high-pressure sales techniques.*

5. They understand your goals and objectives. They assist you by either providing or helping you acquire the information you need to accurately evaluate the probability their business will produce the results you're looking for. They demand that you do the same.

6. They have a clear, step-by-step recruitment process. Both you and the franchisor know where you are in the process and what additional steps need to be taken. If they don't have a clear step-by-step recruitment process, they probably

don't have a clear, well-thought-out, easy-to-follow business model, either. Dismiss them as an option.

For instance, Ben and Jerry's Ice Cream franchisor only recruits a select group of the many possible franchisees who apply for their franchise, rather than selling franchises to anyone who inquires. If you were to go through their investigation process, you'd have the experience of being interviewed, qualified, and studied. Not only does Ben and Jerry's believe it's their obligation to protect the integrity of the Ben and Jerry's business model, they also believe their franchise sales department is the frontline protector of the corporate social, economic, and product missions, which are their company's three reasons for being. Having money and skill alone doesn't cut it in the Ben and Jerry's organization. You must have the appropriate financial backing, requisite business skills, desire to become a socially responsible corporate citizen (according to the Ben and Jerry's definition of what that means), and be able to create a fun and exciting environment for others.

According to their website, Ben and Jerry's corporation believes in "leading with progressive values across our business." Therefore, a franchise candidate who is far right politically and believes in more conservative values may not be a fit for the organization, regardless of whether they have the skills and capital to win.

Ben and Jerry's also looks for people who can create a fun experience for their employees and customers. During their interview process at one time they asked franchise candidates such questions as "If you were a Ben and Jerry's ice cream flavor, which flavor would you be and why?" People have responded with such clever answers as "I don't know which flavor I am, but I am working hard to avoid becoming 'Chubby Hubby.'" They pay attention to those people.

Those who blow off that question as irrelevant are redflagged as possibly being boring. Being boring will disqualify you as a Ben and Jerry's franchisee. Why? Ben and Jerry's isn't in the ice cream business. They are in the "fun, excitement, simple pleasure, community, and social responsibility" business. They rely on peak-performing fun, exciting, and socially responsible franchisees to pull this off.

Franchisors like Ben and Jerry's, who recruit franchise candidates who are a good fit and have a high probability of success, typically often grow larger and offer their franchisees more stability than those who don't. Franchisors who accept marginal candidates have a high probability of failing and disappearing—perhaps taking you and your money with them.

Being a brilliant franchisee recruiter is only part of what it takes to become a brilliant franchisor. Brilliant franchisors know how to efficiently and effectively impart the success formula of their business to people with diverse backgrounds.

Developing Peak-Performing Franchisees

Picture two men inspecting a broken-down car. One is a race-car mechanic. Having built drag racers from the ground up, he appears to know everything there is to know about cars. On the other hand, aside from filling up the gas tank and occasionally replacing windshield wiper blades, the second man is helpless around cars. The two are standing next to each other, while looking under the hood of the car, trying to diagnose what the problem is.

Every engine part that twirls, spins, revs, squeaks, grinds, smells, or hisses gives the racecar mechanic information that will help him find the cause of the problem. Why? He has the distinctions of a master mechanic. In contrast, the same sights, sounds, and smells tell the other man nothing. Why? He didn't know anything to begin with.

Therefore, the two are both looking at the same engine, *but aren't really looking at the same engine! Only one has the distinction of a master mechanic.*

It's the same with franchising. Brilliant franchisors don't look at their business, their customers, their industry, franchisees, franchising, or even their brand the same way as those who don't experience the same level of success. Like the racecar mechanic, they also possess the distinction of a master.

Perhaps if you asked the racecar mechanic to teach you how to become a master mechanic, you may see him pause. Perhaps he wouldn't know how to teach you or even where to begin. Why? True masters are "unconsciously competent," meaning they long ago stopped having to think about what they are good at and how they got there. They habitually do things right without much thought and energy. The same "unconscious competence" that makes a racecar mechanic a masterful mechanic may make him a lousy trainer of other mechanics. It's been a long time since he had to think about what he was doing; therefore, he would have a hard time communicating what he does and how he does it to someone who doesn't already know.

Franchisors also fall into this trap.

The Training Trap

Any franchisor worth considering at one time was brilliant operating the same business model they're now marketing as a franchise opportunity. Hopefully, they were so brilliant, like the racecar mechanic, they no longer had to spend tremendous amounts of energy thinking about how to execute their business model. They just executed.

Many companies who choose franchising as their expansion model find themselves in a position of having to train people with no industry experience. The same "unconscious competence" that makes a franchisor a great executer of their business model may make them "unconsciously incompetent" in their ability to effectively transfer their knowledge and experience to people from outside their industry. In other words, the best executers run the risk of being the lousiest trainers. If a franchisor runs highly successful corporate-owned locations, be impressed but don't be enamored. Be enamored only when you've determined that they have a long track record of helping people like you do the same.

What Is a
Franchise?

Peak-performing franchisors know this "brilliant executer–lousy trainer" paradox and have gone to great effort to become competent trainers. They start by remembering what they're good at and committing the success formula of their business down on paper in the form of an operations manual. Then they mastered how to quickly and efficiently transfer the success formula of their business model to qualified people from outside their industry in the form of initial and ongoing training and support.

Why Training Is Overrated

Training is often defined as "knowledge transfer." But knowledge, left standing alone, doesn't make a difference. Why do so many teenagers pick up smoking? Don't they know smoking causes cancer? Why are so many American adults overweight or obese? Don't they know how to eat a salad and exercise? It seems that just knowing doesn't work.

There is often a great divide between what people know and what they do. Peak performing franchisees often don't know more than their average or underperforming counterparts. They simply implement more of the knowledge they all possess.

Knowing What to Do and Doing What You Know

Brilliant franchisors understand your great "knowing–doing" divide and are committed to stand in the gap on your behalf. Through their ongoing training and support programs, they'll hold both you and other franchisees accountable for consistently executing their knowledge to the best of your ability. By helping you to close your gap, they create two positive outcomes. First, you become a peak-performing franchisee who achieves a level of success you couldn't achieve on your own. Additionally, the franchisor maximizes royalty collections, which is the business they are in.

We discuss how to determine whether franchisors are excellent in training and support later in this work. However, the bottom line is this. Right this second, even in this bad economy, franchisees just like you are winning according to your definition of winning.

Knowing What to Do and Doing What You Know

Brilliant franchisors understand your great "knowing–doing" divide and are committed to stand in the gap on your behalf. Through their ongoing training and support programs, they'll hold both you and other franchisees accountable for consistently executing their knowledge to the best of your ability. By helping you to close your gap, they create two positive outcomes. First, you become a peak-performing franchisee who achieves a level of success you couldn't achieve on your own. Additionally, the franchisor maximizes royalty collections, which is the business they are in.

We discuss how to determine whether franchisors are excellent in training and support later in this book. However, the bottom line is this. Right this second, even in this bad economy, franchisees just like you are winning according to your definition of winning.

Building a Strong Franchisee Community

Brilliant franchisors don't stop at building peak-performing franchisees. While your peak individual performance is critical to both yours and the franchisor's success, franchising is a team sport. Brilliant franchisors know how to get fiercely independent franchisees with diverse backgrounds working together as a fully functioning unit. They make decisions based on not only what is in the franchisor's best interest, but what is in the team's best interest. They carefully weigh their decisions against the impact on the franchisee community.

As we already said, like the McDonald's Big Mac, most of a franchisor's million-dollar ideas will come from the franchisees. Brilliant franchisors know this. Their franchisee community becomes their idea farm. Franchisees of brilliant franchisors have the experience of being heard. They see their ideas implemented.

Great franchisors create opportunities to bring franchisees together to share and harvest their collective genius. They do this through such venues as conferences, business meetings, newsletters, conference calls, intranet, webinars, and blogs.

What Is a
Franchise?

Franchisees experience being connected to both their franchisor and the other franchisees. They have an experience of being part of an exclusive community dedicated to their success.

If you read the terms of most franchise agreements, you will see that franchisors and franchisees are under no legal or business obligation to create or join such a community. This community transcends any legal or business relationship that exists. Yet this community brings out the best in what franchisees and franchisors have to offer each other.

For instance, to be a franchisee of one residential home remodeling franchise, you must first pass "The Camping Test." If the leadership team can't picture themselves sitting around the campfire with you, roasting marshmallows, and enjoying a deep personal conversation, you won't be awarded a franchise. Whether you enjoy the outdoors is irrelevant to The Camping Test. Whether or not the leadership team and the other franchisees will enjoy your company is. This franchisor has a community to protect.

Two Men and a Truck, a residential moving franchise, at one time had a similar test called "The Grandma" test. In an effort to upgrade both the franchisee–franchisor and customer relationships, they train each franchisee and home office employee to treat each other and their customers like they would want their grandmother treated.

Summary

As you are beginning to see, although franchisors are in the business of distributing products and services, franchising is a business unto itself. Aside from being brilliant at distributing their brand of products or services, a franchisor must be brilliant in business of franchising. The business of franchising can be broken down into four key areas. The first is franchisee recruitment. Franchisors have to know how to recruit qualified franchise candidates. Second, franchisors must be brilliant in training and developing franchisees into peak performers. The good news is that a franchisor's survival depends on their ability to help you win. Third, they need to build a solid community, where the franchisor can harvest the collective genius of the franchisee community for the benefit of all. Lastly, they have either created a brand that means something to customers, or they have a proven plan for franchisees to follow that will create such a brand. You should only look into making investments with franchisors that get this. At its best, franchising transcends any legal or business relationship that exists between the franchisees and franchisors. A franchise is a community, comprising franchisees, franchisors and their employees, and suppliers, each looking out for the other's best interest and committed to the success of all.

What to Expect from the Next Chapter

You will take a more extensive look at the reasons why people invest in franchises. You will hear stories about people who moved forward with different franchises and you explore what they expected to happen versus what actually happened when they got started. We also compare the profiles and explore the differences between the people who take control over their own future by investing in a franchise versus those who return to the workforce.

2

Why Should I Invest in a Franchise?

People often ask us, "Why should I invest in a franchise? We'll give you the short answer now, and more details throughout this chapter. A 1997 Gallup study showed that 94 percent of franchisees consider themselves successful. Consider this is by the franchisees' definition of success, which would include achieving more of such things as:

► Money
► Time
► Work–life balance

► Flexibility
► Challenge
► Control
► Security and stability
► Equity
► Making a difference in the lives of others
► Personal responsibility
► Personal impact on the bottom line.

Additionally, in the same study 75 percent of franchisees polled said, knowing what they know now, they would make the same decision again. In contrast, if you asked your coworkers and peers the same questions, how many of them would say they're successful? How many of them would choose the same career or company again? The simple answer is people invest in franchises because most franchisees win.

Now we have a question for you: If most franchisees win and most would make exactly the same decision again, why do as many as 99 percent of people who investigate franchising decide not to invest?

The Path of the 99%

Purely, statistically speaking (and nothing personal intended), it is almost certain you won't make an investment in a franchise either. You will probably complain about the way things are, dream about what could be, take a brief stand for yourself by declaring, "I am tired placing my future in the hands of others. Now it's my turn!" Then you'll Google franchise opportunities, visit franchisor homepages, gather stacks of franchisor brochures, research companies, talk to people and professionals you trust, and have conversations with franchisors. You'll feel proactive. You'll tell your friends you're considering buying a business. Chances are they thought about it, too. Some will be happy for you, some will be jealous, some will be afraid for you. Virtually everyone will share their strong opinions with you. You'll dream about what it would be like to be your own boss. You'll think about your customers and employees. You'll make clever little charts such as the T Bar, where you neatly list all the pros on the left side of the page, balanced by the cons on the right side. Then the time will come to make a decision. Fear, doubt, and negative self-chatter (yours, your spouse's, your kids', your parents,' your friends', and your hired professionals') will kick into high gear. Eventually, you probably will make a fear-based "no" decision, backed by the logic of your neatly listed cons.

"The business has fatal flaws," you think, "Employee turnover is too high. Competition is too fierce. The business is too risky. Sure, it may work in some areas, but everyone knows our town is different." And with everything going on in your life, the timing couldn't be worse. Yes, you are being completely responsible with your resources. You didn't work this hard and long and sacrifice this much to lose what you've earned and saved. Moving forward with a franchise would put your family in danger. If you leave your company, you will lose your insurance benefits and 401(k). What if someone in your family had to go to hospital? How would you survive without insurance? Plus, your industry is changing so fast, in a few years your expertise would be obsolete and it would be impossible for you to regain entry if your business didn't make it. Certainly almost every reasonable person armed with the same research and faced with the same personal challenges you have would naturally come to the same conclusion.

And you are right.

99 percent do.

The Path of the 1%

The 1 percent and the 99 percent all start in the same physical place in the franchise investigation process. However, they don't all start in the same clean mental place. Truth be known (and this is going to make some people crazy), the 99 percent have a consistent and persistent career complaint with no real intention of ever doing anything about it. This isn't right or wrong, just the way it is. The 1 percent have the same complaints as the 99 percent, just different future intentions. The 99 percent investigate franchises with the underlying intention of disproving different franchise opportunities so they can dismiss self-employment as a career option, and go back to a career that seems to keep choosing them rather than a career they choose. Conversely, the 1 percent make a firm commitment to put the past in the past and alter the future.

If you are among the 1 percent, with or without *Street Smart Franchising*, you will probably find a way to make your life and career work in franchising (as evidenced by the fact 94 percent of franchisees consider themselves successful).

Starting a franchise is an unreasonable and unnatural undertaking. But the 1 percent refuse to live a reasonable, natural, and compromised life. Their circumstances aren't any different than yours. Many have similar backgrounds, finances, experience, education, and training to yours. They're your age, have the same family challenges, and even live in your neighborhood. They don't have more confidence, skills, education, experience, or capital than you. Perhaps they're more committed to their dreams. Perhaps they simply have more pain.

Whatever their reason, they have come a place in their life where they would rather take a shot and fail than sit in the bleachers and wonder what it's like to play.

Late at night, the 1 percent have fast-forwarded to the end of their life or career and envisioned themselves sitting in a rocking chair in front of their fireplace thinking, "My career didn't make a difference." They have been to retirement parties and seen plaques and gold watches handed out to the retiring department heads and coworkers. They have heard the toastmasters deliver different versions of the same sincere speeches, like "We will always miss you," and "The office won't the same without you." They also saw how these retirees are always replaced and seldom missed. They don't want to end their career in the banquet room at a steak house, with a smiling waiter bringing out a sheet cake with strawberry fruit filling with the words *HAPPY RETIRE-MENT!!!!* neatly printed in all capital letters and punctuated with several exclamation points for extra sincerity. They cringe at the thought of slightly buzzed coworkers breaking out into an out-of-tune chorus of "(S)he's a jolly good fellow." Then it's all over. Their career ends as uneventfully as it started. They think, "All the sacrifice. All the hard work. All the time away from my family. For what?"

This potential future spooks the 1 percent into positive action in the present. They refuse to be the person who ends their career this way. They are going to work and live all out, holding back nothing in reserve.

The Voice of the Inner Critic

The 99 percent are not worse than the 1 percent, nor are they some way they aren't supposed to be. As the song aptly states, they are good fellows—which nobody can deny.

However, the 99 percent are more likely than the 1 percent to listen to the lies of their "inner critic." You know him. He stays in the background, whispering what you desperately wish not to be true, but on some level believe anyway. Your inner critic waits in ambush, ready to emotionally hijack you at your weakest moments and seize control of your decision-making capabilities. Now you're contemplating a life-changing transition. The critic loves such change. Change and ambiguity are the bread and water he needs to survive. Life changes offer the critic an opportunity to create a larger speaking platform. He has been quiet for so long, now it's his turn to shout and he has you convinced it's your turn to listen. Then he hurls new versions of the same old accusations he has always made against you.

- ▶ You aren't good enough.
- ▶ You aren't smart enough.
- ▶ You fail at everything.
- ▶ You're helpless.
- ▶ You're poor.
- ▶ You're worthless.
- ▶ Nobody cares about you.
- ▶ You can't trust anyone.
- ▶ You will never get what you want.
- ▶ You don't deserve it.
- ▶ You don't belong.
- ▶ You don't make a difference.
- ▶ There's something wrong with you.
- ▶ It's all your fault.
- ▶ You'll go broke.
- ▶ You're weak.
- ▶ You can't do it.

"And that's the way it's always going to be until the day you die. So forget it," says the critic.

Since the situation is new, once again, you fear the critic is right and you listen. And in the end, instead of buying a franchise and pursuing a life you desire, you buy the critic's lie and relive some version of the same old past you expressed a sincere desire to leave behind. You'll compromise on your future and a small part of you will die.

Yes, 99 percent of you who are reading this book probably will make a fear-based, critic-inspired decision and back it up with conventional logic. You think such things as "I need the security of a job until my kids go to college. This business has too much competition." Or conversely, "The business isn't proven (because it doesn't have enough competition). Employees will goof off while robbing you blind. Employees will leave you for another 50 cents an hour. I know someone who failed in a similar business. There's too much inventory. My spouse isn't support-ing me." And then you take a pass.

However, you still hold on to the thought, "If I could only find the right business, I could become successful."

The 'Right' Business

You know the right business. The one with little or no start-up costs. You could start it with the loose change you found behind your sofa cushions. There's no inventory. Or if there is inventory, customers will pay you first, and then you go out and buy your inventory with your customer's money. There are no contingent liabilities, such as real estate or equipment leases. There's little risk, a big return on investment, and fast equity build-up. You par-ley your sofa cushion money into a million-dollar enterprise.

Although there's no competition, there's lots of demand for your products and services all year long. People will walk through snowdrifts in bare feet just for the opportunity to buy from you. And your business is safe. No one has ever failed in this franchise before. Your products and services are so unique they

Why Should I Invest in a Franchise?

can't be found anywhere else. Plus the franchisor holds the patent, so no one ever will. Banks think the business is so hot they're lined up to offer you money on a signature with no collateral. However, you don't need banks. Just more old sofa cushions to rummage behind.

And think about your customers! They are happy, repeat customers ... the kind of customers who walk into your place of business with hundred-dollar bills hanging out of their pockets and buy every product you offer. Plus they bring other customers with them. Of course they seek you out based on your reputation alone, so there's never a need to advertise, network, sell, or even leave the comfort of your home to find them.

What about your employees? There are no employees needed! Or if you do need employees, there won't be any turnover. They punch in exactly when they are supposed to, do what you tell them, exactly the way you told them to do it. Therefore, they need little supervision. They open, close, and maintain your operation while creating complete customer satisfaction. You only need to show up to empty the cash register. Unfortunately, the register fills up so often, this may require you to make several trips a day to the bank, which can interfere with your golf game.

If by some freak chance you do have to replace an employee, it'll be a breeze because responsible, cleancut potential employees with positive, can-do attitudes are always knocking on your door, looking to come to work for you.

What's more, this business is easy to run; the learning curve is nearly nonexistent. You come out of initial training a master. You make no costly mistakes. You work 9–5 with no weekends. You finish one year making the same or more than you are earning now. And next year you will double your income.

Plus, all this happens just at the right time in your life to start a business. You know the right time. The 99 percent live in an illusion—the universe is composed of two time periods to start a business: the right the time and the time period they are currently living in, which of course is the wrong time.

The 'Right Time' to Start a Business

Maybe you think your kids have to be "the right age." This means they aren't too old, or they aren't too young. Or they need to get older and moved out. Or you think, "If only I didn't have kids." On some level you believe nobody has ever found a way to have kids the age of yours and succeed in franchising at the same time.

Second, you may believe you have to be the right age to start a business. Either you must be older, more financially secure, and have additional money to risk. Or you wish you were younger, have a little money, and therefore nothing to lose. On some level you may believe it's harder for someone your age to succeed in franchising.

You may believe your parents need to be the right age. You may think they must be young enough so they don't need your support. Or your parents may need to be older and financially secure enough to support you by giving you some money. Or may think you must wait until you no longer have parents. On some level you may think nobody with parents at their stage in life has ever succeeded in franchising.

You have to have the right spouse. He or she earns enough to meet your household expenses and whole-heartedly supports whatever decision you make. Or your spouse will help you in business to keep your overhead down. Or you aren't married and don't have those commitments. You believe it's harder for anyone in your current marital situation to succeed in franchising.

You can make time. Either you need more free time at work in which to explore your options or, if you have been laid off, you have to focus on earning some income to stop the bleeding. Certainly no one with your time demands has ever succeeded in franchising.

So what do the Boogey Man, The Lost Continent of Atlantis, The Right Franchise, and The Right Time to Start a Business all have in common?

No such thing.

Looking for the perfect business to start at the right time is the franchising equivalent of going on a "snipe hunt." Remember snipe hunts? For those of you who don't know, on camping vacations and family picnics, sometimes the adults send kids out to find snipe, a noble quest designed by adults to occupy the kids for awhile so the adults can drink beer, play poker, and swear like sailors.

The Bottom Line

The 99 percent hold on to the fallacy there's a perfect business that can be started at the right time. The 1 percent believe they have to go out and find the right business and make it the right time.

The Differences Between the 1% and 99%

The 99%	The 1%
Wait for the "right time" to start a business.	Declares "Now is the time." And then works to make it the right time.
Try to find the perfect business.	Tries to find a solid business and will work to make it the right business for them.
Look for what's wrong with franchises and reasons they won't work.	Looks for franchises with a strong track record of success, while acknowledging their unique challenges and potential pitfalls.
Are normal and reasonable.	Is exceptional and unreasonable.
Are committed to achieving stability and security and is risk-averse.	Is committed to making a difference with their life and career and is willing to accept risk to do so.
Are afraid of the unknown. Make their fears mean "something is wrong" and back away from creating the future they desire.	Is afraid of the unknown. Doesn't make their fears mean anything. "I am afraid of the unknown," they think, "so what else is new?"
Their future is something which happens to them and they fall into.	Their future is something they design and then live into.

The 99%	The 1%
Listen to the opinions and accusations of the Inner Critic. Lets him impact their decision-making.	Listens to the opinions and accusations of The Inner Critic. Doesn't let him impact their decision-making.
Aren't born into the 99 percent. Become the 99 percent through the decisions they make.	Isn't born into the 1%. Becomes the 1% through the decisions they make.

How to Join the 1%

► Recognize that if you haven't already started a business or franchise, or lived off 100 percent performance-based compensation, you are already in the 99 percent.

► Recognize the 1 percent is not better or worse than the 99 percent, just different. There's nothing wrong with being in the 99 percent.

► Recognize your past is a product of the decisions you made in the past. You may not be happy with your decisions or the results, but you accept the past as a product of your own creation.

► You look into future. What will your life be like if you stay on your predictable course? What will your life and career look like five years from now? 10? 20? What will your life and career have stood for? What will you have accomplished? What would still be left to accomplish? Hang out with this future. Picture it so clearly it's as if you're already living it. Visit this future often. Know what it will be like before you get there.

► Think about what you "must have" in life, where not having these things isn't an option. For example, "My kids must go to college. I must own a home in a safe neighborhood." Identify the goals that, if not achieved, would make you feel your life was a monumental failure. Are you on track to achieve your "must haves?" If not, you're on the road to serious regret.

▶ Think about your "want to haves," those things that, although desired, aren't mission critical and you could find a way to live without them. The evidence is you're living without them now. Examples would include a bigger house, a nicer car, better vacations, etc. Think about which "want to haves" you will predictably have and which you won't.

Creating Your Desired Future

Use the following table as a worksheet to start designing your future.

Prioritize according to the following 5-point scale.

1   **2**   **3**   **4**   **5**

I could live without, I wish for but could live without, I can't live without

My future desires	Rate from 1-5	Assuming nothing changes, what is the likelihood I will achieve this desire in the future? (impossible, not likely, very likely, almost certain)	Am I OK with this likelihood? (Yes/No)

Make a decision as to whether your predictable future is acceptable or unacceptable.

If the future is acceptable, *more power to you*. You're winning! You're living a fabulous life. What more can you ask for? You may not have everything you want, but clearly you're realizing your high priorities and maintaining the integrity of your values. A new business may or may not improve the quality of your life. Investigate franchises carefully. Evaluate how a franchise will impact your future. Make sure your "must haves" in life are intact and a franchise will deliver more of your "want to haves" than your current course. Investigate franchising as a strategy to possibly win bigger.

If your future is unacceptable, you are faced with two decisions.

1. **Make a decision to accept the unacceptable.** Let go of your future desires and accept the life and career you have. Accept the results of this decision because it's your decision, nobody is doing it to you. It's through your acceptance that the unbearable will become bearable. If you accept the results of your decision as the result of your decision, you won't feel like a loser.

2. **Make a decision to no longer accept the unacceptable.** This is a transformational, life-changing decision, one of the most powerful decisions you can make. Your decision to put the past in the past will immediately alter and enlarge your future. This decision will energize you, calling you forward into committed action, altering what is possible for you today and in the future.

If you decide to no longer accept the unacceptable, you are on the path to greater success, meaning, and achievement. Before you begin down this path, we will equip you with the following:

▶ Greater self-awareness of your style and gifts and your predictable value to a franchise opportunity (chapter 3)

Why Should I Invest in a Franchise?

- ▶ Clearly stated and well-prioritized personal goals (chapter 4)
- ▶ A greater understanding of exactly what it takes to win in franchising (chapter 5)
- ▶ Knowledge and understanding of the learning curve franchisees go through as they take on a new venture. Strategies to accelerate your learning curve (chapter 6)

Only after you have read these chapters and developed a clear understanding of franchising in general will we take you through a process of identifying and investigating your options (chapters 8 and 9). Remember our agreement and read chapter 3 next and resist the temptation to jump around. Franchising is about producing great results by following proven processes and systems. Although you may not know where we are going with every chapter, we have a 30-year track record of getting people there! Have faith! Take one step at a time. Congratulations on taking this powerful step.

3

Understanding Your Behavior Style

Behavior Styles

In the early 1920s an American psychologist named William Moulton Marston sought to create a model that would allow him to predict and explain how emotionally healthy people react to both situations and other people. To test the accuracy of his new theories of behavior, Marston needed to create a system of measurement. Incorporating some of famed psychologist Carl Jung's personality theories stating that there are four distinct personality and behavior styles, Marston created an assessment tool that measured the following behavior characteristics:

1. **D**ominance
2. **I**nfluence
3. **S**teadiness
4. **C**ompliance

Dominance measures how people respond to challenges and problems. People who are high on dominance will attack problems head on and will seek out potential problems before they occur. People who are low on dominance display a tendency to let events unfold and see what happens.

Influence measures how people respond to interactions with others. People who are high on influence are outgoing and have a need to build strong personal relationships and influence others with their views. People who are low on influence appear as more distant and private.

Steadiness measures how people respond to the pace of their environment. People who are high on steadiness desire predictable and slower-paced environments where they can see projects from the beginning through to completion. People low on steadiness desire change and like to multitask.

Compliance measures how people respond to structure or rules created by others. People high on compliance thrive in highly structured environments where they know exactly what to do and what's expected of them. People low on compliance like to make their own rules and prefer to be self-managed.

Take a wild guess where entrepreneurs are on this scale. Most entrepreneurs are a "don't tell me what to do" waiting to happen.

It's from these four characteristics that the DISC theory and assessment tool was named. Marston proved that those who possess similar characteristics also happen to speak, listen, process information, make decisions, and produce results in similar fashion.

DISC has become one of the most widely used, statistically validated, and universally accepted behavior assessments companies use to help determine whether the skills people possess match what's required for particular positions, including franchised ownership. We believe that the DISC theory is among the best available tools to help you evaluate whether your skills match a franchisor's profile of a successful franchisee. We explain the DISC theory in a moment.

As you contact franchise companies and get further into their franchise sales process, you will find some highly skilled and sophisticated franchisors have already used DISC or a similar instrument to statistically measure and help create their composite profile of a successful franchisee. They have figured out who wins and who doesn't. They will profile you on the same instrument and compare your results against their composite of a successful franchisee and examine the deviations. They will discuss the deviations with you and talk about how these deviations may play out positively or negatively in your own business. For instance, they may see that you are more introverted than their profile of a successful franchisee and they may discuss if you are willing to cold call for customers. Some franchisors put so much emphasis on these instruments they will use them as a qualifier or disqualifier for a franchise. Other franchisors take a more balanced approach, using their findings alongside other information they gather, such as interviews, applications, past results, résumés, and financial statements.

Many smaller chains have too few franchisees to make a statistical sampling relevant. Larger, more unsophisticated franchise chains may assume they already know and therefore may not see the value in using instruments. Expect them to supply you with anecdotal evidence, which we urge you to listen to, but not entirely trust. Not that these franchisors are knowingly misleading you or doing anything wrong, it's that they're making an educated guess using observational data which may or may not be accurate. People have a tendency to see what they want to see and ignore the rest. Create your own profile using the information in this chapter. The genius of DISC theory is that it's both easy to learn and apply.

DISC theory states the obvious: Normal and healthy people display consistent, predictable patterns of behavior. Taken one step further, people with similar styles within the same franchise system have a tendency to produce similar results. Put another way, the top performers generally display one style and underperformers display another. Seldom will you find style similarities between top performers and underperformers.

Before we get into styles, understand we are not saying one

particular style of performance is better than another style as it relates to franchising in general. We are, however, asserting that franchise systems are typically set up to support certain styles of performance and not others, which is one reason why franchisees' performance varies within the same franchise system.

Think about it. Franchise systems are typically created by the successful entrepreneurs who invented these systems. Put another way, every *franchise system* at one time was an entrepreneur's *personal system,* usually started with a single business unit. Unless the franchisor's systems have undergone years of development, evolution, or transformation, the franchise system will still be reflective of the entrepreneur's original personal system. Since each entrepreneur will be dominant in one style or another, doesn't it stand to reason that franchisees whose behavior styles most resemble the original entrepreneur's style will also be the ones most likely to master this system? Additionally, many franchisors simply don't take into account style differences when they create systems and develop training programs. They create, train, and develop according to their own dominant style the same way other people act according to their own dominant style.

Certainly there are other mitigating factors that impact a franchisee's performance that you'll also need to take into account, such as demographics, market penetration, brand awareness, competition, location, capitalization, and general economic conditions. However, don't discount style. Behavior styles do play a role in determining results. If your style more closely matches the profile of an underperformer rather than a performer, all other things being equal, regardless of your past successes, you run a high risk of being an underperformer yourself. Why? Because the role the franchise plays in a particular business may not offer you your ideal work environment or the "highest and best use" of your talents.

Have you ever had a job that didn't fit you, where your weaknesses were exposed and your gifts weren't used? Chances are you produced mediocre results at best and went home exhausted. Work was hard and frustrating. You felt like you were always pushing a rock uphill. Each morning, when your alarm clock sounded, you probably threw a shoe at it and fought the urge to bury your head in your pillow and go back to bed. And when you finally did get out of bed, pity the poor souls who were unlucky enough to cross your path or get in your way.

Conversely, have you ever worked in a job that seemed tailor made for you? Work became play. Chances are you produced great results with seemingly little effort. You lived and worked in a perpetual state of forward momentum. After the workday was over, you actually went home energized. When your alarm went off in the next morning, you jumped out of bed, ready to take on the day. Sometimes you even beat the alarm clock up, in anticipation of another great day.

Isn't this what you're looking to recreate with a franchise? Don't you want work that's so interesting and challenging that you welcome every day you are called forth into action? Don't you want work to feel like play? Don't you want to inspire your friends, family, and associates to find their own nirvana?

Use the information in this chapter to help determine whether a particular franchise opportunity will provide you with your ideal work environment, setting you up to win.

Again, don't expect every franchisor to know who wins and loses and why. Most have a high belief level in their program and are sold on their own opportunity. Additionally, many will chalk up franchisees' wins to brilliance of the franchise system and franchisees' losses to the shortcomings of the franchisees. Conversely, many franchisees will chalk up their personal victories to their own expertise and their failures to failures in the franchise system. Reality is usually buried somewhere in the middle. By learning and applying the simple techniques you'll learn in this chapter, you'll gain keen insights into what it takes to succeed in any given franchise system.

While your style can't be relied on to pick which particular industries you should be looking at inside of franchising, your style will help you determine which specific companies, cultures, and work environments you should and shouldn't consider. Put another way, you can't use this information to determine whether you should be in foodservice or the hair care business, it will help you determine if you're a fit for such specific chains as Subway or Great Clips.

How Does DISC Work?

As we said, DISC validates that people are consistent in how they speak, listen, and react to people and situations. So consistent, in fact, that people have essentially become typecast actors in their own movies, playing the same character again and again. Although people and events is unpredictable, the way people react to other people and events are predictable and can even be measured with a shocking degree of accuracy. To assist you, we've applied movie characterizations to each of the four styles.

In this chapter, you will identify which one or two of the four possible typecast characters both you and others play. This will help you to predetermine which characters excel and which underachieve in any given franchise system. The four typecast actors are as follows:

- ▶ The Action Hero
- ▶ The Comedian
- ▶ The Faithful Sidekick
- ▶ The Private Eye

You Are an Action Hero If ...

You are an outgoing, hard-charging, risk-taking, task-oriented, efficient, disciplined, organized, results-oriented, and take-charge character. You make quick, emotional, instinctual, or gut-based decisions rather than information-based or logic-based decisions. Attaining goals, assuming control, achieving results, accepting personal challenge, and creating efficiency drives you. You speak pointedly and directly, telling it like it is. You possess strong opinions and are often closed to any new facts and information that may contradict your formed opinions. Like Action

Understanding Your
Behavior Style

Heroes who don't need or seek much information to make quick decisions, you have difficulty listening to details, preferring instead to listen to headlines, highlights, or the bottom line. Therefore, Action Heroes are often perceived as poor listeners. Since you're such a strong personality, you can easily bowl over weaker personality types, creating conflict in the process. Since you may fear being taken advantage of, you may often question the personal motives, integrity, and loyalty of others, creating issues around trust.

Your Value in Business

You are results oriented and goal focused. You seldom lose sight of your goals or the big picture. You know what you are looking to accomplish and generally are keyed into how to get there. You seldom deviate from your stated objectives. You get others around you focused and organized also.

You are strategic and tactical. You know to chunk problems and situations down to their simplest forms and create a plan of attack quickly. You effortlessly know how to simplify everything.

You are visionary. You can see past the minutia of the day-to-day operations of a business and hold on to your original vision. You are excellent at stating your vision to others in simple terms so they get it also You always seem to have one eye on what is occurring and another eye on the bottom line. Others will follow you because of your commanding presence and clear and simple ideas of what's required to win.

You are an efficiency expert. You know how to trim the fat and cut the waste. You are always identifying and pushing for the quickest, easiest, simplest, and most efficient way to produce results. You will quickly identify and spend time executing the activities that drive results. You know which buttons need to be pushed and when and can be counted on to push those buttons.

You are responsible, self directed, and self managed. You do what you say you are going to do. As long as you know what the

43

results need to look like at the end of the day, you have an uncanny ability to make things happen. Against all odds, you seem to invent ways to produce results and win.

You are a natural-born leader. You have a forceful personality and appear to others as an authority figure. People naturally follow your lead.

You get involved. You see it as your duty to look beyond what's occurring in your little franchise and contribute on a regional or national level. You desire to be heard, and your opinions are generally worth listening to.

You have a strong operational focus. You know how to implement processes and systems that produce results.

You possess excellent multitasking abilities. You know how to juggle people and tasks without dropping any balls. You have a natural ability to keep multiple ideas front of mind without having to write things down.

You create win–win solutions. You are skilled at identifying what winning looks like for yourself and others and will work to create solutions where everyone gets what they want.

You have great problem-solving ability. You don't shrink from, avoid, or deny conflicts and challenges. You attack head-on without reservation. You will be the first to identify where potential breakdowns are occurring or may occur in the future and are often ready with a solution.

You are action oriented and quick to implement. Once you decide what to do, you don't let grass grow under your feet. You are in perpetual motion. You get more done than most people in less time.

You aren't afraid to take risks. As such, yours is the most entrepreneurial behavior style. You aren't afraid to spend time or money when necessary to create long-term gain.

You are a strong decision maker. You move quickly and decisively and aren't prone to second-guess yourself or waffle in the face of making important decisions. Once you decide, it's full steam ahead.

You have a commonsense approach to business. You can easily frame any given situation and quickly formulate a plan of attack. You're brilliant at looking past symptoms and getting to the heart or source of the matter.

You put forth a heroic effort and play to win. You expect and demand the same of others. No one working with you is allowed a free pass.

What Will Kill You If You Aren't Careful

You have a tendency to resist external controls. You may not value being held accountable to follow a system. You resist following certain operational procedures if you deem them inefficient or cumbersome. You will be tempted to deviate from a franchise system, increasing your risk and decreasing the franchisor's ability to offer you meaningful support. You don't always respect boundaries.

You form strong opinions and resist checking out perceptions against the facts. You may make poor decisions because of lack of information. You aren't always open to receive information that's contrary to what you believe. Because you like to rally others to your point of view, you can be labeled by the franchisor and other franchisees as a "rebel" or "trouble maker" and lose credibility with the franchisor. Because you stop listening once your mind is made up, it can be difficult for a franchisor to train and support you and point out problem areas in your business.

You seek control of a situation or interaction. You often resist following other leaders. You may butt heads with franchisor leadership and alienate yourself from the franchisor and other franchisees.

You attempt to gain the upper hand in negotiations. You may be perceived as selfish and not a team player, which would get in the way of others wanting to help you.

You tell others what's on your mind without a thought as to how it might land on others. You can damage key franchisee–franchisor relationships if others aren't comfortable with your directness or bluntness.

You have a tendency to challenge, confront, and make others wrong, which can diminish your franchisor's ability to provide you with leadership.

You possess a tendency to change systems, processes, and procedures you did not create or that you don't agree with. You run the risk of changing the franchise system before you ever learn the system, which could create costly mistakes and extend your learning curve.

You're a notoriously poor listener. This can get in the way of your training and development and create personality conflicts with a franchise support staff.

You're a strong leader and have a tendency to bowl over weaker personalities. Many franchise support and training professionals possess those weaker personalities, damaging key relationships.

At times, you will at times risk damaging key relationships to get what you want since you're more about achieving great results than building powerful relationships.

You have a tendency to dominate and micromanage others, which may create employee turnover, halting forward momentum.

You have a tendency to delegate without effectively training others, setting employees up to fail.

You have a temper. Employees with weaker personality types may hide mistakes and information that indicate problems to avoid setting you off. You are so intolerant of mistakes, you may not give your employees the safe space necessary to make mistakes and learn their roles.

You like to be in control and make decisions with little feedback. You may not effectively harness the collective genius of your employees.

You take a "ready-fire-aim" approach to business. You may impulsively act without thinking about all the ramifications of your actions.

You are a natural risk-taker, which will help you. You may take foolish chances, which can hurt you.

You are impatient and want things now. You sometimes will force a result rather than let it naturally happen. You err on the side of aggressiveness.

You forget to give others positive affirmation for a job well done. You have a tendency to communicate to your employees only when you spot a problem, giving some the experience of being unappreciated, which will create turnover.

Your ideal franchise ...

Has freedom to make unit-level strategic decisions. The franchise system isn't completely button-downed and handed down from the top.

Contains business systems that are clearly articulated, efficient, and well thought out.

Offers a work environment that's efficient and well organized.

Involves multitasking and change. Every day is a bit different.

Includes a workday that allows flexibility.

Requires great personal challenge and working on the big picture. May appreciate a smaller franchisor that doesn't have it all figured out yet. Would appreciate a smaller, more entrepreneurial franchise where you have direct access to the decision makers.

Is a proven, replicable business model, not just a good idea.

Searches for businesses with strong management information systems and clear key measures of success.

Isn't loosey-goosey, where key management doesn't have the skill or experience to continue on a growth track.

Offers customers a unique product or service that demonstrates value, one that will produce great results for customers or clients and something they can sell with integrity.

Is cutting edge or leading edge.

Is a system that provides easy access to data and key indicators of the business.

Offers access to the franchisor's decision makers and a forum to voice opinions.

If successful, can continually be grown.

Is run by executives with a participatory leadership style.

Leaves you alone and won't be overly involved in their business.

Fits the profile of a higher-risk franchise, offering you the possibility for growth and higher return.

Gives you choices and wiggle room, not mandates.

You Are a Comedian If ...

You're a fun-loving, outgoing, empathetic, risk-taking, people-oriented, charming, affable, creative, enthusiastic, talkative, optimistic, trusting, and highly influential character. Like Action Heroes, Comedians are also instinctual, emotion-based, or gut-based rather than information-based decision makers. However, where Action Heroes are more task oriented, Comedians are more people oriented. Building quality relationships, having fun, and attaining social recognition drive them. Comedians look for reasons to believe in, trust, and like others. Like Action Heroes, they listen more attentively to headlines, highlights, the bottom line, and the big picture rather than the details. They have trouble saying "no," and have a tendency to over-promise. They struggle with detail, are known to become disorganized, and have trouble managing their time effectively.

Your Value in Business

You have creative problem-solving ability. You're an out-of-the-box thinker. You can find new ways to look at problems and find solutions. You're resourceful and can find what has worked in other businesses and industries and synthesize a solution for their business.

You're visionary; you see the big picture. You can look beyond the status quo and see what's possible. You're skilled in enrolling others in your vision of the future.

You build consensus and will work hard to avoid conflict and build powerful relationships with the franchisor and other franchisees.

You're goal-oriented. You'll work hard to attain your goals.

You influence others. You know how to rally the troops and inspire others into committed action.

You work well with others and function well on a team. You will work to build synergies and bond with franchisor's employees.

You are a great communicator and easy to talk to, relate to. You know how to make customers and employees feel right at home. You build powerful, life-long relationships with customers and employees.

You are optimistic and put forward positive energy. You maintain a healthy can-do attitude in the face of adversity.

You are trusting and can create trust in customers and employees.

You are outgoing and exhibit mastery in sales and marketing. You are a natural-born salesperson and promoter. You aren't afraid of getting out into the community and telling others why they should be doing business with you. You know how to drive sales.

You make work and shopping fun for employees and customers. Their energy is contagious.

You have good customer service skills. You know how to keep customers satisfied and coming back.

You are a democratic manager, good at soliciting feedback. You'll work to create a positive experience for clients and customers.

You are entrepreneurial and a risk-taker. You aren't afraid to spend money to achieve your objectives.

You are quick to make decisions or to implement.

You like change and you move fast. You can get much done in a short time.

You have a high degree of confidence in your own abilities.

You keep one eye on the bottom line of the business.

What Will Kill You If You Aren't Careful

You move quickly and don't always think about the total impact of your actions before you take them. You are a "run out in traffic before you look both ways" decision maker, which can cost you precious money and time. You need to learn to solicit feedback from the franchise support staff so you don't get flattened in traffic.

You may resist following processes, which can dramatically increase your risk in business. You'd rather be unrestricted in your movements to create a result. This will make it difficult for the franchisor to be able to support you properly as you'd rather create your own system.

You seldom do the same thing twice. You are so creative that you are constantly inventing new ways to serve your customers. You run the risk of changing the winning formula, making yourself less effective. You need to learn how to create a business rhythm.

You form strong opinions and resist checking out perceptions against the facts. You just assume you're right and take off.

You are trusting and people may take advantage of you.

You are optimistic and may overlook information that indicates a problem; therefore, you miss opportunities to head off problems before they occur. You can confuse "feeling good" with creating great results.

You don't always say everything that's on your mind in order to avoid a conflict. You tend to hold back "negative" information from people who can help you.

You make gut-based or feelings-based decisions and may dismiss facts if facts contrast with "feelings." You don't always check opinions against facts.

You will go off on tangents and waste time. You are so creative that you can lose your focus.

You are probably highly disorganized and typically weak with details and financial numbers. Your motto is "Data Schmata! Let's go sell!"

You love spending money and may struggle with budgeting and containing costs.

You may have a tendency to focus on the top line (revenues) and ignore the bottom line (cash flow).

Your Ideal Franchise ...

Is known for building rock-solid franchisee–franchisor relationships. Join a franchise that gives you ample opportunity to network with and learn from other franchisees.

Offers a product or service you're passionate about, that you can enthusiastically market and sell.

Leverages your creativity and ability to build repeat customers.

Is your idea of a fun time.

Is informal in nature, highly entrepreneurial, possibly resembling the culture of a family business.

Is led by a CEO with a democratic leadership style where you have the opportunity to voice your opinion.

Isn't a low-margin/high-transaction business "penny profit" (such as fast food) that relies on an owner's ability to tightly manage the cost the side of the business. Your strengths are driving sales, not containing costs.

Is simplistic, structured, and methodical, compensating for your weak organizational skills.

Possesses a competitive point of difference that relies on your natural abilities to sell, promote, and network within the community (such as the "quick sign" industry).

Is a "flashy" franchise with great "country club" appeal, which appeals to your ego.

Offers freedom from tight external controls; a franchise that lets their franchisees find their own way while at the same time maintains the integrity of the brand.

You Are a Faithful Sidekick If ...

You're a warm, dependable, good-natured, structured, methodical, systems-oriented, open-minded, consistent, persistent, level-headed, pragmatic, objective, sincere, and empathetic team player. Like Comedians, Faithful Sidekicks are people-oriented, but unlike Comedians, are more introverted and less emotional. Where Comedians are driven by having fun and attaining social recognition, Sidekicks are driven by the need for security, stability, and belonging. Sidekicks need to see how they fit into the inner workings of a franchise and what role they'll play. Resistant to change, they make slow, informed, and emotionally agonizing decisions about whether or not to start a business. Having a natural tendency to "play not to lose" rather than "playing to win," they seek to eliminate risk and miss opportunities in the process. They're known to be highly detailed, organized, slow-paced, and patient. Having the gift of objectivity, they can see both sides of an issue. They are the best listeners and the easiest to get along with of all the four characters. Since they are introverted and prefer a predictable environment, they're often seen as timid, possessive, risk-averse, and resistant to change.

Your Value in Business

You are objective and you can see all sides of issues. You make level-headed and carefully thought-out business decisions.

You are methodical and process driven. No one has probably ever accused you of being a rebel. You will spend more time memorizing a franchisor's operations manual than trying to rewrite it ... which will be welcomed by most franchisors.

You function well within a structured environment. You will follow the franchise system as it was written.

You have great listening skills and a good memory.

You are empathetic and people like you.

You are a team player and an excellent team builder. Members of your team see their own value.

You are a communicator. You keep others in the loop.

You are a servant leader. Customers will go away satisfied and happy.

You're easy to talk to and relate to.

You are highly analytical and you will study the numbers and performance criteria of a business.

You are persistent and consistent. Once you tap into the "winning hand" of a business, you will play that hand again and again, without getting bored or feeling like you have to change it.

You know how to build quality relationships with your customers, employees, and franchisor.

You have strong customer skills or aptitudes. Being good at soliciting feedback, you will listen to your customers needs.

You are a "Steady Eddie," and your business will function with precision.

What Will Kill You If You Aren't Careful

You struggle with multitasking. You like to do one thing at a time and complete a task before you start the next one. Unfortunately, small businesses are typically not linear and every day new stuff happens. You have to be able to change your daily action plan on the fly, which doesn't play into your strengths.

You experience a high degree of fear of the unknown. Fear can sometimes paralyze you. You have to learn how to walk with fear as a companion much in the same way a recovering alcoholic walks with urge to drink but doesn't act on it. You will need to learn not to make fear mean anything or allow it to stop you from plowing forward.

You have high security and stability needs and are uncomfortable in ambiguity. In business, you will face many ambiguous moments requiring you to assume more risk than you are comfortable facing.

You need time alone to decompress. You may find it hard to decompress.

You prefer a slow-paced environment. The goal in business however, is to create a fast-paced environment where the cash register is ringing constantly.

You can be overly persistent and possessive. You have to learn that there are times to cut and run.

You're quiet and diplomatic. With most franchisors, the squeaky wheel gets the grease. If you aren't receiving the support you need, you'll need to overcome your natural tendency to avoid a conflict and either get loud and angry like an Action Hero or get up on your soapbox and preach like the Comedian. Franchisors, of course, don't like this, but many franchisees do this because it works.

Your Ideal Franchise ...

Is a stable business and not prone to dramatic swings because of seasonality, the economy, or other conditions outside your control.

Sells products or services that are necessities rather than luxuries and is stable rather than trendy. Examples would include such things as house cleaning and dry cleaning.

Plays into your customer service strengths, like specialty retail.

Is a repeat customer business, allowing you to build rock-solid relationships, like hair care.

Allows you to pace your day like automotive care, and isn't prone to customer rushes, like flower shops on Valentine's Day.

Has an established and identifiable brand. Let's face it, you aren't a promoter. You are more comfortable behind the counter than outside on the sidewalk. Look for a business where the Comedians and Action Heroes have already built the brand and you do what you do best: maintaining the integrity of the brand.

Has an outstanding reputation for maintaining excellent franchisee–franchisor relations. You enjoy being a member of a high-performance team.

Generates fewer transactions but does generate high ticket/high margins. You may not multitask well or fare well in a fast-paced environment. You need a "tortoise business" where slow and steady wins the race.

Creates happy customers. You may not enjoy a business such as transmission repair where many customers feel like they are being ripped off. You would do better with a business like ice cream where everyone is smiling all of the time.

Is either advertising or location driven, meaning your customers come to you. You aren't exactly the type who will wear holes in your shoes from beating the streets cold calling.

You Are a Private Eye If ...

You're a precise, exact, focused, detailed, neat, systematic, polite, logical, professional, open-minded, and slow-paced character. You are the most analytical, compliant, and methodical of the four characters. Private Eyes are driven by an internal need for perfection and want clear instructions about what's expected of them. Your motto is "Tell me how you want it done and I'll do it." You are task oriented and once you are clear about what's expected, you become self-directed. Unlike Action Heroes who seek control over others, you prefer to work alone. You pride yourself on being informed, pouring through information, and analyzing data prior to making any type of decision. Because Private Eyes are introverted and prefer to work alone, you can be seen as aloof, critical, and antisocial. Because Private Eyes need more details and information than the other three characters before being able to make a decision, you also can be seen as missing the big picture, fearful, risk-averse, and resistant to change.

Your Value in Business

You are objective and open to new information.

You are methodical and process driven.

You are quality driven. Your customers will be amazed at your level of conscientiousness and pride of service. They will have a hard time finding a business that cares about each transaction the way you do.

You function well within a structured environment. You follow the franchise system, even if you aren't in total agreement with the structure or system. You adapt well. No one has probably ever said about you, "You know that [insert your name]. He/she is always bucking the system!"

You have great listening skills and you remember details. You're a genius with detail. You categorize everything like the library's Dewey Decimal System and know where everything is.

You seem to know everything about everything. And what you don't know, you know where to go to find out.

You find holes in any system, and have the uncanny ability to spot what's missing. You are brilliant at creating processes and procedures that plug these holes.

You are diplomatic. You walk and speak softly.

You are highly analytical and an Einstein with numbers.

You are persistent and consistent. People can count on you to do what you say you are going to do by when you said you were going to do it.

You work at a steady pace and are self directed.

You gather information and make data-based decisions.

What Will Kill You if You Aren't Careful

You struggle with many of the same issues as the Faithful Sidekick, so refer back to their list. Additionally:

You prefer to be alone. Your ideal franchise business would be "light housekeeper," but they don't have one. Being alone means *you are the business*. If you aren't working, you aren't getting paid. And when you are working delivering a product or service, it means you aren't marketing for new customers. By your nature, you resist building a team.

You struggle with multitasking. You like to do one thing at a time and complete one task before you start the next one. As we said with the Sidekick, small businesses are typically not linear and every day new stuff happens. You have to be able to change your daily action plan on the fly, which doesn't play to your strengths.

You struggle with fear. You have to learn how to walk with fear as a companion much in the same way a recovering alcoholic walks with urges to drink but doesn't act on it. You need to learn not to make fear mean anything or allow it to stop you from plowing forward.

You need time alone to download. You may find it hard to download during the day.

You can get so caught up in the details, you miss the big picture. You can lose sight of what the details add up to and what the details mean.

Because you are a perfectionist, you can spend too much time on a given transaction. You need to learn what is "good enough to satisfy the customer" rather than always trying to achieve inner perfection. Once you have the quality required to satisfy the customer, move on. It is better to be high volume and excellent than low volume and perfect.

You may be seen as aloof, anti-social, and difficult to do business with.

Your Ideal Franchise ...

Is highly structured and systematic. All you need to do is execute.

Is advertising driven, not direct sales driven. Let's face it. You aren't going to cold call. You need a business where customers are finding you through advertising, the Internet, or the Yellow Pages.

Has few or no employees. You prefer to work alone.

Has limited customer interface. As long as you get the job done well, on time, and on budget, that's enough. You aren't the one who's going to schmooze your customers at the bar during happy hour.

Gives you the down time you need to decompress and allows you to mentally prepare for each customer interface.

Differentiates from its competitors by the quality of products and services offered. You are meticulous and quality driven. Make this work for you.

Tracks and offers easy access to all key performance indicators of the business. You manage by analysis. You need the data to analyze.

Specializes in one product or service. You pride yourself as an expert, not a generalist. Find a franchise that is well known for one particular product or service.

Is technical in nature. You are a technical genius; make it work for you.

Has fewer transactions, but is high ticket and high margin. You are built for comfort, not for speed.

What Character Do You Play?

We described these typecast actors like you were all one character and none of the others. While most people tend to act according to one dominant style, they typically exhibit the characteristics of two styles. Also, people's style varies in intensity from individual to individual. Chances are when you read the descriptions, you found at least one character you completely identified with and another that you sometimes do and sometimes don't. You probably also identified one or more characters whom you regularly have conflicts with. For instance, Faithful Sidekicks and Action Heroes struggle to get along. Private Eyes and Comedians also have difficulty relating. When you study style differences

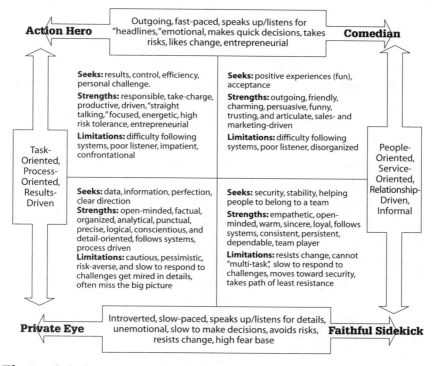

Figure 3-1. Summarizing behavior styles

you will typically discover two things.

1. People whose typecast actors are different than ours have skill sets (or a particular genius) we don't have. If you start a franchise it's wise to surround yourself with different actors who possess different skills and have a different take on the business. They will contribute to you in a way you can't begin to imagine. However ...

2. We are too busy conflicting with or judging others whose style is different from ours to appreciate their gifts and getting around to bringing them on our team. As a result, we mostly hire and surround ourselves with people just like us, killing diversity and limiting what's possible.

When interacting with the same characters as their own dominant character, Action Heroes, Comedians, Faithful Sidekicks, or Private Eyes can communicate effectively. However, communication breakdowns occur when one character converses with a *different* kind of character. Let's look at an example.

Imagine that we're in an office and about to watch an Action Hero department head interact with a Faithful Sidekick subordinate. Let's assume the Action Hero has just returned from a meeting with his vice president to discuss reorganizing his department.

The Faithful Sidekick, who seeks a stable environment and likes to prepare mentally for change, asks, "What happened during the meeting?" and listens for the details about what was discussed. Being an Action Hero, however, the manager doesn't offer any details, just "headlines." The Action Hero responds, "We talked about some changes in our department."

Because the Faithful Sidekick doesn't receive the details he was listening for, he probes by asking more questions, such as "What types of changes?" "Who will be impacted?" "What are you looking to achieve?" "When will changes occur?" "What do we need to do to prepare?" and so on.

The Action Hero, who likes to control conversations and has difficulty listening or explaining details, becomes frustrated with the Faithful Sidekick, making a melodrama called "I'm Being Bombarded by Stupid Questions!" Since the Action Hero is quick to exhibit impatience, he snaps and says, "Don't worry about it. When I'm ready to announce it, I'll announce it!"

Since the Faithful Sidekick seeks stability, security, and belonging, he makes a melodrama called "My Stupid Hothead Boss Just Singled Me Out and Put Me Down!"

Since the Faithful Sidekick usually shrinks from conflict instead of addressing it head on, he doesn't go back to his manager to communicate how he was offended. He waits for the Action Hero to recognize his improper treatment and apologize.

Because the Action Hero is more task-oriented than people-oriented, he is oblivious to the fact that a personal issue now exists with the Sidekick, and therefore never resolves the issue. The Sidekick, who values relationships, remains dumbfounded as to why the Action Hero never apologized for his outburst. Rather than confronting his manager, he harbors a grudge and gossips about the Action Hero to other employees, which creates a disruption in the office.

Both parties share a profound negative experience because neither party was responsible for the impact of their typecast actor on the other.

If the Action Hero understood the needs of the Faithful Sidekick, he would have taken the time to explain the necessity for change and given the Sidekick ample opportunity to ask questions and acclimate.

If the Faithful Sidekick understood the needs of the Action Hero, he would have made an appointment to speak to the Action Hero, set an agenda for that conversation, and prepared the Action Hero in advance with the concerns he had and the types of questions he would ask during that meeting. The Sidekick would have also had a direct conversation with the Action Hero explaining how he was offended, not expecting the Action Hero to already know. Since Action Heroes are responsible people, the Sidekick would have then received the apology he wanted and the situation would be resolved.

What if ...

The Action Hero built a powerful relationship with the Sidekick and regularly consulted him to hear both sides of issues, to check out opinions against the facts, to get feedback on issues involving how to approach different types of people, and other areas where the Action Hero is weak. How much more effective would the Action Hero be with the Sidekick's help and support?

The key to effectively communicate with any of these characters is to understand and speak to their individual communication styles. The key to performance is to know your characters' genius and weaknesses. Align your genius to what's required to succeed in any given franchise and compensate for your weaknesses by hiring other characters. Respect and celebrate these differences and you'll build a high-performance team.

How Can I Predict Others' Styles?

You can predict someone's style with a high degree of accuracy by asking yourself two basic questions.

Question 1: Does this person appear outgoing, emotional, and expressive or introverted, distant, and reserved?

- ▶ If they appear more outgoing, emotional, and expressive, then you know your candidate is either an Action Hero or a Comedian.
- ▶ If they appear more introverted and reserved, then you know your candidate is either a Private Eye or a Faithful Sidekick.

If your candidate is outgoing, emotional, and expressive, then ask

Question 2: Is the candidate informal and friendly or professional and businesslike?

- ▶ If the candidate is professional and businesslike, you're probably dealing with an Action Hero.

▶ If the candidate is more informal and friendly, you're probably dealing with a Comedian.

In Summary

There are no "right" or "wrong" styles; styles just are. However, you'll have a false experience that your style is right and other styles are less effective, which is why, left to their own resources, franchisees will hire employees just like them. This diminishes their ability to build a high-performance team, decreases their results, and increases their risk.

Consider there are no right or wrong styles for franchising in general, *but there are right and wrong styles* for individual franchise opportunities. As you investigate franchises, you'll see that top performers have similar styles as other top performers and underperformers have a tendency to exhibit similar styles as other underperformers. One predictor of how you'll perform in any given franchise system is to determine how people just like you perform. You'll have a high probability of achieving similar results.

Many franchisors use behavior or values profiles to help them evaluate whether a candidate fits the profile of a successful franchisee or is a culture fit for the company. Don't be surprised if you're requested to complete a profile. Others use "gut instincts" or don't care either way. Let the buyer beware. When talking to franchisees of the systems you'll be evaluating, use the information in this chapter to help you identify the commonalities between your and top performing franchisees.

4

What Does Winning Look Like?

ome from another long business trip, Ken dragged himself out of the car, pulled his suitcase out of the trunk, fiddled to find his house keys, and opened the door to his home. "Home at last," he thought. As he walked into his kitchen, his two-year-old son Mitchell stared at him in horror. Terrified of "the stranger" who unexpectedly "broke into" his home, Mitchell ran and hid behind his mother for safety. In that moment Ken made a

bold decision. "I will not be a stranger to my children." With that decision, Ken was one step closer to owning a franchise. Months later, Ken was franchisee of a home-based consulting business.

Remember how Zig Ziglar said, "People don't buy drill bits; they buy holes"? Ziglar asserts that people don't want the tool; they want the results. Carrying that point forward, it's our opinion that people don't buy franchises, they invest in a desired future. Ken didn't want a business. Ken wanted to be a dad. His franchise was the drill. Before you even think about a franchise, you must ask yourself, "What am I drilling for?"

In his landmark book *The 7 Habits of Highly Effective People,* Stephen Covey saw that before highly effective people engage in activities, they create a clear vision of their desired outcome. Their tasks and conversations are then designed to bring that vision about.

Makes sense. Would you ever consider hiring a remodeling contractor who tells you he doesn't work from a set of blueprints or drawings? Instead, he says, "I just wing it. Our crew just shows up one day, rips down some walls, hammers nails into boards, slops some paint on the walls, and sees what happens from there."

Yet isn't this exactly how most people live and work? We engage in so many conversations and feverish activities that we lose sight of what we want to accomplish. We forget to pause to see if we are heading toward the destination we desire.

Franchising is all about producing results and creating a desired future. Investing in a franchise affords you an opportunity for deep personal and career transformation, allowing you to make a clean break from the past and create a new, safe, and sustainable asset and income stream for yourself and your family.

When franchisees are *not* producing great results (assuming they have the necessary knowledge, skills, and capital to potentially win), the culprit is usually one of two things: They don't have specific goals, or they have goals but don't allocate enough (or any) time to achieving those goals. Thus, by learning effective goal-setting and time management techniques now, you can prevent most performance issues from arising in the future. Goal setting and time management are essential building blocks of successful franchising.

Goal Setting and Benchmarks

Before you research any franchises, you should set three- and five-year goals. Goals must be both financial and "quality of life" (or nonfinancial) in nature. Financial goals should take into account cash flow, savings, net worth, equity build-up, and spendable income. Quality of life goals should take into account lifestyle issues that are important to you, like having dinner at home three nights a week, being able to take vacations, attend soccer games, make a difference in the community, and so on. Don't overlook quality of life goals or you're setting yourself up to be sorely dissatisfied. Quality of life goals are more important than financial goals. Why? Because many people who invest in a franchise have already made a decent living in the past. Aside from earning a paycheck, however, they couldn't find a compelling reason to go to work in the morning. Money alone was not enough to keep them going, and money won't hold your interest long either. While you'll have some minimum threshold of earnings that you won't dare venture below, once that threshold is exceeded, you'll find that your quality of life then becomes the driver.

Virtually all franchisors have key performance criteria that help you and them determine whether your business is winning. You'll no doubt be taught how to track sales, labor cost, cost of sales, and other statistical measures. Franchisors design their business and support systems to help you structure your business to achieve these measures and monitor results. However, we know of no franchisors that measure and track how many meals you've eaten with your children or how many of the kids' soccer games you've attended, nor should they. Franchisors measure your success by their definition of success, not yours. Most franchisors have no clue as to whether or not their "successful" franchisees are living the life they originally desired when they invested in the franchise. Franchisors follow the money.

So it should be clear that it's solely your responsibility to create a clear definition of the financial and quality of life goals that outline what winning looks like for you. Use your definition of winning as your criteria to compare franchise opportunities. The franchise where you have the highest probability of attaining both your financial and quality of life goals is the franchise you invest in.

Perhaps at one time you've participated in a goal-setting exercise and you may be thinking about glossing over this chapter. Pause for a second. Often in times of loss or radical change, like the loss of a previously secure job or collapse of the stock market, one's outlook changes and therefore goals change. The right goals will call you forward into action and fill your day with purposeful inspiration.

It's easy to lose sight of your goals. Prospective franchisees often get caught up in their perceptions of the problems and challenges of the business rather than if the franchise can help them achieve their objectives with a high degree of probability.

For instance, you may be investigating a residential home cleaning business and from talking to franchisees you hear there's high employee turnover. Afraid that you may get stuck cleaning houses, you think, "My mother didn't send me to college so I can clean toilets and vacuum carpets." Or you think, "Anyone can push a vacuum. In this economy, people will return to cleaning their own houses." Your knee-jerk reaction may then be to dismiss the opportunity. However, whether there's employee turnover or how many people vacuum their own homes isn't the real issue at hand. Given employee turnover and the current state of the economy, your focal point should still be whether your goals can be achieved with a high degree of probability. Therefore, goal-focused prospective franchisees will dig deeper and ask such questions as ...

- ▶ What are the franchisor's hiring and retention strategies?
- ▶ What's the impact of turnover on the business?
- ▶ How long does it take to find replacement help?
- ▶ What training programs are in place to train replacement labor?
- ▶ How long does it take a new hire to be productive?
- ▶ What's the trajectory of existing franchisees' businesses?
- ▶ How is the economy impacting sales and profitability?

What Does
Winning Look Like?

Every franchise has its unique challenges that must be overcome. Franchisors either have proven systems and a demonstrated track record for overcoming these challenges or not. Dismiss those that don't. Investigate those that do by asking questions like the ones above. The most important part of your investigation is to thoroughly interview and visit many existing franchisees. We show you how in detail in chapter 9.

Goals Schmoals! Why Should I Care About Goals!

Mark McCormack, in his book *What They Don't Teach You at Harvard Business School*, tells of a Harvard study conducted between 1979 and 1989. In 1979, the graduates of the MBA program were asked, "Have you set clear, written goals for your future and made plans to accomplish them?" Only 3 percent of the graduates had written goals and plans. Thirteen percent had goals, but not in writing. And 84 percent had no specific goals at all.

Ten years later, in 1989, the researchers found that the 13 percent who had nonwritten goals were earning twice as much as the 84 percent of students who had no goals at all. And most surprisingly, they found that the 3 percent of graduates who had clear, written goals when they left Harvard were earning, on average, 10 times as much as the other 97 percent of graduates all together!

Keep in mind, there are no dummies in Harvard, so students' intelligence level was a constant, not a variable in this study. The variable was whether clear, written goals were set with plans to accomplish them.

Clear goals, whether financial or quality of life in nature, must pass the S.M.A.R.T. test.

Specific. Goals need to be clearly articulated and written down. "Making a lot of money" is not specific. Making $200,000 is specific. "Having more money for retirement" is not specific. "Building a business asset worth $500,000" is.

Measurable. You have to be able to create a tracking system, a method of keeping score. This lets you know if you're on track and if you've hit your goals. If your goal is to make $200,000 by the end of the year, on June 30 you should have earned $100,000 or you may not be on track. On December 31, you either hit your income goals or not. It isn't open to opinion or speculation. Using the previous example, if you attended 11 Little League games, you won. If you went to 6, you fell short. It isn't open to interpretation or opinion.

Attainable. Goals must be considered both possible and a worthwhile pursuit, or you won't be motivated to achieve them. For instance, you may say your goal is to make $1 million a year, but if you have never made more than $100,000 a year, you may not really see this goal as possible. Therefore, you won't really take aggressive steps toward achieving it.

Relevant. Goals must speak to your current situation, be consistent with your values, be worthy of attainment, and inspire you into action. As a franchisee you may want to experience a 20 percent increase in sales, but if you think it is going to take working 90 to 100 hours a week to achieve that goal and the reason you started the business was to spend more time with your family, you may not consider it a worthwhile pursuit.

Time Bound. Goals have to have a deadline ... a hard, cold "by when" date. Goals without a deadline don't inspire commitment. It's human nature not to take action on anything you wish to achieve "some day." Think of how long you have thought about starting a franchise. Do you have a deadline as to when you will be open by? If not, other more urgent activities will take precedence and your dream will be pushed back further and further.

If you don't have deadline as to when you're going to start, then you may have a good intention, but you don't have a plan or a goal. A wise person once said, "The road to hell is paved with good intentions." Good intentions don't make a difference; committed action does. You will never be called forward into committed action without a specific, measurable, attainable, relevant, and time-limited goal that's worthy of being achieved. Activities with deadlines attached to them grab your attention and create a sense of urgency and action. For instance, you know you have to get your taxes done by April 15. If your goal is to get your taxes done on time, April 14 will be a very productive day for you!

Goals with deadlines that are too far out also don't inspire action. Think about something in your life that you wish would occur within the next 20 years. Are you taking action now? Think about when you bought your home. Did you think, "Here is where I am going to live for the next 30 years," or did you think, "This home is ideal for now." You aren't wired to think more than three to seven years out. Goals with extended timelines are as useless as goals that you want to achieve "some day" because they don't inspire action. As it relates to franchising, consider setting long-term goals with a three- to five-year time limit.

Making Your Desired Future S.M.A.R.T

Go back to the worksheet in chapter 2 entitled "Creating Your Desired Future." You were challenged to identify and prioritize your "must haves" and "want to haves" in your life and career. Now is the time to tie down your desires and make a commitment.

My "Must Haves" (highest-priority objectives and absolute necessities)	By when do you commit to achieving this?
My "Wish to Haves" (high-priority objectives but not necessities)	By when do you commit to achieving this?

By assigning short deadlines as to when you will achieve your goals and objectives, you create urgency. Urgency creates action and commitment. Action and commitment generate results.

> Remember the Harvard study. Your goals need to be clearly articulated, written down, and revisited constantly!

As a franchisee, it still isn't enough to have S.M.A.R.T. goals. Goals must be broken down into monthly, weekly, and daily targets.

> We can't overemphasize the importance of having daily targets.

Thinking about annual or even monthly goals can be intimidating for many franchisees. A franchisees' day moves fast and furiously. Sometimes it's hard to carve out enough time to think beyond one day.

But when goals are broken down into daily chunks, even the biggest annual goals seem more doable. Business appears less daunting when you work a daily plan for attaining daily targets. Franchisees who approach business this way have the luxury of working one day at a time without having to look too far into the future. They go into the day knowing that their daily targets are aimed at attaining their monthly benchmarks; their monthly benchmarks are aimed at attaining their year-end goals; and their year-end goals are aligned with attaining their three- to five-year goals. Therefore, by attaining today's targets, they are attaining their three- to five-year goals. All they need to do is wake up and do it again.

For instance, a franchisee may have a goal of increasing sales $50,000 this year by increasing its customer base. Assume each customer is worth $100. Therefore, the franchisee knows they must find 500 new customers this year. On the surface, this appears to be a daunting task. However, when looked at weekly, the franchisee must find about 10 new customers. When looked at daily (assuming a Monday through Friday–type of business) the franchisee must find two customers per business day. When chunked down to daily targets, the $50,000 increase all of a sudden doesn't seem as daunting or unattainable. The franchisee is left empowered to design activities to bring two more customers in the door or make the phone ring two more times. Once the second customer calls or walks in, the franchisee has achieved the objective. If they choose, they can stop for the day and focus on something else. Tomorrow, all they need to do is to wake up and do it again.

Many people, as they investigate starting a franchise, look out and see all the things that have to make happen just to get started and then look further and see all the things that need to happen to become successful. They become intimidated by what appears to be an impossible, Herculean task.

How Do You Eat an Elephant?

Taken as a whole, a big goal can appear to be impossible, just as eating an elephant would seem impossible. Big goals need to be approached one bite at a time. If you keep taking one bite at a time, eventually the elephant disappears. You will look back thinking, "Where did the elephant go?" It's the same with franchising.

A great franchisor understands that, left to your own resources, you will try to eat the elephant of business success all in one bite and choke. The franchisor presents the goals in bite-sized pieces and feeds you one bite at a time. If you get too far ahead of yourself worrying about such things as, "What about the ears? What about the legs? What about the trunk? What about ..."

"Shhh," they will say to you. "It isn't polite to talk with your mouth full. After you swallow what's in your mouth, take another bite."

Weak, unskilled, and unsophisticated franchisors will just show you the whole elephant and hand you their version of a knife, fork, and bib. "Have at it!" they say, "You have my number. Call me if you choke." A franchisor whose only value to their franchisees is that from time to time they perform the Heimlich maneuver and dislodge elephant chunks isn't earning their franchisee fees or royalties.

Effective Time Management

Chances are, at some time in your life, you've taken a time management class, read about time management in books, and learned to use either an electronic or paper-based day planner to organize, prioritize, and schedule your day. "Why, with this knowledge, and these gadgets," you ask yourself, "do I still feel like I can't get everything done I need to?" The answer is simple. Everything you ever learned about managing time is a complete waste of time because it doesn't work.

You have bought into time management gadgets and systems the same way other poor souls have been suckered into buying worthless swamp land in Florida or toll bridges in New York. We aren't saying time management gurus are dishonest people who are out to take your money. They are noble men and women who no doubt seek to make a difference in the lives of others. But if you were to have an honest conversation with time management and other self-help gurus, you'd find that they don't get everything done either.

So, you're waist deep in the middle of the muck and mire of a massive time conspiracy that you're just waking up to. The good news is that in this chapter you'll learn how to pull yourself out.

Before you can even begin to manage time, you must find know what time is. It would seem logical that you can't manage something if you don't know it when you see it. So, what is time?

Merriam-Webster's dictionary defines time as "the point or period at which things occur." Put simply, time is when stuff happens.

There are two types of time: clock time and real time. In clock time, there are 60 seconds in a minute, 60 minutes in an hour, 24 hours in a day, 365 days in a year, and so forth. All time passes equally. When someone turns 50 years old, they are exactly 50 years old, no more or no less.

In real time, all time is relative. Time flies or drags depending on what you're doing. For instance, two hours at the Motor Vehicle Department feels like 12 years. And yet our 12-year-old children seem to have grown up in only two hours. If you were to ask a person who just turned 50, "How old you would be if you didn't know how old you are?" chances are you would hear a number that's less than their actual age.

Which time describes the world in which you really live, real time or clock time?

The reason time management gadgets and systems don't work is that these systems are designed to manage clock time. Clock time is irrelevant. You don't live in or even have access to clock time. You live in real time, a world in which all time flies when you are having fun or drags when you are visiting your in-laws. Additionally, real time is mental; it exists between your ears. You create it. Anything you create, you can manage. In this chapter we dispel clock time myths and teach you the seven truths about real time. We wish to remove any self-sabotage or self-limitation you have around "not having enough time," or today not being "the right time" to start a business.

The Seven Truths About Real Time

Truth #1: Everything happens now.

Chances are, you now relate to time as if you are standing in the middle of a timeline.

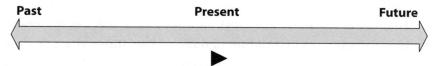

Past   **Present**   **Future**

You think you are here facing this direction

You "look back" on the past, like the past is somehow behind you. You "look forward" into the future as if it is in the distance, and you are marching toward it. You relate to the future as if it's a destination, like a city on a map, like it is a place you have to get to.

However ...

The past is in the past. It is gone; you will never have that moment back. The past is a spent resource.

The future is an illusion because the future as the future never occurs. Eventually, the future will be now and then it will be past. Every past moment once occurred as a present moment. The future will enter the universe as a present moment. You can't live in either the past or the future. Therefore, all you have is now. All you ever had was now. All you are going to have is now. All life happens, all work occurs, all results are achieved now. Whether you succeed in franchising is a direct result of how you choose to spend this very moment ... and the next moment ... and the next moment after that. If you aren't taking action now to achieve the life and career you desire, you are designing a future now that assures that this life and career never occurs. The time line is a time lie. Wake up! Stop living and working a lie and start living and working now!

Once upon a time there lived a true time management master named Christine. Christine had not always been a time management master. Most of her life she struggled to manage clock time just like us. She spent most of her life engaged in thoughts, activities, and conversations, which, looking back on it, really didn't matter. But one day, Christine had to go the hospital to have a routine gall bladder operation. After the operation, the surgeon informed her that although her gall bladder operation was a success, in the process he discovered that she had cancer. The cancer had advanced, attacking and destroying most of her major internal organs. There was nothing more that the doctor could do. He projected that Christine had about two more years to live.

After a period of brokenhearted shock, Christine quickly regrouped, committing to do the most with the little time she had left. She spoke simply and directly, for miscommunication wasted time. She spoke openly and honestly, for pretense wasted time. She loved and forgave, for judging and resenting wasted time. Rather than wallow in self-pity, Christine invested time in being present to the simple joy of being alive.

Christine did not invest her time brooding over what her life could have been. Instead she lived moment to moment, accepting and making the most out of what was.

Because Christine was so accepting of her disease, someone once asked her, "What is it like for you to wake up every morning knowing that you are so close to death?"

Without thinking she lovingly responded to that person by asking another question, "What is it like for you to wake up every morning pretending that you aren't?"

She went on to say that when she finally accepted and embraced death, she experienced life. She saw life as a priceless and precious gift that other people were afraid to open. She possessed a screaming desire to tell people to rip open the box and enjoy what's inside. She said that when she tried to get that message across to people, they didn't seem to get it.

Make sure you aren't one of them.

Consider for a second that your life is like a basketball game. You are standing on the court and your game clock is ticking. God is the timekeeper and He will not stop the game clock. At some point the buzzer will sound and your game will be over. Take a look around and see how others are playing their game.

Some people play as if they're frozen; they hold the ball and are afraid to shoot. Others pass the ball, hoping someone else will shoot the ball for them. Still others simply sit on the bench, either living inside the empty promise of "I'll get into the game someday," or waiting for their clock to run out with no expectation of ever playing.

Make sure that none of them is be you.

Don't waste your life watching the clock tick or pretending there is no clock. Don't hold the ball or pass it off to anyone else. Certainly don't sit on the bench, waiting for someone to give you permission to play your game.

This is your game to win or lose, so take a shot.

Franchisees Take a Shot

As their ball soars through the air toward their intended target, they experience the fullness of their life and work. Others hold the ball, pass the ball off, sit on the bench, or take their ball and go home. They experience a sort of death by compromise.

Consider that your game has only two certainties. The first certainty is that you will miss 100 percent of the shots you don't take. The second is that your game will end. If you were going to take a shot with your life and career, what would that shot be?

Consider that if you take that shot, you must learn to live with risk. If you hold or pass the ball, you must learn to live with regret. If you sit on the bench or take your ball and go home, you must learn to live with apathy.

Of risk, regret, and apathy, which do you choose to live with? Christine chose risk. By doing so, she reaped a mental and emotional wellness and spiritual fulfillment that far exceeded the limitations of her physical illness.

If you choose a career in franchising, you are choosing a life with risk ... delicious, exciting, nerve-racking, nail-biting, life-altering, "I can't wait to see what today brings" kind of risk. Risk, while certainly scary, may be the least scary of all the available options in the end.

Take a moment and fast forward to the end of your game ... the end of your life. Consider a life in which you never took your shot. Will you have peace or regret?

Truth #2: We Fill 'Now' With Three Things

There are only three ways to spend time: thoughts, conversations, and actions. Regardless of the franchise system you choose, the system will be composed of three things: thoughts, conversations, and actions. A masterful franchisor is one who has taken the time to identify and document all the thoughts, conversations, and actions a franchisee must be engaged in to win. Additionally, these franchisors know how to give these thoughts, conversations, and actions away to new franchisees, eventually helping them think, speak, and act expertly for themselves. Let's look at thoughts, conversations, and actions individually.

Thoughts. What do peak-performing franchisees think about? How do they view their businesses? What do they think about their customers? How do they relate to their products or services? Suppliers? Other franchisees? The franchisor's support staff? Themselves? Their future? Winners have similar thoughts as other winners. Underperformers also think alike. They focus much of their mental energy worrying about things outside of their control, like state of the economy. If you identify with the mindset of a winner and make their mindset your mindset, you're positioned to win, too.

Conversations. What conversations do winning franchisees need to be engaged in? Whom should they be talking to? About what? What should they be listening for? What needs to happen as a result of those conversations? Peak-performing franchisees have conversations that matter with customers, employees, and other people who can further their business.

Sales calls, for instance, are a conversation. Management and delegating are also primarily done in the form of conversation. Regardless of the franchise system, most top-performing franchisees are excellent communicators. They may not all be charismatic, but they all know how to listen with understanding and how to be understood. They know the high-priority conversations that drive the business, such as networking conversations. Underperforming franchisees waste time engaged in meaningless conversations with people who don't impact their business or about topics that don't make a difference. When you investigate franchises, find out whom those high-priority conversations are with and what they're about in each system you consider. If you don't consider yourself a good communicator, consider that great communicators weren't born great communicators. Up to the age of two, they all said, "Goo-goo, da-da, bah-bah" and a host of other nonsense syllables. Great communication requires great training. Nonprofit organizations such as Toastmasters and for-profit companies like Dale Carnegie (a franchised company) offer training to help you build your skills.

Actions. What do peak performers do that average or underperformers don't do? What are the high-priority activities that drive results? What are a winner's habits? Find out how peak performers spend their day and replicate it in your business. Peak performing franchisees know what the leverage points of their business are and spend their time focused on the key activities that drive all results. Underperforming franchisees get mired in the minutiae of the business and trap themselves by doing busy work that doesn't have a major impact on results.

Consider all actions and conversations have one thing in common: They all originate in thought. Thoughts drive conversations and actions, which means thought is the most important of the three ways to spend time because it generates the other two. We aren't saying you should climb to the top of a mountain, sit in a lotus position, stay there all day and expect to be successful. However, we are saying you will never speak and act like a peak performer within a particular franchise until you learn how to think like a peak performer.

However, most franchisors will only train you in how their winners speak and act. The majority of franchisors won't train you in how their winners think. Most simply don't know how important that piece is. Therefore, on completion of the franchisor's training programs, you probably will only have little more than two-thirds of the franchisor's total winning formula. Most likely, you'll be left to your own resources to put that missing critical-thinking piece in place. But putting this piece in place will be less difficult than you think. All you need to is to ask a winner, "What do you think about your customers? What do you think about your products and services? What do you think about when you plan your day? What do you think about your employees? What do you think about [fill in the blank]?" Then chose to think like they do. Make their belief system yours and their results will most likely also be yours over time.

What Does
Winning Look Like?

Truth #3: It's Never Finished

When is the last time you went to bed saying, "I got everything done. There is absolutely nothing left to do. I will now enter the restful sleep of a fully completed day."

What do the Loch Ness Monster, Easter Bunny, and fully completed days have in common? No such thing.

It's a given that there is simply not enough time to finish everything you'd like to do each day. And who says you have to? Is there some local ordinance that requires you to get everything done? Are you subject to fines or imprisonment if you don't? As we already stated, no one gets everything done every day, especially time management gurus. Do you know what Thomas Jefferson, Albert Einstein, Thomas Edison, Abraham Lincoln, Jack Kennedy, Ghandi, and Mother Theresa all have in common? None of them got it all done either.

Part of being human is to have stuff on your to-do list at the end of every day. As a franchisee you aren't going to get it all done either. But you do need to get the important things done. You need to identify and complete those high-priority activities that generate all the results.

Once, a small business owner was complaining that his sales were flat and he was overwhelmed with all the moving parts of his business. Taking an inventory of everything he did during the course of the day, he saw he accomplished at least 15 things a day, sometimes more, but always at least 15 things. His biggest challenge was he always had 25 things on his to-do list. Furthermore, most of what he accomplished had little or nothing to do with generating sales.

Not wanting to work 24 hours a day to accomplish the 25 things on his list, he decided to work smarter. When he finally accepted that he would go into every day accomplishing only 15 things without pretending he could do more, he regained his focus. Before he started every day he identified at least eight high-priority activities to generate. By only planning eight instead of 15 he realistically left time for employee and customer interruptions. He learned how to prioritize and delegate the low-priority activities that were consuming him. He regained his passion for his business and starting driving results.

Truth #4: You Waste Time

As we already stated, most of what you do, say, think about, and worry about doesn't matter. That sounds harsh, but it's accurate. Famed management consultant Dr. Joseph Juran studied what executives did every day. He found that 20 percent of an executive's activities, thoughts, and conversations produced more than 80 percent of the person's results. What's more, he found this premise held true across people and across industries. This principle applies to franchising also. Acknowledging similar research by Italian economist Vilfredo Pareto, Juran named his concept The Pareto Principle, which is also known as The 80/20 Rule.

According to Juran's hypothesis, only 20 percent of your current activities produce 80 percent of your total results. And 80 percent of your time is typically spent generating less than 20 percent of your results. Put another way, 80 percent of all time is wasted on thoughts, conversations, and activities that don't make much of a difference.

If you buy this concept, then it becomes obvious that if you become a franchisee you should identify and master those "20 percent thoughts," more "20 percent conversations," and more "20 percent activities." In his book *The 7 Habits of Highly Effective People*, Dr. Stephen Covey stated effective people make a distinction between what is urgent and what is important, and then focus on the important. For instance, answering a ringing telephone may be seem urgent, but unless the franchisee knows a customer is on end of the phone, the conversation may have no measurable impact on the financial health the business. What if the franchisee picks up the phone and finds a telemarketer who is selling vinyl siding? The conversation becomes one of the 80 percent of activities that waste a franchisee's precious time and take away from time dedicated to driving results. Compare that to handling a customer complaint in such a powerful way that the complaining customer now becomes a lifetime customer. Both may take the same amount of time, but each produces materially different results.

Regardless of the franchise you investigate, it will have a version of the 80/20 rule. There are a small number of thoughts, conversations, and actions that drive the entire business and seemingly a million thoughts, conversations, and actions a franchisee will get sucked into that chew up time and don't make a difference. Each is identifiable. As you research different franchises, keep this in mind. One strategy is to keep a simple chart.

You can best gather this information by talking with top performing franchisees of a particular system. Ask franchisees such questions as "Where should I be spending my time? What are the high-priority activities that drive most of your results?" and conversely "What activities suck you in and consume you if you aren't careful? Where can you really waste time if you aren't paying attention?"

The 20% thoughts, conversations, and activities that produce more than 80% of franchisees' results	The 80% thoughts, conversations, and activities that produce less than 20% of a franchisees' results
What are the 20% thoughts?	What are the 80% thoughts?
What are the 20% conversations?	What are the 80% conversations?
What are the 20% actions?	What are the 80% actions?

Street Smart Franchising

When we address franchisees during national conferences, seminars, or workshops, we like to ask them the following questions:

1. Given where you're spending your time right now, assuming you change nothing, in three years...
   a. How much money will you be making?
   b. Will you hit your financial goals?

2. If you spend 50 percent of your time focused on the "20 percent that produces 80 percent of the results," in three years ...
   a. How much money will you be making?
   b. Will you be working more/the same number/fewer hours?
   c. What would you do with the extra time/money?

3. If you spend 80 percent of your time focused on the "20 percent that produces 80 percent of the results," in three years ...
   a. How much money will you be making?
   b. Will you be working more/same/fewer hours?
   c. What would you do with the extra time/money?

This is an empowering exercise for a franchisee to complete. Franchisees get to say how much time they put in and where it's spent. If you become a franchisee, you will, too. You can spend your moments strategizing about how to take your business to new levels, executing brilliant conversations, and engaged in focused activities, or building expert business skills. You also can waste time in a million ways accomplishing little. Every franchisee's future results are a function of the skill and quality of the franchisee's and franchisor's thoughts, conversations, and actions taken now. Furthermore, a franchisee's current results are a direct function of the skill and quality of a franchisee's and franchisor's thoughts, conversations, and actions taken in the past.

Franchisees get to say what they did then and what they do now. Therefore, every franchisee is responsible for their own results and the author of their own life and business. And their results aren't random. Results are a function of what they're doing right now.

Truth #5: There Is No Such Thing as Multitasking

Have you ever tried to have a conversation with someone who you knew had their mind on something else? How did that make you feel? Was it a powerful and productive conversation or did you have the experience you were merely being tolerated? Did you get the results you were looking for or were you left dissatisfied?

Conversely, did you ever have a conversation with someone who gave you the experience that you were the most important person in the world right then and the entire outside world would have to wait for a moment? How did that make you feel?

Whom would you rather do business with?

What separates the first person from the second? Is it their communication skills or is it their singular focus?

Another way people deceive themselves is by believing they multitask. Computers multitask. People are only wired to hold one thought at a time. The person in the first conversation above heard about multitasking and bought that thought hook, line, and sinker. The person in the second conversation knows the truth and sees multitasking as a version of being distracted while pretending to be efficient. If you're to be a peak-performing franchisee you must:

▶ Choose to be in the conversation you are in, and
▶ Be present to the thought or activity you are currently engaged in.

Furthermore, you can practice the skills it takes to become a peak-performing franchisee right now, long before you make an investment. Practice doing one thing at a time. Master being in one conversation at a time. Pay attention to people.

With smart phones, netbooks, laptops, Facebook, Skype, and other technologies that give others instant access and competition for our attention, entrepreneurs need to learn how to hunker down, unplug, and stay focused executing the high priority activities that drive results.

Truth #6: You Determine Your Future Now (or, Why Didn't I Do This Sooner?!)

Your future is determined by the quality of your thoughts, actions, and conversations, done now. The future isn't random. It's a simple function of the quality and results of the thoughts, actions, and conversations you have every day.

When a franchisee rigorously watches what they think, say, and do, and builds on the skills with which they think, say, and do, they know exactly what their future holds in store. Their success is not random. Regardless of the economy, success and failure are functions of how franchisees choose to spend this moment and the next.

For instance, think about how long you've been thinking about starting a business. You have the inkling, but then you fill "now" up with other thoughts and activities, designing and creating some other future than the one you profess you want. When people who are thinking about starting a franchise give up on their dream, they usually blame the timing. "It's not the right time," they say. They desire more freedom and control, but only if external events are aligned to give it to them. Where is the freedom and control in that?

Conversely, the people who start franchises are generally not faced with any fewer pressures, commitments, or obligations than those who never pursue franchising. But they understand that all they have is now. "If I don't do this now," they think, "then perhaps I never will." They make a decision that this *is* the right time because they accept the responsibility for making it the right time.

Starting a franchise is much like starting a family. Originally, you want to have a nest egg, have a stable job and home, and be positioned to give your children a great life. However, as time passes, the nest egg never seems big enough, the job never seems secure enough, and so on. You realize that perhaps there is no right time. Eventually, you just throw your hands up in the air and say, "I can always find an excuse not to have children. We will find a way to make it OK." And then you start a family. You took responsibility for making it the right time, even in the face of not knowing how to do it. Somehow, you survived and things turned out OK. You look back and wonder why you waited so long.

It's the same in business. If you start a franchise, most likely you'll have to take responsibility for making now the right time, regardless of what the economy is doing. The stars typically don't align. Good timing typically doesn't randomly create itself. You can always create reasons, either real or imagined, that you'll use to convince yourself this isn't the right time. Then you'll most likely fill up your day with activities designed to make sure tomorrow isn't the right time either. Then one day, you'll look back on your life and say, "What happened? Where did my life and dreams go?" Or you can start new today. You can take matters into your hands and declare today is the right time because this is your life and you have a say in the matter. Like having children, you may not know how everything is going to work out. And like having children, you will most likely survive and look back one day and say, "Why didn't I do this sooner?"

Truth #7: Nothing Happens Exactly as Planned. Plan on It!

Think about the last time you planned an event. You covered every detail, you planned for every contingency, you thought of every angle, and then you executed your plan. Then, as the plan unfolded, people, events, and stuff started happening that you didn't plan for. You thought you planned for it all, but somehow things you didn't plan for still found their way into the equation. You adjusted what you were doing, went with the flow, and chances are although things didn't go as planned, the results were still what they needed to be. Management expert Tom Peters once said he felt much time spent on planning was overrated as nothing seems to go as planned. It either goes better or worse.

We aren't saying you shouldn't do your due diligence, develop a business plan, or create a cash flow analysis before you invest in a franchise. All these exercises are critical to developing a thorough understanding of the franchise you choose. We are saying your planning should allow for things not going as planned. For instance, most new entrepreneurs don't exactly hit the sales, cost, and cash flow projections they make when going into a business. They do better or worse.

In addition, as a franchisee you will frequently be interrupted and pulled in different directions. While you can't eliminate interruptions, you do get to say how much time you will spend on them.

You can practice the following techniques now that will position you to win as a franchisee in the future.

► Any activity or conversation that's important to your success should have a time assigned to it. To-do lists get longer and longer to the point where they're unworkable. Appointment books work. Schedule appointments with yourself and create time blocks for the high-priority thoughts, conversations, and actions. Schedule when they will begin and end. Have the discipline to keep these appointments.

► Know how long these important thoughts, conversations, and actions take. Then design them into your day.

► Schedule time for interruptions. Plan time to be pulled away from what you're doing. Take, for instance, the concept of having "office hours." Isn't "office hours" another way of saying "planned interruptions?"

► Consider carrying around a schedule and recording all your thoughts, conversations, and activities for a week. This will help you understand how much you can get done in the course of a day and where your precious moments are going. You'll see how much time is actually spent producing results and how much time is wasted on unproductive thoughts, conversations, and actions.

► Plan to spend at least 50 percent of your time engaged in the thoughts, activities, and conversations that produce most of your results.

► Take the first 30 minutes of every day to plan your day. Don't start your day until you complete your time plan. The most important time of your day is the time you schedule to schedule time.

▶ Take five minutes before every call and task to decide what result you want to attain. This will help you know what success looks like before you start. And it will also slow time down. Take five minutes after each call and activity to determine whether your desired result was achieved. If not, what was missing? How do you put what's missing in your next call or activity?

▶ Put up a "Do not disturb" sign when you absolutely have to get work done.

▶ Schedule a time to answer e-mail. Practice not responding to e-mail just because it came in, unless you are in a business where immediate response is a competitive advantage.

▶ Practice not answering the phone just because it's ringing, or text messages and e-mails just because they show up, unless you are in a business where human response is a competitive advantage.

▶ Disconnect instant messaging. Don't instantly give people your attention.

▶ Block out other distractions like Facebook and other forms of social media unless you use these tools to generate business.

▶ Remember that it's impossible to get everything done. Also remember that chances are 20 percent of your thoughts, conversations, and activities produce 80 percent of your results. Since most of what's left undone is a waste of time anyway, who cares? Get the important things done first.

5

What Does It Take to Win as a Franchisee?

s you research fran-
chise opportunities you
are faced with the diffi-
cult task of answering five
questions with great clarity:

1. What are the key ingredi-
    ents in the franchisor's
    recipe for success?
2. Which of the key ingredi-
    ents do I possess?
3. Which of the key ingredi-
    ents am I missing?
4. What is the franchisor's
    track record of helping
    others like me acquire
    these missing ingredients?
5. Am I willing to do what it
    takes to acquire these
    ingredients?

This requires great dis-
cernment on your part. As you
investigate franchising, you
will most likely work with a
franchise sales representative
(or development representative as they are sometimes
called) who may not know all
the ingredients needed to succeed in the particular franchise you are investigating.

Few have actual experi-
ence operating a franchise and

therefore have limited or no real-world experience running the franchise business format they are marketing. That doesn't mean their feedback isn't useful and shouldn't be trusted, but it does mean you need to conduct a thorough investigation on your own.

They will generally know enough about operations to be competent in their roles as ambassadors to people investigating their franchise, but not to the extent where they could train and support new franchisees or run the franchise business competently themselves. And since their role is not to train and support new franchisees or run an operation, this is perfectly acceptable. While they can explain on a high level what it takes for you to succeed as a franchisee, they may omit, gloss over, or not take into account certain skill sets or habits required for your success. Some of the shadier or less competent franchise sales representatives will just answer what you ask, either not knowing or not caring if you're investing in a business with carefully managed and realistic expectations about what the business is and isn't.

Most franchise salespeople are of high integrity and desire to look out for both your and the franchisor's best interests. They'll take an interest in you as a person and will facilitate your investigation process. But many franchise salespeople don't invest enough time in interviewing and screening you properly to accurately determine both the transferable skills and abilities you possess and those you are missing. If you were to examine the background of franchise salespeople, most are indeed salespeople and approach their positions as a salesperson would. They are "hunters," and you're looking at the business end of their gun. They'll push the features and benefits of their franchise and move you toward closure, meaning a "yes" or "no" decision as expeditiously as possible.

The law of averages has proven that the longer you take to move through the process the more likely it is that either fear or a lack of passion will keep you from ever moving forward. "Time kills deals" is their mantra. Sometimes you'll feel pressured to make decisions before you feel you have conducted a reasonable investigation.

Keep in mind, only one or two out of every 100 people who inquire about a particular franchise actually move forward. The others fall away for reasons we discussed earlier. Franchise salespeople are under enormous time pressure to expeditiously sift through the 100 to find the one or two who'll move forward in order to spend most of their time with them.

So you must beware. Earlier we told the story of the vice president of franchise sales of a large national automobile body repair franchise who once said, "It isn't my job to qualify franchise candidates. I will give anyone their God-given right to fail." If your skill sets don't line up with the core competencies required to be successful in the business, some will turn a blind eye and attempt to coerce and manipulate you through their sales process anyway. They're not concerned with your heightened risk or how financial failure may impact your family. Nor are they concerned with how your failure will impact their customers or their brand.

They are more concerned with "closing the deal and getting one on the scoreboard." They're like the slick used car salesperson who once tried to sell a man a used SUV. "Whether or not you purchase this car from me," the salesperson said, "I can tell we will become great friends!" A month later (after the man *did not* purchase the car from the salesperson), he sarcastically mused to his family, "Gee, it's been a month and I haven't heard from my new friend yet. That's not like him. I hope he's OK!"

However, more sophisticated and enlightened franchisors not only look for franchise salespeople who can sell, but those who have the ability, vision, integrity, and discipline to accurately qualify and screen potential franchise buyers. Peak-performing franchisors will employ franchise salespeople who take time to get to know you and compare your skills and aptitudes against their profile of a successful franchisee. They'll communicate what it takes to win and check to make sure you understand them properly. If your skills don't match up, they may not immediately disqualify you from the process. They'll inform you of your weak areas and how those weaknesses may impact your business. They'll ask you what training you'll take or what you're committed to do to improve in those areas. For instance, you may have weak computer technical skills. They'll inform you that unless you take computer training, they can't award you a franchise. They may even be at the ready with some recommendations of good computer classes you can take that will fill in your knowledge and skill gaps. These are the true professionals. Unfortunately, right now they are in the minority. However, they are getting attention within the franchising industry.

We expect more franchisors to adapt their best practices. With the tightening of the credit markets, lenders are looking as hard at a franchise candidate's qualifications to own a business as they are their credit score. So current lending practices are forcing franchisors to interview and qualify candidates more, which is good for you, your family, the franchisor, and the lending institutions. Any franchisor that sends lenders a steady stream of franchise candidates who are a poor fit for the business runs the risk of losing their financing sources and cutting their own throats.

Another problem in franchising is that franchise salespeople's compensation and bonus structures are tied to whether you join the franchise, not whether you perform well once you are open. Their compensation is tied to their ability to move you through the sales process, regardless of whether you match the profile of a successful franchisee. Few franchise salespeople have final say as to whether you are approved as a franchisee, so checks and balances exist. But the problem remains that most franchise salespeople's compensation is incongruent with both yours and the franchisor's goals for your personal success within their system. We don't expect most franchisors to suddenly awake to the idea that their franchise salespeople's compensation plan is incongruent with the long-term best interests of both the franchise candidate and franchisor. They seem to already know this. As a general rule, there appears to be no immediate motivation for change.

However, professional franchisee recruitment is a hot topic right now with franchisors. More attention is being paid to the long-term benefits to both the franchisor and potential franchisee of recruiting highly qualified franchise candidates and declining everyone else. They are also waking up to the negative financial and emotional costs of selling franchises to people who simply aren't positioned to win. So this dynamic is changing slowly. The old ways will most likely still be in place with most of the companies you'll be looking at.

This issue will remain until franchisors completely change the way they view their franchise sales departments. Even the words "franchise sales" is a tip-off as to why there is a problem. If you were applying for a key position within the franchisor's company, most likely you would be taken through a series of several hard interviews and interface with Human Resources. What would you think of working for a company who named their HR department the "Vacant Position Sales Department?" If a franchisor has a key management position open, they interview and screen. They have open and frank discussions with potential management candidates about the responsibilities of the job and what it takes to win. If the candidate is thinking the position isn't right for them, they wish them well, and terminate future interviews. They understand the risks of making a bad key management hire and will work hard to find the right person.

However, many franchisors don't consider franchisees "key management" and therefore don't put in the time or energy to make sure they're finding the right franchisee partners. Again, they are more keyed into the quantity of franchises sold than the quality of franchisees they award to.

For a franchisor, "quantity" of franchises sold versus "quality" of the franchisees are opposing forces. Franchisors are pushed and pulled by these forces and struggle to find the right balance. This isn't good or bad, just the way it is. Most franchise salespeople are high-integrity, knowledgeable salespeople who accepted this position because they have a genuine love of people and want to see others win. They are just generally not compensated if you do or held accountable if you don't.

Expect these salespeople to ask you highly personal questions, such as what you have in the way of personal assets to finance a business. While this may put you on edge, it's in your best interest to answer these questions openly and honestly. Since one of the leading causes of failure in business is undercapitalization, it's reasonable to ask such questions and in your best interest to answer completely and without reservation.

As we discussed in a previous chapter, many franchisors will use tools such as behavior profiles and personality inventories. They will spend the first several meetings and conversations getting to know you and qualifying you, much as if you were interviewing for a senior management position within their organization. Once they're clear you match their criteria of a successful franchisee, watch the salesmanship begin! A skilled franchise salesperson will know you fit the profile of a successful franchisee before you do. Take their salesmanship as a compliment. They want you!

While the franchisor will help you identify what it takes to win, their feedback will be incomplete for the reasons we discussed earlier. You can count on franchise salespeople to give you a good overview of what it takes, but most don't know all the details. Therefore you'll have to gather your details from other sources. We show you how in a later chapter.

The KASH Model of Success

As you gather data, you'll find successful franchisees of particular franchise systems have a tendency to think and act alike. They view their customers, employees, business, competition, products and services, and the franchisor the same way. They know the same things, possess similar skill sets, and engage in the same high-priority activities each day. Underperforming franchisees view their customers, employees, business, competition, products and services, and the franchisor the same way also.

The success formula for every franchise opportunity is composed four key ingredients:

1. Knowledge
2. Attitude
3. Skills
4. Habits

This recipe for success has been coined KASH, after the first letter in each word. Here's how we define each KASH element:

Knowledge: Peak-performing franchisees have high levels of product, service, and operational knowledge and are students of their business and industry. They know the business model inside and out and execute it consistently well over time. Plus, they understand the nature, dynamics, and leverage points of their business, meaning they've identified all the activities that produce the greatest results.

Attitude: Franchisees with appropriate attitudes have a realistic and healthy view of their business and the franchisor. Their results may not always be great, but they know why—and are working with the franchisor to continually improve. It's often said that attitude (or thinking) drives all action. Given the same external event (such as a potential conflict), some attitudes, such as problem solving, generate greater results than others, such as fighting. Few franchisees create outstanding results without first generating winning thoughts. Attitude, or mental management, is one of the keys to achieving peak performance in any franchise system. When franchisees learn how to manage their minds, their bodies follow.

Skills: Skillful franchisees exhibit polished and effective behaviors on the job. They know how to accomplish their jobs and manage their customers and employees with great effectiveness. They possess and refine the skills required to be effective franchisees. They execute their knowledge with freedom and ease.

Habits: Franchisees with good habits produce results easily and naturally. They are almost unconsciously competent. And they tend to produce more results than other franchisees do with the same time, money, and energy. They know what the high-priority activities are that produce the greatest results and they spend more time engaged in these activities than underperforming franchisees.

Remember, KASH elements are very different from each other. For instance:

► Knowledge consists of the "mental maps" that show us what to do and how. Writing a service order in an automotive franchise depends on knowledge of automotive repairs and of the front-desk order system. Skill is the way the service writer uses this knowledge. It's how the person writes up the order and conveys it to the shop mechanics. Or how the person handles a customer complaint. In short, knowledge is invisible, but skills are observable. Usually, good skills rest on a foundation of good knowledge. So both elements are equally important.

► Attitude is the lens through which franchisees view the world. It's the meaning they place on events and how they respond to them. A particular franchisee's business results may be subpar, especially during the start-up of their business. Rather than blaming the franchisor, responsible franchisees are more apt to engage in problem solving. Merriam-Webster's defines attitude as a "mental position" or "state of mind." Attitude is often linked with "good" or "bad," but that isn't what the definition means. Attitude is defined in terms how we relate to people or events as we experience them. For example: In the face of a customer complaint, one franchisee's attitude might be: "This customer is the lifeblood of my business." This franchisee will then design a solution congruent with that attitude, hopefully creating a lifetime customer in the process. Another franchisee facing the same complaint might harbor the attitude, "This customer is a pain in the neck." Chances are, the customer will go away dissatisfied and perhaps take other customers with him or her.

► Habit is the cement or glue that combines knowledge, skill, and attitude into long-term peak performance. It occurs over time with practice and refinement, with learning from mistakes, and through sheer hard work. Athletes call habit "being in the zone." It's the point at which people produce results almost unconsciously. And franchisees with good, strong habits usually produce more than do franchisees who are still forming habits. Performing at the level of habit is your ultimate goal as a franchisee.

Let's take a look now at the importance of peak-performing franchisees to every franchise system. You'll see that without these stellar performers, the world of franchising might quickly go dark.

The Importance of Peak Performers

The survival of every franchisor lies in their ability to recruit and train peak-performing franchisees. Here's why peak-performing franchisees are indispensable.

To themselves: The rewards of peak performance are easy to see. First they receive the obvious rewards of greater revenue, profits, and personal income. Next, they experience the intangible satisfaction that comes from doing a great job. Finally, their strong results tend to confirm the reasons they entered the business in the first place. This encourages them to produce even greater results in the future.

To the franchisor: Peak performers produce the greatest royalties and usually consume the least of the franchisor's time and money. This makes them the financial bedrock of any franchise organization. Because they produce the lion's share of franchisor's profit margins (remember, most franchisors rely on royalty collections), they subsidize the support provided to weaker franchisees. Royalties generated by peak-performing franchisees pay management salaries, fund new initiatives, pay the franchisor's rent, and keep the franchisor's lights on. And because these franchisees are so competent, they help the franchisor validate its business model and show other franchisees what it takes to win. Peak performers don't just bring financial advantages. They also help franchisors achieve a competitive edge in the marketplace because they are able to capture a disproportionate share of the market. This makes it difficult for competitors to stake out and hold a position. So, whether you view them from a financial or a marketing perspective, peak-performing franchisees are crucial to a franchisor's success. A franchisor will never succeed unless their franchisees are successful.

To other franchisees: Peak-performing franchisees are seen as leaders within their franchise system. They serve as a constant reminder to other franchisees of what's possible if they stay on course. Many assist the franchisor and other franchisees as mentors and coaches, helping newer or underperforming franchisees discover the success formula for their business also.

To customers: Peak-performing franchisees generate higher levels of customer satisfaction and repeat business than do lower-performing ones. That's because customers prefer to deal with people who know what they're doing. And when they find someone who performs well, they tend to stick with that person and generate referrals.

The Costs of Poor Performance

It's a statistical fact of life that for every peak-performing franchisee, there are also average, below average, and failing franchisees. And for every franchisee that underproduces or fails, there's a financial cost and a human cost that affects everyone in the franchise system.

To themselves: Franchisees who fail can and often do lose substantial sums of money. If they put their homes up as collateral, some may lose those homes. If they invested all their savings, they may lose their retirement security and children's educations. With these losses come stress-related illnesses such as heart attacks and depression—or worse.

To the franchisor: Franchisee failure makes it increasingly difficult for a franchisor to recruit new franchisees, halting forward momentum. Prospective franchisees want to invest in a franchise that's flying high, not crashing and burning. Thus, the chain doesn't grow and eventually starts to decline. The franchisor will lose its ability to negotiate positive terms with vendors, receive choice locations, obtain favorable financing rates, and hire and retain good employees. Lastly, successful franchisees don't sue. Many failing franchisees may look to recapture some of their lost investment by suing the franchisor. This forces the franchisor to spend money on attorney fees to protect the franchise system rather than on making investments that produce results for the other franchisees

To other franchisees: Failure pulls other franchisees down. Franchisees develop a "fox hole" mentality and see fellow franchisees as "brothers in arms." It's emotionally devastating for other franchisees to watch one of their own fail. One franchisee's failure can halt forward momentum in an entire market. In addition, franchisee failure allows the franchisor's competition to create a beachhead, emboldening them to go after more markets, and attacking the livelihood of other franchisees.

To customers: Franchisee failure leaves existing customers doubting the quality of the products and services and value of the brand. You can almost hear the customer thinking, "If this product or service was any good, they would have made it. I had better shop their competition."

In short, a franchisee's failure breeds more failure, creating a vicious downward cycle. Conversely, a franchisee's success breeds more success, creating a virtuous upward cycle.

In this economy, pay particular attention to what cycle franchisors and its franchisees are in. It will be difficult for a franchisor and franchisees in a clearly vicious negative cycle to pull out. If sales are flat or slightly down, this isn't a huge red flag. Many of the business pundits say "flat" is the new "up." Watch the companies who appear to be bleeding and losing customers. Don't assume they know or have what it takes to turn it around. Instead, align yourself with companies that are proven adept at navigating the minefields of low consumer confidence and belt tightening.

Many virtuous and viscious cycles are not caused by external influences such as the state of the economy. They are caused by the success or failure of a company's response. Most franchisees' success or failure is not random. Success and failure are a direct result of the KASH balance. If a wide gap exists between your personal KASH and the KASH required to succeed in a franchise business, then you are at risk. If your KASH is consistent with the profile of a successful franchisee, then most likely you're positioned to win.

All KASH is acquired. No doctor ever presented a newborn baby to his or her mother proclaiming, "Congratulations, you have just given birth to a future successful automotive repair franchisee."

The KASH Deficit Analysis

Identifying whether you'll succeed within a particular franchise system requires personal detachment and rigorous self-examination.

- ► Start with your existing KASH.
- ► Identify the KASH required to succeed
- ► Then subtract that KASH, and you'll know what is missing.

If your KASH deficits are too high going in, you run a higher risk of failure. If your KASH deficit is low, you're a more natural fit for the business. While franchisors have training and ongoing support aimed at building your KASH balance, they aren't miracle workers. If your KASH isn't already in reasonable alignment with a particular franchisor's KASH formula of success, take a pass. There are thousands of franchise options available to you. Find one that fits. We show you where can go to explore your options later in this book.

Once you have identified your KASH deficits, ask yourself, "Am I willing to do whatever it takes to acquire my missing KASH?" If you are one who works hard to achieve your goals, most likely you will work hard to acquire your missing KASH. If you are one who likes to get by, most likely you will lose your investment. If you like to coast, or if you simply struggle with learning new things, find a franchise whose KASH formula of success is a mirror overlay to your personal KASH balance. We show you where you can explore your options later in this book.

While you need to develop your own KASH model for each business you explore, we have included a self-assessment to help you create a baseline to use when exploring franchises.

Greg Nathan, corporate psychologist, franchising expert, and founder of The Franchise Relationships Institute, helped us develop the following worksheet for you to use to identify your starting KASH balance.

Fill out the survey to the best of your ability. Don't over-analyze the questions, just go with your gut and circle the first answer that comes into your head.

My Starting KASH

Name		Date		
Trainability		**Always**	**Sometimes**	**Never**
I adapt well to change		3	2	1
I invest money in my personal development		3	2	1
I am open to feedback on my weaknesses		3	2	1
I am open to trying new ways of doing things		3	2	1
Total for Section				

Marketing/Sales Aptitudes	Always	Sometimes	Never
I am skilled at influencing others with my viewpoints	3	2	1
I am comfortable talking to strangers	3	2	1
I am a creative problem solver	3	2	1
I am a confident presenter	3	2	1
Total for Section			

Motivation	Always	Sometimes	Never
I have clear goals	3	2	1
I achieve what I set my mind on	3	2	1
I honor my commitments	3	2	1
Faced with a problem I can create a proper solution	3	2	1
Total for Section			

Working with Others	Always	Sometimes	Never
I compromise to comply with the wishes of the majority	3	2	1
I get along well with others	3	2	1
I resolve differences with others without creating arguments	3	2	1
I listen to other viewpoints	3	2	1
Total for Section			

Leadership	Always	Sometimes	Never
I achieve my goals through the efforts of others	3	2	1
I will spend money developing my employees' skills	3	2	1
I positively impact others	3	2	1
I can get a diverse group of people moving together in the same positive direction	3	2	1
Total for Section			

What Does it Take to Win as a Franchisee?

Health	Always	Sometimes	Never
I have high energy	3	2	1
I know how to handle stress	3	2	1
I exercise regularly	3	2	1
I eat properly	3	2	1
Total for Section			

Personal Responsibility	Always	Sometimes	Never
I will use my full-time best efforts to drive the business	3	2	1
I accept responsibility for my results	3	2	1
I accept responsibility for my failures	3	2	1
I accept short-term pain for long-term gain	3	2	1
Total for Section			

Family/Friends Support	Always	Sometimes	Never
My famiy/friends support my decision to start a business	3	2	1
My family/friends understand the risks involved	3	2	1
My family/friends understand the time commitment involved	3	2	1
I have stable, positive relationships with my family/friends	3	2	1
Total for Section			

Systems Orientation	Always	Sometimes	Never
I am comfortable following processes and systems others create	3	2	1
I adjust my methods/habits to comply with existing procedures	3	2	1
I am organized and good with detail	3	2	1
I am willing to comply with systems, even if I am in personal disagreement with the methods	3	2	1
Total for Section			

Entrepreneurial Drive	Always	Sometimes	Never
Even when at first I don't know how, I find a way to make things happen	3	2	1
I take risks	3	2	1
I am comfortable with ambiguity	3	2	1
I multi-task well	3	2	1
Total for Section			

Small Business Acumen	Always	Sometimes	Never
I create and achieve budgets	3	2	1
I use technology	3	2	1
I read financial statements	3	2	1
I create and achieve strategic plans	3	2	1
Total for Section			

Time Management	Always	Sometimes	Never
I use my time wisely	3	2	1
I do high-priority activities first	3	2	1
I create a daily plan and work my daily plan	3	2	1
I guard my time	3	2	1
Total for Section			

Communication Skills	Always	Sometimes	Never
I speak clearly	3	2	1
I say what needs to be said	3	2	1
I listen with understanding	3	2	1
I communicate well in writing	3	2	1
Total for Section			

What Is Your Starting KASH Balance?

You have completed the first step in assessing your KASH. But it's hard for anyone to completely assess themselves. Ask friends, family, and coworkers you trust to assess you also.

What Does it Take to Win as a Franchisee?

Compare your answers with theirs and see what you learn. Where you have great disparities, say, for instance, you rated yourself a "3" and they rated you a "1," discuss their answers with them. In a nonjudgmental manner, ask, "How did you come up with that answer?" See yourself through their eyes.

Pay particular attention to any section where you or others rated you a total of "8" or below. You may be at risk in these areas. This doesn't mean you won't succeed in franchising, but it does mean you need to plan to improve your skills in these areas.

Pay attention to the particular line items where you or others rated you a "1." What are you prepared to do to improve in these areas?

Pay attention to particular line items where both you and others rated you as a "3." How can you capitalize on these strengths?

Help Franchisors Help You

When you begin contacting franchisors, consider forwarding the franchisor's representative a copy of this completed assessment. This will help them identify who you are and if you match the profile of a successful franchisee, which protects both your and the franchisor's best interests.

Take Responsibility

This assessment will help you determine your personal KASH balance. We can't overemphasize the importance of completing the survey and having several people close to you complete it for you, too. In selecting and running your own business it's vital to know yourself. Take responsibility for identifying and shoring up your weak areas. Personal responsibility is the key.

6

The Learning Curve of a Franchisee: From the Launch to the Zone

Just as humans evolve as they enter different stages in life, franchisees also evolve as they enter different stages in business. In fact, franchisees move through five distinct phases in linear order: The Launch, The Grind, Winning, The Zone, and The Goodbye (see the chart on the next page). Each stage is marked by changes in franchisees' results and satisfaction level.

This chapter identifies each stage and gives you proven strategies to accelerate through the learning curve. It's one of the most important chapters in this book—the one you will reread, mark up, and return to often. We discuss how franchisees' KASH (knowledge, attitude, skills, habits) fluctuate within each stage. We also show you how to help the franchisor tailor their support to your specific needs within each stage.

As a franchisee, you will go through emotional fluctuations, from the joy at opening

(The Launch), to the frustration of putting forth a huge effort for modest results due to the distressing frequency of your mistakes (The Grind), to satisfaction from succeeding in your business (Winning), to your mastery of the model (The Zone). The illustration that follows lays out the five stages and shows what happens to franchisees' results and satisfaction in each stage. Pay particular attention to the inverse relationship between franchisees' results and satisfaction in the first two stages of the learning curve.

In this chapter, we answer four important questions.

1. What is the predictable learning curve and lifecycle of my franchise and what happens during each stage?
2. What are the three modes a franchisor will use to support me?
3. How do I accelerate through the learning curve toward The Zone?
4. What is the proper combination of franchisor support that will help me accelerate through each stage?

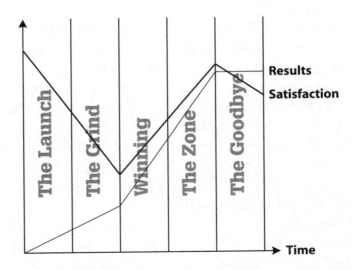

Figure 6-1. The performance/satisfaction curve of a franchisee

The Learning Curve
of a Franchisee

Let's look at The Launch from the franchisor's perspective. As we discussed, many franchisors make little or no money from their franchise fee. Franchise fees usually cover the cost of running the franchisee recruitment department. Your franchise fee was probably spent on salaries, recruitment advertising, benefits, supplies, and other departmental expenses for the purpose of trying to find you. Therefore, most franchisors are completely reliant on the royalty income (and product sales for those franchisors that are also suppliers to their franchisees) for the survival of their businesses. Peak-performing franchisees pay the highest royalties and purchase the most products and, therefore, drive the most revenue for the franchisor. Additionally, because peak performers fully realize the success formula (KASH) of the business, they also consume fewer resources than their counterparts. They pay the most and consume the least, making them (in business terms) the franchisor's highest-margin customers. In addition, they are also the brand's standard bearers, proving how the model works and showing everyone what's possible.

Conversely, franchisees in The Launch and The Grind understandably generate the lowest royalty revenue and product sales for the franchisor because they're still ramping up. If they are being adequately supported, they also consume most of the franchisor's time and management resources. Looking at the franchisor's profitability on a per-franchisee basis, many franchisors lose money on franchisees until they grasp the KASH success formula of the business. Established franchisees (those who are in Winning or The Zone) subsidize the ongoing support and training of new franchisees. Therefore, the success of a franchisor depends on their ability to give franchisees the necessary KASH as quickly as possible. If mature franchisees (in business three years or more) aren't winning, then the whole franchise system may implode. Before we dissect the five stages of the learning curve, let's look at the three ways franchisors give their KASH to franchisees.

Three Modes of Franchisor KASH Distribution

The three ways franchisors will help you accelerate you through the learning curve of your business are training, consulting, and coaching. When used in combination and at the right point in your business lifecycle, these modes work together to achieve the same goal: your peak performance.

Some franchisors instinctively support their franchisees correctly. They may train, consult, and coach their franchisees at the right time and in the right combination without even knowing the difference or what to call it. Others understand the differences and the timing, and have a proven system for supporting franchisees. A third group, consisting of unskilled franchisors, doesn't know the differences or the timing and may never bother to learn. Let's take a moment and identify these three modes just in case you are unfortunate enough to align yourself with an unskilled franchisor. If you're left alone to acquire your KASH, you'll at least know what you need, when you need it, and where to look. Additionally, many unskilled franchisors want to do the right thing … they just don't know what the right thing is. If you know, you can train them to provide what you need to succeed.

Franchisee Support Mode 1: Training

Training is about teaching you *how* to perform. It's about conveying the knowledge you need, modeling the skills (behaviors) required, and providing opportunities to practice, refine, and lock in what you learned (habits). Here's what differentiates training from consulting and coaching:

► Training involves teaching you "how to fish." The first step is to describe a fish. Franchisee training should be highly structured and remedial, assuming franchisees know little. Many franchisors will send remedial information ahead for franchisees to digest *before* they come into the franchisor's training program. Don't be offended by franchisors that design remedial programs for franchisees, offering knowledge you already possess. It's much better for a franchisor to assume you know nothing and offer you everything than to assume you know something, leaving you with critical knowledge and skill gaps.

▶ In training, the assumption is the trainer knows more than those being trained. The "trainer knows–you don't" dynamic creates a hierarchical relationship between you and the trainer. This isn't a bad thing, just the dynamic of the trainer/trainee relationship. Training is an acceptable forum for a franchisor to "talk down" to their franchisees.

▶ When you are being trained, communication typically flows downward from the trainer to you. Very little flows upward, and very little *should* flow upward. For example, picture being in a franchise training class where a new franchisee says, "In our CPA firm, we didn't do it your way; we did it [such and such] way," and the trainer responds sweetly, "That probably works great in a CPA firm, but we are learning how to run a muffler shop, not an accounting practice. Do it our way. Thank you for sharing." You are there to acquire, not offer knowledge. It's time to put much of your past in the past.

▶ When in a training mode, the franchisor assumes a more directive role. Expect them to do much more speaking and showing than listening.

▶ When in training, the franchisor will focus intently on building knowledge and skills, while providing opportunities for you to build winning habits. The mantra of a trainer is "Learn, learn, learn, practice, practice, practice!" Remember, practice does not make perfect, practice makes permanent. Only perfect practice makes perfect. Make sure you only do business with a franchisor that regularly monitors your practice, making sure you engage in perfect practice designed to create permanent winning habits.

▶ Trainers often mistakenly assume that if they show franchisees what to do and how to do it, they will do it unaided in the future. However, there's often a gap between what people know and what they do. Again, a skilled trainer will monitor your practice and close that gap!

- Skilled franchisors will develop your business and technical skills. Remember, you're not joining a franchise to learn how to do such tasks as unclog a drain; you are joining a franchise to learn how to make money and create a desired lifestyle by unclogging drains. You need to learn how to deliver the product and market, manage, and promote a business. Only do business with a franchisor that understands your business skills are as important as your technical skills.

- Just as franchisees don't need to re-invent the wheel, neither does a franchisor. Smart franchisors often use outside vendors to deliver certain components of their training program and adapt their franchise systems to the vendors' products and training. For instance, Dale Carnegie or Sandler Sales Institute (both franchises) offer excellent sales training programs that would be difficult to improve upon. Don't be surprised if a franchisor requests or even requires you take outside training programs.

Again, the goal of training is to transfer knowledge and skills. This can be hampered by several common mistakes.

- Systems are not properly documented, leaving knowledge gaps.

- Training programs are "data dumps," offering too much information in too little time.

- Knowledge is offered but modeling skills are not. David Sandler, founder of Sandler Sales Institute often said, "You can't teach a kid to ride a bicycle in a seminar." Nor can you in a classroom or with a book. Kids get balance by falling down a lot and scraping their elbows and knees. During the "getting balance" process, a responsible parent is right there, ready to offer coaching, hugs, and bandages. Then, unpredictably, almost magically, the kid gets it. He may wobble, but he doesn't fall. He may narrowly miss trees and mailboxes, but he doesn't hit them. The frustration of falling is replaced with the thrill of the ride, a sense of winning, and an empowered feeling called "balance."

The Learning Curve
of a Franchisee

So it is with franchising. Exactly when a kid finds their balance is unpredictable, especially if you are the kid. Getting balance over time however *is predictable*. The kid gets it when they get it and it's pointless to force the issue. So it is with franchising. Franchisees get KASH when they get it. Although you can't predict when they will acquire KASH, a franchisor should have a demonstrated track record that shows franchisees get it eventually, before they run out of the other kind of cash.

▶ More emphasis is placed on training than on consulting and coaching. Knowledge is overrated. For instance, why do so many people smoke? Don't they know it causes cancer? Why are so many adults obese? Don't they know how to order a salad and exercise on a treadmill? Knowledge, on its own, doesn't make a difference. A franchisee's consistent and skillful implementation of their knowledge is what produces great results. Many franchisors assume that if franchisees know what to do, they'll do it. They forget that even with peak performers, there is a great divide between what is known and what is implemented. Skilled franchisors hold franchisees accountable for closing the gap.

Franchisor Support Mode 2: Consulting

Consulting is about fixing problems. After initial training, competent franchisors consult with their franchisees on an ongoing basis, identifying and eliminating obstacles to growth. While the same person may provide initial training and ongoing consulting, consulting and training are materially different modes of support and are used at different times in the learning curve to produce different results. We discuss why and when each is used later in this chapter. For now, let's just distinguish the differences. Consulting differs from training in the following ways:

▶ In consulting mode, the support person's job is to throw you a fish, not teach you how to fish. They help you fix problems fast, not increase your knowledge base. The franchisor takes the responsibility of identifying your problems and crafting a solution. Your role as a franchisee is to execute the solution. Often franchisors will train franchisees after the fact; helping franchisees learn how and why a breakdown occurred and showing ways to prevent a similar breakdown in the future. This is ideal because it will also help get a deeper understanding of the unique dynamics of your business; what does and doesn't work and why.

▶ With consulting, as with training, communications flows downward.

▶ When a franchisor's support staff is in consulting mode, they take an even more directive role than when they train. They will probably tell you "do this and that," but they may or may not get into the rationale behind the directives.

Franchisor Support Mode 3: Coaching

Coaching is about pure execution. Coaching assumes you know what to do; now it's time to get it done. In the face of inaction, coaching is also about discovering why franchisees aren't doing what they already know or using solutions that are readily available. Here's what differentiates consulting from training and coaching:

▶ When the franchisor's support staff is in coaching mode, they address situations in which a franchisee knows what to do, but isn't doing it or doing it effectively. They hold franchisees accountable for implementing what they've learned and crafting their own solutions. They hold franchisees accountable for waking up early and "getting some fish in the boat," because they already know how to fish.

▶ When coaching, franchisor support staff operates in partnership with franchisees. There's no hierarchy. The coach's job is to coach. The franchisees' job is to execute. Each has clear roles and responsibilities.

▶ In coaching mode, the franchisor's staff focuses on driving franchisees' results. And if results are already good, they drive them higher.

The Learning Curve
of a Franchisee

▶ When there's a breakdown in performance, the coach will immediately start asking questions about what happened, instead of telling franchisees what to do like a consultant or trainer. The coach assumes franchisees have the solution inside them, waiting to come out. By asking the right questions, the coach will assist franchisees in diagnosing their own problems and creating and implementing their own solution. In the process, franchisees will put in structures or safeguards that will prevent the same problem from occurring again.

> In coaching, the solution resides with the franchisee, not with the coach.

Coaching places greater emphasis on asking questions, goal setting, action planning, implementation of the plan, and accountability than do the other two modes. It places relatively little focus on knowledge/skill acquisition or technical solutions, because coaching assumes franchisees already possess the knowledge and skill. All that's missing is proper implementation. How do these modes differ? Let's assume a franchisee isn't growing their sales as budgeted.

Franchisee: "My sales are off this month ... "

The Trainer	The Consultant	The Coach
"Let's hold a sales training program for your salespeople. "The problem is identified as a lack of training. It's assumed if the salespeople knew more, they would perform better. **The solution resides with the trainer.**	"Let me follow your salespeople around and hear what they are doing wrong and figure out a solution. "The consultant assumes the salespeople or franchisee cannot identify the problem or craft a solution. **The solution resides with the consultant.**	The coach asks, "How many calls are you making? What are customers telling you as to their reasons for not buying? What changed from last month? What do you need to be doing differently? "The coach assumes that by prompting the franchisee with questions, the salespeople or franchisee will identify their own problem and create their own solution. **The solution resides with the franchisee.**

The trainer, if all he knew was training, would jump right into a training solution, assuming that if the franchisee knew what to do, he or she would do it and achieve results. The consultant, if all she knew was consulting, would try to identify and fix the problems herself, many times bypassing franchisees in the process. This is a good short-term fix, but doesn't empower franchisees to identify and craft solutions themselves. Aside from disempowering franchisees, this will lead to more dependence on the franchisor in the future. The coach, if all he knew was coaching, would help franchisees identify and resolve their own problems, assuming there is a gap between what they know and how they implement this knowledge. The coach helps the franchisee bridge their own gap. "The system works," the coach says, "Now where are you not working the system? What do you need to do to get back on track?"

The point is this. If you're to be successful, the franchisor needs to be prepared to mix and match training, consulting, and coaching at the right times. Your role as a franchisee is to internalize the training, and execute the consulting and coaching as it's offered. Let's look at how to successfully navigate the learning curve.

The Launch

When a franchisee signs the franchise agreement, they are filled with mixed emotions. While there is some fear of the unknown, they are mostly filled with a sense of joy and empowerment. It's as if they can look out across the learning curve and see the life they are designing for themselves and their families as if it's already occurring. They know they just made the necessary step to make it happen. This "knowing" fills them with a sense of wonder and awe. Still excited, they move feverishly through the start-up activities such as setting up a corporation, securing financing, finding and securing a location, purchasing opening inventory, and so on. They hang on to the training instructor's every word during initial training. They've left training charged up and ready to make their mark.

Eventually the franchise opens and the franchisee wakes up every morning ready to take on the day. They eagerly serve customers and treat themselves and their employees gently, seeing rookie mistakes as productive learning opportunities. While money is tight, they prepared for it to be tight, and they are right on plan.

However, because they are not yet skilled at what they do and customers may not know the brand, their results are poor ... as poor as they will ever be. Despite the weak initial results associated with starting a business, they recognize this is temporary and they give themselves permission to learn. They know their results will be there eventually if they diligently do what it takes to learn the success formula of the franchise.

In this and the previous chapter we harp on the KASH model of success (knowledge, attitude, skills, habits). Successful franchisees seem to usually possess the same KASH as other successful franchisees in the same franchise system. Unsuccessful or underperforming franchisees seem to reflect the same KASH as their counterparts. Many underperforming franchisees become arrested in their KASH development, never acquiring the necessary KASH to successfully navigate the learning curve into Peak Performance. In this chapter you will see how your KASH will fluctuate during each stage of your franchisee evolution, and learn what it takes to successfully graduate to the next stage.

Knowledge

When you launch your franchise, much of your past business knowledge becomes irrelevant. Truth be known, when you sign your franchise agreements and write the check for the franchise fee you have invested in the right to be incompetent. What you don't know about your new business could fill an encyclopedia. However, you are confident that this knowledge exists within the franchisor and franchisee community and is properly documented. You are confident in both the franchisor's ability to teach you their system and your ability to learn it. You go through the franchisor's training program and so much knowledge is crammed into your cranium that you are afraid your eyes will pop out.

Attitude

Life is good. The grass looks a little greener, the sky a little bluer, and birds are singing. Each day is filled with excitement, adventure, and awe. For the first time in a long time, you feel as if you're being called forward into action. Instead of throwing shoes and curses at your alarm clock, you often wake up before it rings, charged up with the electricity of an exciting new day. You're on fire. Work becomes play. Aside from attitudinal changes, you may experience physical changes. Although you may be sleeping less, you appear rested and relaxed. Although your business may not yet be making money, you experience peace. People may even begin remarking on how much younger or fitter you look. They also complain about your frequent gleeful whistling of *Zippity Doo-Dah* and *The Andy Griffith Show Theme Song* while they're trying to work. For the first time in a long time, your life and career are working together in balance and harmony.

Skills

Let's face it. You will probably stink. This is not a bad thing, because, as we already discussed, you know you've invested in the privilege of being incompetent for a short time. The launch is a time of unconscious incompetence, meaning that you don't know what you don't know. And because you've given yourself permission to learn, you aren't torn up about it. Like a famous motivational speaker once said, "Anything worth doing is worth being lousy at for a little while." Unless you're one of those rare prodigies or your background closely matches the skills required to succeed in your new venture, your skills at best will be unrefined. Some skills will transfer over from your past career and some won't. The Launch is a time for deep personal development.

Be mindful that franchisors are typically skilled at imparting knowledge to their franchisees, but often ignore their skill development. Therefore, you may be left on your own to develop your skills.

For instance, in most franchise businesses, successfully selling your product or service is critical to the success of your business. A franchisor may have documented and taught you the steps of the sale, the benefits of the product or service, and the differentiating factors between your products and services and those of your competition. However, they may have no systematic ongoing program to develop your sales skills.

Sales are typically done in the form of oral communication. Put another way, sales is a conversation and good salespeople are expert communicators. Expert communication requires such refined personal skills as:

- ▶ **Interviewing skills.** The ability to ask pertinent questions to determine another's needs.
- ▶ **Problem-solving skills.** Ability to correctly identify needs and problems and craft effective solutions.

- ▶ **Empathetic listening skills.** The ability to put yourself where the customer is standing and see their needs from their perspective.
- ▶ **Speaking and being understood.** Being able to relate information to a customer in a way that's relevant to the customer's needs.

While you will find many franchisors that have correctly documented their sales process, you will find few franchisors that have the ability to correctly identify your missing personal skill sets and have programs in place to fill in your skill gaps. For instance, we don't know of any franchisors that have training programs to teach franchisees how to listen. If you have deficits in this area, most likely you are going to be left on your own to develop that skill. The good news is that there are plenty of outside courses and training programs that can help you develop specific skill sets. Make sure you have correctly identified which skills sets are necessary to succeed in business as you investigate the business. Furthermore, take a personal inventory and identify which of those skill sets you possess and which you are missing. Budget money, perhaps even several thousand dollars, to invest in seminars and training programs to fill in your skill gaps. Perhaps you are thinking, "Why should I invest my money? Isn't that why I pay royalties? Shouldn't the franchisor train me?" Some franchisors are, indeed, brilliant sales trainers and coaches. Some are good enough to get by in a good economy and thriving industry where the rising tide lifts all ships. However, in a bad economy there is intense pressure to grow sales and in many franchise business models it's incumbent on the owner to do so. So if you aren't already a proven rainmaker, it's time to learn ... and when starting a new business, time isn't always your friend.

Habits

The second you open your doors, your habits will start forming. At the beginning of The Launch, you have few good or bad habits.

The Learning Curve
of a Franchisee

However, during The Launch you will either begin the good habit of spending more time executing the high-priority activities that generate the most results or formulating the bad habit of wasting time on busy work that produces little. Carefully document and observe where you spend your time. A key habit to develop during The Launch is to *budget time for learning and skill development.* How quickly you develop your knowledge and skills will determine how quickly you ramp up your business and generate positive cash flow.

Strategies for a Successful Launch
More Training

Training isn't a one- or two-week event that occurs after you sign your agreement, but an ongoing process, continuing well past the grand opening of your business. Remember, many franchisor's training programs are a massive data dump, the training equivalent of trying to take a sip of water from a fire hose. Also, initial training programs are typically done in the vacuum of a classroom setting. You will have little real-world experience. If the franchisor doesn't offer continuation training three to six months after you open your doors, ask to take the initial training program a second time, even if this means paying additional fees. Once you're in the real world executing the business model, you develop the context you didn't have in the initial training program. By attending training again after three or six months, you'll get the franchise training program on a much deeper and more meaningful level.

Not all franchisors offer meaningful training programs beyond their initial classroom instruction before you open. Depending on the complexity of their business model, they should have a three-month to one-year training, skill development, coaching, and mentoring program designed to accelerate you through the learning curve into competent levels of performance. Not all do; so beware. Most likely, beyond an introductory point, you will be forced to train and develop yourself, taking total ownership of much of your learning curve. While the world is full of self-taught musicians, artists, and businesspeople, attending music, art, or business schools would make learning faster and easier. However, beyond some entry-level initial training program, many franchisors may not offer you additional opportunities. Most franchisors have regular regional and national conferences that do offer additional training programs, networking opportunities, and panel discussions. However, these forums may or may not address your specific business needs at the time you need it. Again, these conferences, while valuable, dump more data. Most offer little opportunity for role-playing, skill development, or additional on-the-job training.

When you launch your business, don't focus on profitability. Focus on learning. Identify and acquire the KASH necessary to survive ... and then thrive.

You will know you have completed The Launch when you find yourself becoming frustrated and disillusioned with the learning curve of your business. Put another way, your attitude goes in the tank. Instead of whistling *Zippity Doo-Dah,* you now hum B.B. King's classic *The Thrill Is Gone.* Don't despair. The thrill isn't really gone; it hides for a little while.

The Grind

Think about the last time you picked up a new hobby. Let's use golf, for example. Adults who picked up golf later in life were thrilled with the decision to learn the game. They got fitted with clubs and shoes, went to the driving range, signed up with a teaching pro and learned the basics of the game. Some were so giddy, they even bought silly hats, bright sweaters, and loud, plaid pants. Learning was fun, and at first, they didn't take mistakes so seriously. They let themselves hit pop-ups and ground balls, and took out Texas-sized divots. Hitting into the woods, trap, or lake, although not desired, was really no big deal ... it was a given part of the learning process.

Then something happened. Somewhere in the learning process,

The Learning Curve
of a Franchisee

golf stopped being fun. In fact, it became infuriating … to the point that when a golfer's ball splashed into the lake the offending golf club, or perhaps the entire bag, was flung into the lake right behind the ball. The permission they had given themselves to make mistakes was revoked, replaced by a demand for results equal to the money, effort, anguish, and loud plaid pants they'd invested in.

The golfer, like the entrepreneur, insists on a proper return on their investment. The golfer has entered The Grind.

Golf, once explained in terms of heavenly virtue, is now described in a steady stream of hellish obscenities. The golfer, once in awe of everything that is right with golf—the beauty of the course, the peace of the surroundings, the camaraderie of their peers—now focuses on everything that's wrong with their swing.

From your vantage point as an objective third party who's watching this golfer, ask yourself the following question: Has the game of golf really changed or has *the golfer's relationship to the game* changed?

This phenomenon occurs in franchising, too. In the eyes of the franchisee, the game changes.

If you take an objective look at golf, the game probably wasn't as good as the golfer originally made it out to be, nor as bad as it seems now. As a matter of fact, golf isn't good or bad. Golf is whatever the golfer makes out of it.

It's the same with franchising. However, as franchisees move through the learning curve, they change their relationship to their business. They revoke their own learning privileges and demand a return on their investment. Work is no longer play. Work becomes hard, frustrating, excruciating work. The glee of the The Launch disappears. The frustration of The Grind now occupies that space.

As you read this, check your experience. Chances are, just like franchisees mired in The Grind, you're relating to the pain and frustration of The Grind as a bad thing. We invite you into a new, more powerful perception.

The Grind is a good thing! The Grind is a sign of progress, because after The Grind comes Winning. You can't jump from The Launch to Winning without experiencing some Grind.

Some franchisees in The Grind may feel they have halted their forward momentum. Others may even experience failing. However these experiences can't be trusted. Just like the game of golf doesn't change as the golfer moves through the learning curve of golf, the game of franchising doesn't change either.

Once, a franchisee of a business service franchisor became visibly distraught during the franchisor's initial training program. Picking up on this, the astute trainer took the franchisee aside during the next break to check in and see what was happening. The franchisee confided, "I am upset because I know the other franchisees are getting the business quicker than I am. I'm behind the rest of the class."

The trainer gave the franchisee an assuring smile. "Do you think that when you leave here, you are going to know everything you need to know to become successful, or do you think your real training begins when you leave here?"

"I know I will have a ton of work to do when we leave here," replied the franchisee.

"Will you do what it takes?" asked the trainer.

"Absolutely!" declared the franchisee.

The trainer paused to choose his next words carefully. "Consider for a second," he continued, "that not only are you not behind the rest of the class, *I am secretly declaring you the valedictorian!* Everyone else is reveling in the joy of their start-up. You have already moved into the frustration of the learning curve. Congratulations. You're at the head of the class."

The trainer knew that pain meant progress.

Consider for a second that there are two types of pain. The first is like headache pain. We relate to this pain as if it is something bad ... something that shouldn't be. We then do whatever it takes to make this pain go away.

However, there is a second type of pain, like exercise pain. During exercise, muscle burn or fatigue becomes a desired result.

The Learning Curve
of a Franchisee

We take steps to manifest this pain. We invite it into our bodies. "No pain, no gain!" we say. We relate to exercise pain as a sign of progress, a sign of winning. This pain is good.

For whatever reason, a franchisee experiences the pain of the learning curve of a business as headache pain rather than exercise pain.

Earlier, we stated that franchisors, even those whose systems produce outstanding results, report that 99 percent of the people who investigate their franchise end up not moving forward. Why? Many prospective franchisees are terrified of The Grind. They relate to it as if it were a permanent state instead a temporary part of the learning curve. Remember the kid riding the bike? When he's sprawled out on the sidewalk, bleeding from the elbows and knees, what would lead him to believe that in the next ride he will get balance? But then, one magical, unpredictable time, this is what happens. While baby-soft skin may seem to be preferable to cuts and bruises, you can't get balance without first experiencing falling down.

The Grind ends with an empowering "Now I get it!" series of experiences. Just like the kid who gets "balance" when learning to ride a bike, once a franchisee gets the business, they will always get it. The KASH formula becomes part of their identity.

When polled, most franchisees of most franchise systems report that they are winning by their own definition of winning. When asked, "Knowing what you know now, would you make the same decision again?" most answer a resounding "Yes!" If most franchisees win (and they do) and most are satisfied with their decision (and they are), then why don't more people invest in franchises?

They are making their pain go away.

It's hard to describe The Grind to anyone who has never experienced it. However, try the following exercise to get a snapshot of what it's like.

Start by crossing your arms. Notice which arm is on top. Leave your arms crossed and notice what you experience. You know this position because you've crossed your arms this way for years. It's natural and easy for you. You don't feel stress or experience any need to make a change. Got it?

Now uncross your arms. Re-cross them, but this time putting *the opposite arm on top*. Chances are, on the first attempt you couldn't even do it. Now that you finally figured out how, leave your arms crossed that way for a few moments. What are you experiencing? You probably have some deep-seated feeling that you're crossing your arms the wrong way. There appears now to be a right way and a wrong way to cross your arms, and you're now crossing them the wrong way. It's so wrong, in fact, that it's making you crazy. So crazy, you can't wait to uncross them. Take a second and watch yourself make yourself crazy over something as silly as crossing your arms. Welcome to The Grind.

Comedian Steven Wright once explained it a different way. "Ood you remember how you felt when you leaned too far back in your chair, and you think you are going to fall, but suddenly you catch yourself?" he said. "I feel like that all the time."

While Wright may experience living there all the time, we assure you your stay in The Grind will be temporary.

Going back to your arm-crossing adventure, what if you were to cross your arms that way every day? Would your "I am crossing my arms the wrong way" experience eventually change? Would you become more comfortable? Over time, isn't it reasonable to assume you will have the freedom of choice as to which way you cross your arms?

Franchisees eventually get it and the The Grind disappears. It is the franchisor's job to accelerate the "getting it" process. And it's the franchisee's job not to take themselves so seriously. One time I was experiencing a particular level of frustration with a task I was trying to complete and I was visibly upset. My young, happy-go-lucky, blond-haired, blue-eyed son Michael walked up to me and said, "Dad, get over your funky bad self, yo!" I laughed ... and then got over my funky bad self. Getting through The Grind requires a two-pronged approach. First, learn as fast as you can. Second, get over your funky bad self.

Shifting gears, let's take a look at a franchisee's KASH when in The Grind.

Knowledge

Knowledge is steadily increasing, however, gaps still exist. Franchisees are still dependent on the franchisor, because they don't know what they don't know. Where The Launch is a time of unconscious incompetence, meaning franchisees don't know how bad they really are, The Grind is a time of conscious incompetence. They get how bad they are and how much further they need to go to win. In addition they see precious dollars going out the door not knowing when they'll grow the business into a sustainable, profitable business. This ambiguity can be disempowering, terrifying, and frustrating.

However, fearing The Grind is like fearing the Boogey Man. When a child realizes there is no such thing as The Boogey Man outside their own imagination, darkness loses its power over the child. When franchisees get that there is no such thing as The Grind outside their own imagination, the disempowerment, fear, and frustration of the learning curve dissipates also. It's during this stage that a franchisee's ability to manage their attitudes and emotions is mission critical to their success.

Attitude

To quote an overworked cliché, "The bloom is off the rose." Most franchisees are results oriented and often results simply aren't to the franchisees' satisfaction or expectations. Here is where franchisees and franchisors disconnect.

> This disconnection occurs when franchisees need franchisors the most.

An objective look at results and key performance indicators would often show a steady increase in franchisees' performance.

Franchisees will typically produce marginally better results week after week, slow and steady. However, franchisees often get caught up in the frustration of the almost superhuman effort it takes to produce those results. Most franchisees have been solid producers in the past. Producers like to produce. They have a demonstrated track record of competently and consistently hitting their personal and corporate objectives. Many can't remember the last time they struggled. They forgot how hard they had to work early in their careers. They only remember and still relate to their past mastery. Because they're struggling to achieve the results they do achieve, many get sucked into *the false experience of failing* although they may actually be on or ahead of plan!

I remember once getting a call from a new franchisee in a panic, telling me they were closing down their consulting franchise, which had been open less than a year. The franchisee had a full pipeline of potential clients and showed competency in new-client lead generation. Like anyone in a learning curve, he had a breakdown converting potential clients to paying clients. I asked him to consider giving the business more time and he agreed to continue for three more months. So his regional director and I focused on honing his sales skills and closing the potential book of business that was already in his pipeline. Within six months he generated almost $100K in new business and later went on to be Franchisee of the Year.

Being mired in the learning curve, he couldn't see the progress he had already achieved. His regional director and I only provided finishing touches, the few missing pieces that created a tipping point. The franchisee couldn't see that he had already done the heavy lifting himself, nor could he experience how close he was to his tipping point where the business became self-sustainable.

Franchisors don't measure false experiences, just results. They aren't living inside the franchisees' phantom failure experiences. Many of the franchisor's support personnel have never owned a business before and don't get what it is to be in The Grind so they don't understand the emotional toll of The Grind on a franchisee. Therefore, often they don't offer the emotional support franchisees desperately need to successfully navigate this stage. Many franchisors are reactive. If the numbers don't show a problem, there is no problem. They assume franchisees will call if there is. Franchisees respond to The Grind generally one of four ways.

1. **Fighters fight.** These franchisees create monumental problems where either no or perhaps tiny problems exist. They cry wolf every time something doesn't go off as planned. They blame the training, products, competition, support, marketing, pricing, and even their customers. They think, "I'm working the system, but the system isn't working." They blame and complain, creating a strained relationship with the franchisor support team at the time they need this team's best efforts. They become like the child who is sprawled out on the sidewalk who kicks their bike yelling, "Stupid bike! If only I bought another stupid bike I wouldn't have fallen!" The franchisor support team responds to their anger with a "what does this ungrateful $*#! franchisee want now!" kind of attitude. They become either curt or make efforts to dodge the calls altogether. Because franchisees think the system isn't working, they start changing the system to coincide with what worked in their past business or career.

   These changes often don't work, prolonging the learning curve, miring the franchisee in The Grind, creating more complaints and changes, which in turn creates more Grind. Some franchisees get so caught up in a death spiral, they never acquire the necessary KASH and produce marginal results. Others simply get it over time.

   If you're the type of person who pushes off responsibility on others or fights before problem solving, remember, it's probably not the bike. If you've never ridden a bike before, you'll jump on a $2,000 custom-built titanium bike and probably still wipe out. Be gentle with yourself and others. Learn humility and let others contribute to you. Don't kill off the people who are trying to help you. Own your results and learning curve. Trust the learning process and over time you will achieve balance.

2. **Overly optimistic franchisees get caught up in false hopes.** They hope things will get better, although they have no plan of attack to acquire the necessary KASH to make things better. When the franchisor calls asking, "How are things going?" the franchisee responds, "Just peachy!" They don't dare admit to "negative thinking," although that's where they spend much of their day. Lynn Giulianni of The Summit Group, a business coach who works with both franchisees and franchisors, says, "Hope is a beautiful thing. Never lose hope. However, hope is a lousy business strategy." Many franchisors aren't going to pick up on when you are operating inside of "false hope without a plan." They're going to assume when you say you are "peachy," you are indeed peachy, instead of pretending to be peachy when you're really petrified. If you're prone to false positive thinking, learn how to shoot straight and say what you're really experiencing so the franchisor can offer you support.

3. **Overly pessimistic franchisees will have a Chicken Little "the sky is falling" experience.** Don't expect franchisors to confuse falling acorns with the collapse of the world as we know it. These franchisees begin expecting failure, and can easily gather the data to support their conclusions. "Just look at my past results!" they say. In a learning curve however, past results *are no indication of future failure* because every day new franchisees acquire new KASH, which alters the existing state of their business and what they are capable of achieving in the future. Again, they are like the little kid who is sprawled out on the sidewalk, who screams "I will never, ever ride this stupid bike!" Remember that one time

The Learning Curve
of a Franchisee

the child will get it if the child continues to give himself or herself permission to keep pedaling.

Unlike The Launch, where a franchisee can clearly see across the learning curve into the land of milk and honey, in The Grind, the learning curve becomes a blind curve in which franchisees can't see past the bend. However, when the franchisor examines the franchisee's results, they see a steady progression of results. Franchisees in The Grind have a tendency however to dismiss data and results, preferring instead to believe the sky is really falling. Again, the franchisor will typically miss the franchisee's false failure experience, examining the data according to plan. If you are pessimistic by nature, trust the data and discount your interpretation of the data. Give yourself permission to learn, letting others contribute to you also. Commit yourself to the learning process and you'll eventually ride the stupid bike, and ride it expertly.

4. **Emotionally mature and balanced franchisees manage their emotions,** don't buy the false experiences, and give themselves permission to learn. They treat themselves and others gently. Although they aren't crazy about mistakes, they learn their lessons and move on. They know that slamming into the pavement is part of learning how to ride a bike and they don't have false expectations otherwise. They know there will be bruises and bleeding and they know they will scab and heal. They remember that the last fall didn't kill them so they will probably survive the next fall also. They don't blame the bicycle, the bicycle manufacturer, the pavement, or the entire biking industry for their decision to learn to ride a bike. They know they will be fearful. But they know they will survive the fear because they also remember being afraid in the past, and they didn't die from that fear either. They know there will be frustration, and their frustration won't be fatal. They will take the business *one day at a time* with a full understanding that whatever happened yesterday is already in the past and can't be changed.

Just as balance seems to find the child who continues to pedal the bike, they know success will find them even if they commit to acquiring the necessary KASH of the business. They invested in the privilege of getting to say what happens today and for the ability to own their results, whether or not those results meet expectations. For these franchisees, The Grind is a temporary nuisance, not a permanent nightmare. They know it is a mental state that they create. They don't blame others for their Grind. They know that if they just own their thoughts and emotions for one more day, and do what they are supposed to, tomorrow will take care of itself.

Asking what causes The Grind is like asking what causes The Boogey Man. Franchisees make up The Grind the same way children make up The Boogey Man. The Boogey Man isn't good or bad, just a figment of a child's imagination. The Grind isn't good or bad either, just a figment of a franchisee's imagination. Having a conversation about the Grind with a franchisee who currently is in The Grind is like having a conversation with a child who is certain the Boogey Man is under their bed.

Turning the light on, the adult says, "Look under the bed. There is no Boogey Man. The Boogey Man is pretend."

"He's real!" the child replies. "The Boogey Man turns invisible when you come in the room!"

Just as the child can always find evidence to believe in the Boogey Man, franchisees can always find evidence that keeps them in The Grind.

The Boogey Man is a child's fear of the dark manifested. The Grind is a franchisee's fear of failure manifested. Kids aren't bad or wrong for believing in the Boogey Man; they are just being kids. Neither are new franchisees bad or wrong for being in The Grind. They are just being new franchisees.

Someone once said a hero is an ordinary person, under extreme circumstances, who puts forth an extraordinary effort and produces outstanding results. Don't think that we're diminishing new franchisees by equating them with children. On the

The Learning Curve
of a Franchisee

contrary, we equate them with heroes. They are up to creating something extraordinary with their lives and careers. This takes guts. And a fierce, rigorous, and continual grasp of reality.

Skills

Throughout The Grind franchisees are usually getting better at what they do. But because progress is slow, steady, and many times undetectable, they may lose sight of the progress they are making. It is kind of like watching grass grow or paint dry. Eventually it happens, but too slowly to see.

Skill development is what carries franchisees past The Grind and into Winning. Hopefully your franchisor is helping you identify areas to work on. If not, take it upon yourself to identify the skills you lack and create a plan to acquire these skills. Depending on the business and support level of the franchisor, an ideal scenario would be to budget several thousand dollars and at least one day a week to focus solely on skill development.

Does that sound excessive? Well, you can chop down a tree with a dull axe. It just takes a lot more swings, effort, and energy. Or you can stop chopping and invest time and money to sharpen the axe. Chopping becomes easier, your swing's more efficient, and you have energy left over to chop more trees. By developing your skills, you're sharpening your axe.

If this make sense to you, it's because you aren't in The Grind. Logic and reality are suspended in The Grind and misperceptions rule. Many franchisees in The Grind think, "I can't afford to sharpen my axe right now. When the tree finally falls, I'll cut it up, sell the firewood, and then sharpen the blade." Others think, "If I stop swinging the tree will never fall. I can't take the time to stop swinging." Some franchisees have spent such little time in skill development that they don't recognize there isn't any blade left at the end of their axe handle. "What is that thud?" they ask as the wood of the handle meets the wood of the tree. "I must not be swinging the axe handle hard enough!" *Thud, Thud, Thud ...*

These are not stupid people. These are extraordinary people

who've invested a lot of money for the right to create outstanding lives and careers. They simply forgot what it takes to learn and become masterful. It has been a long time since they had to build their knowledge and skills from the beginning. Since many of the franchisor's staff have never owned a business, they can miss or fail to appreciate their franchisees' needs—and heroism.

Habits

In The Grind habits are beginning to gel. This is a critical time in the learning process, because as we said, "Practice doesn't make perfect, only perfect practice makes perfect. Practice makes permanent." Bad habits form as easily as good habits. Each business has high priority activities that produce most of the results. Each business has minutia; those activities that suck a franchisee in, chew up time, and ultimately don't make a difference.

Forming winning habits will propel franchisees to a breakthrough in results and into the stage we call Winning. If the franchisee forms bad habits, they continue "grinding it out," feeling decreasing satisfaction, and dramatically increasing their chance of failure. Most franchisees get into the flow of the business, find the right rhythm, and acquire the necessary KASH to experience Winning. But don't leave it to chance. Keep reading!

Strategies to Successfully Navigate the Grind

Work your business one day at a time. Plan your day and work your plan. Forget what happened yesterday. Deny yourself your right to worry about tomorrow. Today has enough worries of its own. Chances are you have the capital, desire, and energy required *today* to work toward creating your desired future. Focus today on developing the necessary KASH you need to succeed. Once today is complete, make a commitment to wake up tomorrow and do it again.

Get emotional support. Find someone in your life who instinctively knows how to pick you up when you're down. Call them 10–15 minutes every morning to get you ready for the day. Let them be your emotional anchor. Tell them what you plan to achieve that day, and make it happen. Do it again tomorrow.

Acquire KASH.

Stay out of "survival." If you think you are failing, instead of playing to win, you are going to play not to lose. In baseball, when a pitcher is pitching not to lose, he starts aiming the ball and being too cautious. He loses velocity, becomes error prone, and gets creamed. Eventually, his fear of losing is manifested as losing. Make decisions you would make if you were playing to win.

> Play to win. Don't play not to lose.

Before you are in The Grind, think about the kind of decisions you would make if you were afraid of losing. What expenses would you cut? How would you modify your life or business? Write your answers down. That way, if you find yourself going down that tunnel, you can cut yourself off before you go. Share your plan with your "emotional anchor" and perhaps with the franchisor so they can head you off also.

Treat yourself gently. Mistakes aren't bad or wrong, they just are. Learn and move on. You are supposed to be learning. If you aren't making mistakes, you aren't trying hard enough. If you are the type who, after making a mistake, likes to heap on guilt and blame, cut it out.

Be humble. Reach out for help. Let the franchisor contribute to you, helping you fix your problems fast. Find out how they see and define problems. Find out why they craft the solutions they craft. Get their vision. Stay in regular communication with those supporting you. The Grind comes from the disempowering belief "There is no solution to my problem." You can't be working on a solution and be in The Grind at the same time.

Trust the learning process. Remember, you weren't born competent in your last position. No doctor ever removed anyone from their mother's womb, spanked their little butt, wrapped them in a blanket, and handed them to their mother proclaiming, "Congratulations, you just gave birth to an eight-pound-three-ounce Vice President of Human Resources." No one gave your previous KASH formula to you. You earned it. You found a way to make it happen. The best predictor of future performance is always past results. If you found a way to make it happen in the past, chances are you will find a way to make it happen now. You are resourceful. You can trust you. Don't forget it.

Work with the franchisor to get training to increase your knowledge and skills, consulting to fix your problems fast, and coaching to hold you accountable for executing the knowledge you do possess and to help you manage your emotions.

How Franchisors Can Help You

More Training

Have the support people watch you, monitoring your on-the-job performance. Have them focus on developing good habits, improving skills, and continuing to develop your knowledge base.

More Consulting

Don't be afraid to burn up the franchisor's phone lines. Keep close track of the key performance measures of your business (such as labor cost, cost of sales, etc.—the franchisor will train you as to what they are and mean). Get these measures to the franchisors' support staff. Ask them what it means and get strategies to fix problems fast. If you disagree with the franchisor's solution, execute it anyway. Remember, your disagreement is coming from your past, and much of your past will be irrelevant in your new business model. Follow the franchisor's instructions closely until results prove otherwise.

More Coaching

Remember, your attitude is going in the toilet. You need consistent reminders of what your goals are and why you started your business in the first place. You need constant reminders that things will turn out fine over time. You need help moving through worry and you want the franchisor's support team to help you move through your stress in order to make better business decisions.

Winning

As franchisees acquire the necessary KASH to succeed, they begin to experience the ability to create positive outcomes. In The Grind, outcomes were something that happened to them; in Winning, outcomes are something designed by them. Like a man pumping water, franchisees in The Grind spend a tremendous amount of time, money, and energy pumping and pumping, disheartened by the mere trickle of water their pumping creates. What they don't see is the pipeline full of water that has yet to make it to the nozzle. Once the water starts flowing, it takes less and less energy to keep it going. Less pumping produces more water. This is what Winning looks like. Winning isn't produced by a singular event, just like water doesn't flow by one mighty pump. Winning is a process. You enter Winning through little victories, by learning to do the little things right, by steadily acquiring the KASH formula of success.

Winning creates a feeling of empowerment. Franchisees in The Grind feel trapped and powerless, like somehow *the business owns them*. In Winning, franchisees experience being able to produce positive outcomes by design. Keep in mind, all the time, *the business itself never changes*. The franchisees change! Their relationship to their business also changes. While in The Grind, owning businesses used to be something these franchisees did. Now it is who they are; they are entrepreneurs. They have made a successful personal transformation from a newbie to a competent professional, like a caterpillar to a butterfly.

Now for the million-dollar question: Was it worth it?

Asking franchisees who are winning is like asking a mother of a newborn baby if the labor pains were worth it. "Sure, it was worth it," the new mother smiles as she answers. She wouldn't have it any other way. The pain becomes a distant memory, replaced by the joy of being Mom.

Franchisees who are winning will probably smile before they answer, too. "Yeah, it was worth it," they will most certainly respond. The pain of The Grind was replaced by the joy of being an entrepreneur.

Once the caterpillar becomes a butterfly, it is never a caterpillar again. It also seems that once employees become entrepreneurs, few will ever become employees again.

Keep in mind, there is nothing wrong with being an employee. Franchisees need and value employees. Without faithful and committed employees, most franchisees will never enter Winning. We are merely talking about personal transformation. Getting franchisees to return to employee status is like getting a butterfly to return to caterpillar status. Being an employee is not wrong, the same way being a caterpillar is not wrong. A butterfly is not better or worse than a caterpillar, just different. Entrepreneurs are not better or worse than employees, just different. The transformation process however, moves in one direction.

Franchisees in Winning see their desired future as occurring. The freedom, challenge, flexibility, control, and other rewards they desired when they started their business are now becoming reality. It's no longer a question of if they'll succeed, as they're already succeeding. It's now a question of how high they can fly.

Franchisees enter Winning as a combination of their own personal effort and the franchisor's skill in imparting their KASH formula of success. Using a poker analogy, these franchisees are holding a Winning hand. However, they are not yet out of the woods; they can still fall back into The Grind. How? By folding the winning hand.

A franchisee of a vitamin retail chain once told a funny story about some of his customers. "When my new customers start taking our vitamin supplements, they feel 10 times better. Some think, 'If I take 10 times that original amount, then I should feel

The Learning Curve
of a Franchisee

100 times better!' But instead of feeling better, they pollute themselves and feel 10 times worse."

Why? They changed the winning formula. They folded the winning hand.

It can be the same with franchisees in Winning. Many feel compelled to make "minor adjustments" like emphasizing certain aspects of their business, de-emphasizing others. Because they haven't completely grasped the KASH success formula of their business, they may not fully realize the synergistic relationships and see the full impact of these decisions. They tamper with the Winning formula and in the process, fold their Winning hand. Then it's back to The Grind until they can figure out what went wrong.

When franchisees are in The Grind, a sophisticated franchisor focuses on training and consulting, imparting knowledge and skills as fast they can, making sure franchisees are focused on building winning habits. They coach franchisees on maintaining a positive and healthy attitude. They encourage learning.

When franchisees enter Winning, a sophisticated franchisor shifts the support strategies to making sure franchisees *change nothing*, drumming the Winning formula into the franchisee's memory through sheer repetition. Franchisors should keep a watchful eye on these franchisees, but many franchisors don't understand this dynamic. Therefore they don't remain vigilant. They assume these franchisees will just keep doing what works and the world will be as it should be.

Because many franchisors don't understand this dynamic of human performance (the Winner's unwitting drive to fold the winning hand), they aren't on the lookout. Therefore, as you enter Winning, make sure someone is watching your back, documenting what you do, and holding you accountable for not changing anything!

Some franchisors offer competent, ongoing coaching and support to their successful franchisees. Other franchisors spend most of their time and resources supporting franchisees in The Grind and less time with franchisees in Winning. If you're among the latter, consider hiring a professional business coach to make sure you don't change the winning formula.

Franchisees in Winning face a second risk. Although the business is growing, one person can only do so much. Steady growth will eventually cause an organizational breakdown unless franchisees develop their teams. The business needs to be more dependent on processes and systems and less dependent on entrepreneurs. The value entrepreneurs bring to the table must decrease and the value their teams bring must increase. Additionally, God forbid if something unfortunate happens and the Winning franchisee becomes incapacitated. If the franchisee's team lacks the KASH to step up and continue in this franchisee's absence, the business may still fail.

So, once it's clear the business will survive, it's imperative that franchisees impart the franchisor's KASH formula of success to their team. However, franchisees that have successfully completed The Grind have difficulty letting go; they're afraid of going backward. Some hold on too tight, micromanaging, disempowering staff, and creating turnover. Others continue to work "medical residency" kind of hours and physically and emotionally burn out. Because they haven't fully developed their teams, some can't handle the growth and the business implodes. They become a casualty of Winning.

> Franchisees in Winning should work with the franchisor to be trained as a trainer.

Knowledge

Franchisees in The Launch are unconsciously incompetent. They don't know how incompetent they really are, so they're happy. Franchisees in The Grind are consciously incompetent. They know how bad they are and how far they need to go. Their joy turns to frustration. Franchisees in Winning are consciously competent. They know what they're good at and what they need to do to produce results. They are empowered with the experience of being able to make things happen. Their frustration turns to self-confidence. Yes, there is always more to learn, but they know enough to drive results. Their success depends more on how they skillfully execute their existing knowledge than on learning new knowledge.

Attitude

Winning franchisees are empowered franchisees. They are re-engaged in the reasons they started their business in the first place. The future they desired when they started their business is now occurring. They have successfully navigated their learning curve and can see the finish line. All they need to do is to keep their foot on the gas, keep the wheels straight, and keep looking ahead.

Franchisees in The Grind drive their businesses by looking in their rearview mirror, fretting about costly mistakes in the past. Franchisees in Winning spend more time looking through the windshield, focused more on the road ahead. They only throw occasional glances in the rearview mirror as a reminder of where they have been.

Additionally, many franchisees in Winning start developing genuine humility. The success formula of their business will shift again, this time becoming more dependent on contributions of others and less dependent on the entrepreneur. Franchisees simply can't do it all, so they should stop trying. It's time for these "Superman" franchisees to retire their cape and red tights, put on their horn-rimmed glasses and to return to Clark Kent status. Let Lois Lane and Jimmy Olsen shoulder some of the load.

Skills

They have developed and refined their personal skills. They are good at whatever they need to be good at to win. They have the ability to produce positive outcomes and handle whatever the business throws at them. Their next step is to become skillful trainers, having the ability to successfully impart the KASH formula of the business to their employees.

Habits

Franchisees know the high-priority activities that produce the greatest results and spend their time engaged in them. They've gotten into the rhythm and the flow of the business. They're generating greater results with more ease and a high degree of predictability. One habit they probably need to drop at this point is self-reliance. It's time to include professional development and nurturing of staff into their day and groom themselves as a manager ... transitioning from doing to delegating.

Strategies for Successfully Navigating from Winning to Peak Performance

Don't fold the winning hand. Train and develop your staff, giving away the KASH success formula of the business. Make sure everyone has the Winning hand. Refine your systems and document your processes and procedures. Let employees step up and contribute. Decrease your value so your employees may increase their value.

Get training from the franchisor on how to become a trainer and coach.

Request coaching from the franchisor, having them hold you accountable to staying the course and not folding your Winning hand.

An out-of-the-box strategy to drive performance is to volunteer to mentor another franchisee or to act as an assistant trainer in the franchisor's initial training program. Medical school professors have a saying called "See one, do one, teach one." They teach surgery by first letting the medical student observe (to build their knowledge), they do (to build their skills), and *then* *teach* (to build winning habits). This is a brilliant way to permanently cement the Winning KASH formula in your memory.

How Franchisors Can Help You

Less Training

You already know what it takes to win. Now it's about executing what you know. You do, however, want to be trained as a trainer so you can develop your staff. You also want to make sure you have a solid understanding of all the key performance indicators of your business and what they mean.

Less Consulting

You want to start developing a healthier sense of independence from the franchisor, building your skills as to diagnosing your own problems and having both you and your staff creating your own solutions. The knowledge is now within you. Exercise it.

More Coaching

Work with the franchisor to help with goal planning and strategic planning. Request the operations support team to take on your goals as their goals. Since you're no longer concerned with simply surviving, it is time to re-engage in designing and realizing the future you originally desired for yourself and your family. Use the franchisor as your accountability structure, holding you responsible for executing your plan and realizing this future. Give them permission to challenge you and confront you when you are off track.

The Zone

When franchisees enter The Zone, they produce outstanding results as if they were on autopilot. They have fully committed the KASH success formula to memory. They are unconsciously competent, and brilliant execution has now become habit. Keep in mind, most of what franchisees are looking to accomplish with their business will occur in Winning. Many Winning franchisees will not enter The Zone, nor is it a requirement for success. Peak-performing franchisees are far to the right of the franchisor's performance bell curve. These franchisees have highly developed teams and manage their businesses according to key performance measures. Rather than dismissing data and buying into the emotion of The Grind, they look past their emotion and take a healthy, daily, objective look at results. They study the key performance measures, such as sales, labor cost, product cost, and others. They know what these numbers mean. If a number is off, they know where to look.

For instance, if labor cost is high, they will look into how they or their employees schedule their labor. They will analyze customer counts during different periods of the day, looking for whether they were overstaffed and for changes in customer's shopping patterns. They will look for fall-off in individual employees' sales productivity and see if the "dollars-per-customer transaction" is falling. Each measure will give them a separate plan of attack. They become an expert consultant of their own business and head off small problems before they become major problems. They play the Winning hand again and again, not feeling the need to fold it.

Just as golf's Phil Mickelson doesn't need to think about the mechanics of his back swing before he tees off, The Zone franchisees no longer need to think about the mechanics of their businesses. Separating them from the KASH success formula of their business would require a lobotomy.

Picture yourself reviewing a detailed financial statement while sitting next to a CPA of a large public accounting firm. You and the CPA are looking at the same financial statement. You see lots of numbers that may or may not mean anything to you. The CPA sees patterns and a story behind the numbers. You may be looking at the same financial statement, but you aren't really looking at the same statement. Only one of you is looking through the eyes of a master.

So it is with peak-performing franchisees in The Zone. They don't see the business the same way as franchisees in The Launch, The Grind, or Winning. They have the distinction of a master.

Transitioning from Winning into The Zone is not about doing more of what it takes to get into Winning. The difference is attitudinal. When in Winning, franchisees need to think about what they must do to win, create a plan, and then they must execute their plan. Winning requires time invested in strategic thinking and planning. Franchisees in The Zone win automatically, with little thinking. They have so committed the KASH success formula to muscle memory, they now perform at masterful levels instinctively, with seemingly little thought or effort.

Knowledge

Peak-performing franchisees are walking encyclopedias, experts in their field. They know their customers and products and they know where their industry is heading. They know the franchisor's corporate structure inside and out and where to go for support. They know what they need to know and stay on top of the changes.

Attitude

These franchisees are empowered with the sense of being able to design positive outcomes. They are winners and they know it. Some become humble, attributing their success to the franchisor, their employees, and their Creator, instead of their own personal greatness. Others become puffed up, reveling in their "rock star" status given to them by the other franchisees.

For some, their relationship to their business evolves again. No longer are they focused on just making money. They are now thinking about how to benefit others and the community. Their desire for success is replaced with a new desire for significance ... profits for purpose. Others get caught up in the trappings of success, like bigger houses, fancier cars, expensive toys, and luxurious vacations.

Skills

They expertly execute their knowledge. They have highly defined personal and organizational skill sets, being able to produce outstanding results with seemingly little effort.

Habits

The KASH model of success is fully committed to muscle memory. Peak performance is now reflex, requiring little or no thinking. These franchisees know what activities produce the greatest results and structure their day to expertly execute these activities.

Peak-performing franchisees are not without risk, however. Believe it or not, their greatest risk comes from winning.

You may be asking incredulously, "Winning? How does winning create risk?"

After conquering the last known civilization, famed military leader Alexander the Great cried out in anguish, "Alas, no worlds left to conquer." Alexander had won. What was he to do next?

Winning, like losing, means your game is over.

The thrill of living occurs in playing to win, not in the actual winning. Winning is overrated. Playing to win is juicy.

Have you ever climbed a hill or mountain? How long did you hang out at the top before you were bored out of your mind? Isn't it more thrilling to climb?

Peak-performing franchisees need to invent a new game to play or create a new mountain to climb, such as running multiple units, mentoring other franchisees, or getting more involved with their communities. If not, they will experience the anguish of having no more worlds left to conquer.

How the Franchisor Can Help You

More Training

Not training for you; but get training for your staff and offer to train other franchisees. Volunteer to train other franchisees, giving you an experience of greater purpose. Allocate some time to mentor employees and at least one other franchisee who's mired in The Grind.

Less Consulting

Start relying on and challenging your staff to identify their own breakdowns and craft their own solutions. Give them decision-making power. Use the franchisor's operational audits as their scorecard, an objective measure as to how your staff is doing.

More Coaching

Get agreement from the franchisor's support staff to never let you win. When it looks like winning is inevitable, have them challenge you to design larger and loftier goals ... goals so large you may never win or lose ... designed to keep you motivated and in the game.

The Goodbye

When you contemplated buying your first home, did you think, "This is a house I will live in the rest of my life," or were you thinking shorter term? When you took your first job, did you think, "This is a good place to work for 40 years and then retire," or did you think it was a good place to cut your teeth, with thoughts of eventually moving on. For whatever reason, many people who look at franchises elect not to move forward because they can't find the business they want to operate for the rest of their lives. If they waited for the right job to come along at which they wanted to work for the rest of their lives, they'd be unemployed. People who invest in franchises shouldn't look more than five to 10 years out.

Many consultants will tell you the time to sell the business is when a business is at its peak market value. This doesn't always hold true in most franchises. That's like saying to a homeowner, "The time to sell your house is at peak market value." From a financial perspective it's true; from a practical standpoint it's naïve. What if you have kids in high school? Do you pull them out and put them in a new school because your house has hit peak market value? What if you simply enjoy your neighborhood and living in your town? Do you sever these relationships because the real estate market peaked? "Who cares about peak market value?" the homeowner thinks. "I like living here."

Just as there's a time to sell your home and change jobs, there will be an appropriate time to sell your business, and it may or may not be when it hits peak market value. There are other considerations. Before we discuss what those considerations are, let's first draw a boxing analogy.

Pretend you're the referee of a heavyweight championship fight. The champion is fighting a brilliant fight, landing combination after combination. The challenger is hurt, and appears dead on his feet. What do you do? You can wait for the champion to knock the challenger out cold, thus ending the fight. Or you can end the fight by declaring the champion the winner by "technical knockout," or TKO as it is called. "The champion will eventually win," you think, "so why prolong the inevitable?"

The same is true with franchising. There are two times to sell, one is not necessarily better than the other. It's your business, so you get to choose which.

1. When you've accomplished what you originally set out to accomplish and there's nothing left in mind worthy of being accomplished. In other words, you won by a knockout. If you aren't inspired to train for your next fight, it's simply time to retire from fighting and choose your next sport.

2. When you know you'll accomplish everything you are looking to accomplish, although it hasn't all been accomplished yet. It's just a matter of time, just around the corner. Sure, you could wait around for those results to occur, but work has lost its challenge and you don't feel like waiting. In other words, you declare yourself the winner by a TKO. If you aren't inspired to train for your next championship fight, it's time to retire from fighting and choose your next sport.

Sell your business when there are no worlds left to conquer ... when you have nothing left to prove. Don't prolong the decision or you'll have the same unsatisfying experience Alexander the Great had after the last civilization fell.

Remember, winning is boring; *playing to win is exciting.* Winning means your game is over. Winning, while certainly more rewarding than losing, is just as sad when you don't have the next game to look forward to. So play a new game! Don't wait for the sadness to come!

Still, many franchisees hang around too long and become bitter. They long for "the good ol' days" when business was fun and they were inspired. They engage in gossip with other franchisees and end up destroying the integrity of the franchisee–franchisor relationship. Because they have no worlds left to conquer, they simply hang around and take cheap shots at the franchisor and suppliers. Regardless of their age, they become like the crotchety old neighbor who sits on her rocking chair on the front porch, yelling at people who walk past. Not that the people walking past are doing anything wrong, but because the crotchety neighbor has nothing better to do. The franchisor becomes a frequent and convenient target for franchisees who have nothing left to win and nothing better to do.

We're not asserting that these franchisees are necessarily doing anything wrong, the same way rocks aren't doing anything wrong when they hit the ground after being dropped. Rocks simply obey the laws of gravity. Franchisees are obeying the laws of behavior. To interfere with law of gravity, the rock has to be caught before it hits the ground. To interfere with the laws of behavior, franchisees must either catch themselves or be caught by the franchisor before their attitude hits bottom. Because few franchisors understand the dynamics of normal human behavior, few look out for Winning or Peak-Performing franchisees to fall. Asking franchisees to catch themselves is almost like asking the rock to catch itself.

Just as it's completely natural and expected for franchisees to generate positive attitudes in The Launch, it's just as natural for franchisees who win to become bitter if they don't create a new challenge. Again, this is not good or bad, just the way it is. However, if they aren't acting responsibly, they'll react to their bitterness by creating problems between the other franchisees and the franchisor. And they won't have a problem finding an audience. The first people they will call are franchisees in The Grind!

Knowledge

Franchisees in The Goodbye stage of their business have expert knowledge. They've seen it all. While there are always knowledge gaps to fill, new products being introduced, new vendors, new industry data, etc., these franchisees know what it takes to succeed and have committed the KASH success model to memory.

Attitude

There's a slow and steady erosion of their attitude. The business has lost its fun and challenge and these franchisees are no longer inspired. Where work was once play, work once again becomes tedious. Often, they start assigning the cause of their frustrations outward. They think, "If my employees were more loyal, the franchisor was more responsive, my vendors weren't squeezing me, and my customers weren't so price sensitive, I would be happy." The business simply isn't fun any more. Since the business is working, there's little motivation to sell. However, their attitude will eventually impact their results, and the business will track downward.

Most franchisors report significant sales increases when such a business transfers, often in double digits. What do these new franchisees have that the old franchisees don't? More knowledge? More skills? Better habits? Certainly not. They have a more productive attitude. Their attitude drives their results. New franchisees are inspired; old franchisees are tired. Over time, their knowledge will become obsolete.

Skills

These franchisees are highly skilled. However, one of their newly developed skills is cutting corners. Some become highly skilled gossipers and complainers. No longer motivated by achieving peak performance, they are more driven by not being hassled by employees, customers, and the franchisor. They become a "don't bug me," waiting to happen. They know how to cut back on the effort and still achieve some minimally acceptable performance.

The Learning Curve
of a Franchisee

Over time, skills will erode and negatively impact performance.

Others learn to delegate and start detaching more from the business. They develop other hobbies and interests that the business funds.

Habits

Many of these franchisees walk the path of least resistance. Chances are they've gotten out of the habit of personal development and continual improvement. They've gotten into the habit of cutting corners and just doing enough to continue to maintain their current lifestyle. As they're no longer focused on perfectly executing the high-priority activities that drive results, results will eventually flatten or track downward.

Franchisees in The Goodbye stage of their business usually say long goodbyes. They're like the last guests to leave the party, oblivious to the fact that the party is over. Because they have no other party to go to next, they just hang out.

These franchisees need coaching. They need the franchisor to sit down with them and revisit what they are looking to achieve. They need to be asked, "What's left to accomplish? What more is there to do? What's next for you?"

However, most franchisors don't track attitudes, just results. They don't measure whether franchisees are winning (or have already won) *by the franchisees' definition of winning*. Most don't know how to career coach franchisees out of their existing business and into an exciting new venture or challenge.

Overall, the franchising community has done an excellent job of developing themselves as trainers and consultants. Coaching is a largely ignored discipline within franchising, often confused with training and consulting.

These franchisees don't need to be trained. They already have the knowledge and skills they need to win. Nor do they need consulting; if they have an occasional operational problem they have the ability to fix it. They lack goals to inspire them. They haven't designed a future that they wish to bring into the present. They're stuck. All the training and consulting in the world won't make a difference.

We recommend franchisees in Winning hire skilled business coaches to supplement the expert training and consulting many franchisors offer. Skilled coaches help these franchisees design, visualize, and construct the future, while letting the franchisor's operational support team help franchisees with the present.

When selling a business, there appear to be two types of franchisees' responses to the resale process. The first group may have sold businesses before or know others who have, and thus have a realistic idea of what their business is worth and what happens next. They sell a business the way others sell used automobiles. They know the business has a certain fair market value, and they research what it is. They calmly contact the franchisor's franchise sales representatives and alert them of their intentions. They also enlist the services of a business broker to generate leads. They exit with dignity and grace.

The second group dismisses the notion of "fair market value," assuming this concept doesn't pertain to their unique circumstance. Therefore, they have no realistic idea what their business is worth. They assign a monetary value to their pain and suffering in The Grind and add that to the asking price of their business, like they're suing the new owners for damages. When the prospective buyers do their due diligence and question them about the business, they experience it as a personal attack. "More pain and suffering," they think. "I'm going to have to raise the price of the business." They exit screaming and yelling, assuming someone screwed them.

How the Franchisor Can Help You
More Training

Get training on how to value a business and what happens before, during, and after the resale.

More Consulting

Find out what have businesses sold for in the past. What is fair market value for your business? What terms should you consider? How will the franchisor support you and the buyer during the resale and transition of your business?

More Coaching

Selling a business is an emotionally taxing process. By then, you have so much mentally and emotionally invested in the business, separation is difficult. Additionally, what are you to do next? Having nothing to do will make you want to hold on to the business longer, although you have somewhat lost interest. Work with the franchisor to help you design what's next, either inside or outside their franchise system.

Chapter Summary

Just as human beings evolve as they enter different stages in life, franchisees evolve as they enter different stages in business. This evolution occurs through five distinct phases in linear order: The Launch, The Grind, Winning, The Zone, and The Goodbye. The franchisees' results and satisfaction level fluctuate from stage to stage. During each stage, franchisees are transformed by the KASH they acquire. Eventually, they experience the sense of control they were seeking when they started the business. Both work and life are good. They have internalized the KASH success formula of the business.

None of these stages are better or worse than any other stage, they simply are. Many franchisees however, resist The Grind and attempt to leapfrog right into Winning. Forcing a learning process seldom works, you get it when you get it. With an intelligent learning strategy, and close contact with the franchisor's trainers and operational support personnel, you will accelerate your learning curve and compress your time frame from The Launch to Winning.

7

The Evolution of the Franchisee–Franchisor Relationship

Back in chapter 2, we looked at the ways franchise candidates and franchisors answer the question, "What is a franchise?" You saw franchising in its lowest and simplest form as a distribution model, where franchisees sign a license granting them the right to distribute the franchisor's unique brand of products and services. Their relationship is defined by the language, intent, terms, and provisions of their agreement. This defi-

nition is impractically simplistic, assuming the relationship is static by not taking into account how both parties grow, communicate, and develop within this relationship.

More experienced and professional franchisors know this relationship is not defined by the language of any contract, much in the same way a marriage relationship is not defined by the marriage certificate. The franchisee–franchisor relationship is a highly personal relationship. All the frailties, foibles, and imperfections of what it is to be a human being become visible in the franchisee–franchisor relationship.

There is love and respect. There is also anger and resentment. There are times of peace and times of war. Hang around franchisees and franchisors long enough and you'll see their relationship break down, mend, break down, and mend again. There will be times of pushing and shoving, blaming and resenting, as well as peace and harmony, acknowledgment and gratitude. Their relationship spans from selfishness and pettiness and to selflessness and heroism, plus everything in between.

All the love, anger, and occasional dysfunction you would witness when you attend a large family gathering also show up in the franchisee–franchisor relationship at one point or another. This isn't bad, the same way large family gatherings aren't bad. It just needs to be anticipated and dealt with powerfully. In this chapter you learn how.

Franchisees and franchisors who master this relationship become as one body, each acknowledging they need the other to win. Franchisees rely on the franchisors to put together marketing strategies and operational processes and systems that will help them generate cash flow to sustain operations. The franchisor depends on the royalty income paid by franchisees. Both the franchisees and franchisors are completely reliant on the success of the franchisees' operations to survive, although they come at it from different perspectives. Therefore, highly competent franchisees and franchisors put aside their petty differences, remembering they aren't each other's competition. The war they need to be fighting is for increased market share and franchisee profitability. Putting their personal differences into perspective, they recognize neither party is going away. Then they find powerful ways to work with each other toward their common goals.

Again, this isn't bad, just the way it is.

World-famous psychiatrist and Nazi concentration camp survivor Viktor Frankl once said, "An abnormal response to an abnormal situation is completely normal." Keep in mind 99 percent of the people who contact a franchisor to learn about their opportunity don't move forward. While the 1 percent isn't abnormal, they aren't normal either. People don't "normally" take the actions necessary to define their lives and careers on their own terms. Franchisees are exceptional. Therefore their relationship with their franchisors also has the tendency of being exceptional—exceptionally good, exceptionally bad, and everything in between.

Greg Nathan, an internationally renowned franchise adviser, corporate psychologist, and founder of The Franchise Relationships Institute, has created a brilliant model that explains and identifies the normal shifting pattern of the franchisee–franchisor relationship. Nathan distinguishes a six-stage natural progression, which he calls the "Franchise E-Factor." Each stage is marked by the franchisee's and franchisor's distinct beliefs, emotions, actions, and levels of dependence and satisfaction of the relationship at that time. As the relationship matures, these beliefs, emotions, actions, and satisfaction levels change. These stages in the franchise relationship are described in two of his books, *Profitable Partnerships* and *The Franchise E-Factor*. With his permission we provide in this chapter an outline of these stages and some tips for managing them. The six stages are:

1. Glee
2. Fee
3. Me
4. Free
5. See
6. We

The Glee Stage

The moment a potential franchisee makes the decision he or she is joining a particular franchise, they enter the Glee stage. They are filled with heightened emotions, ranging from joy to fear of the unknown, but underneath it all is a strong belief that in the end they'll be living the life they are designing for themselves and their families. They may not have even physically signed on the dotted line of their franchise agreement yet, but they have already mentally signed on. Having made a bold move to accept more responsibility for how their lives and career turn out, they feel empowered by the experience of having just altered their future.

The franchisee–franchisor relationship is marked by solid trust. The franchisee thinks, "Hasn't the franchisor done everything I asked them to? Haven't I been dealt with honestly and fairly throughout the investigation process? These are people I trust and respect, who believe I can get the job done and win."

Since most franchisees join franchise systems that are a departure from what they are currently doing, their relationship is also marked by complete and total dependency on the knowledge and experience of the franchisor. In the absence of any training and support by the franchisor, many franchisees will ultimately fail. Therefore, franchisees are vulnerable in the Glee stage. However, they believe their franchisor will successfully impart the necessary KASH (knowledge, attitudes, skills, habits) that will eventually liberate them. They have heart-to-heart discussions with the franchisor about their fears and concerns and have heard back, "We are always here for you. You are our top priority. We can't win if you don't win," and "If you have a problem, we're only a phone call away."

Tips for Managing the Glee Stage

► Recognize it takes time to ramp up a business. Give yourself permission to learn. Most franchisees have been producers in the past. Producers want to produce. However, early in the learning curve of the business, peak production is an unrealistic demand. Treat yourself gently.

► After you open, early on, you will understandably bombard the franchisor with questions about what to do from "My cash register receipt tape is jammed, and I don't know how to fix it" to "My employee didn't show up, now what do I do?" When contacting the franchisor with a question or concern, give them time to respond without creating a conflict. While your issues may appear urgent to you, most of what happens early on in a business is not life threatening. At times, they will need 24 hours to get back to you. Treat others gently also.

▶ If you're lucky enough to have a strong grand opening, don't be put off if you see a lull afterward. Many times franchisees are successful in getting curious customers to try their products and services. These customers come in with a high frequency until the newness of your concept wears off and their number of visits or calls will go down. Then they will shop you with lower frequency, but in a more predictable pattern. This will be offset by your marketing for more customers.

▶ Accept eventually the newness of your business will wear off with you, too. This isn't bad, just the way it is as you get into the routines of the business. So be gleeful about being gleeful.

The Fee Stage

As you saw in the last chapter, "The Learning Curve of a Franchisee," franchisees enter a period called The Grind, where it takes tremendous effort to generate marginal results because they're still learning what it takes to succeed in the business. Just as their relationship with their business goes negative for a period, so does their relationship with the franchisor.

Franchisees in Nathan's Fee stage think, "My employees are getting paid, my vendors are getting paid, the franchisor is getting paid, but I am not getting paid enough for my hard work! If the franchisor is my partner like they said, why do they take their money off the top! Forget what the franchise agreement says; they should make money when I make money! And what am I getting for this money? I have to do all the work!"

Franchisees in the fee stage can become more demanding about the service they receive for their franchise fees. They look to cost justify the royalties they're paying in by demanding more.

As franchisees learn how to survive in business by spending their own money rather than their employer's money, they become more sensitive to where their money is going. Like any businessperson, they want to receive a return on their royalty investments. They raise their expectations of the franchisor, wanting such things as more services, higher quality, greater responsiveness, and more training for their staff. They also become more familiar with normal, everyday personalities and usual character flaws of the people working within the franchisor, and can become frustrated.

Just as in a marriage, the Glee stage of the honeymoon is short lived, replaced by the hard work of creating appropriate boundaries and setting realistic expectations of the marriage. The honeymoon period of the franchisee–franchisor relationship is also over, replaced by the "What have you done for me lately?" attitude of the franchisees present in the Fee stage.

Again, this isn't bad. It's the natural process franchisees and franchisors go through as they work together to create an interdependent win–win relationship. They just aren't there yet.

Franchisees are still not fully competent in their business. So this stage is marked by a dependency on the franchisor, learning what they can count on the franchisor for and what they need to count on themselves for.

Tips for Managing the Fee Stage

▶ Consider your royalty fees cover more than whatever the franchisor has done for you lately. The franchisor has invested tens of thousands, hundreds of thousands, or perhaps even millions to develop the systems to get to where they are. Your royalty payments are the way the franchisor monetizes past investments and provides for future investments to better the system.

▶ Accept employees of the franchisor are only human. Just as they were not as perfect or superhuman as you may have made them out to be in the Glee stage, they're probably not as flawed or incompetent as you may make them out to be in the Fee stage.

▶ Continue to develop the business relationship *without fighting or taking things personally.* Allow time to manage your attitude before and after conversations with the franchisor's staff. Know what you want to take away from conversations and field visits before you have them. Develop a healthy sense of what you can and cannot count on the franchisor for and what you need to count on yourself for.

The Me Stage

Franchisees move into the Me stage when they finally get it, right down to their toes, that the franchisor is not going to make them successful. Their success will be completely dependent on their ability to create results using the franchisor's business systems. Their mantra becomes "If it's to be, it's up to me!"

Now they enter this stage about the time they start generating results and gaining competency. Nathan talks about a negative, self-serving "I did it all myself without help from anyone" kind of bias that can mark this stage. Franchisees may discount the value of the training and support they received, as well as overlook the genius of the franchisor's systems and business model.

When things weren't going as well, it appeared as if it was the franchisor's fault. Now that results are occurring, it appears as the franchisees' victory. "I am succeeding *despite* the franchisor's incompetence," think some franchisees. From the franchisor's perspective, it seems the franchisor can't win.

Franchisees in the Me stage start winning and experience a renewed sense of empowerment. Some will become somewhat egotistical, dismissing the franchisor's and other franchisees' contributions to their success. Some will become more assertive requesting, and sometimes demanding the franchisor fund and implement initiatives they create. Franchisees can inject an "I know more than you do" attitude into the relationship, demeaning the franchisor's support staff and damaging the relationship.

In the Fee stage the franchisor falls off the pedestal franchisees placed them on. In the Me stage the franchisor smashes on the ground and franchisees jump up and down on the pieces.

The Me stage is marked by franchisees asserting independence, a clear departure from their previous dependent relationship with the franchisor. Franchisees may exercise their independence by testing the boundaries of the franchisor's systems or even crossing the boundaries. Franchisors may respond to these challenges by using command-and-control techniques, like sending violation letters, demanding compliance, and correcting violations. Franchisees respond to these techniques by rebelling and pushing back more. The relationship breaks down further.

Franchisees in this stage are similar to rebellious teenagers. In the teen years, parents appear stupid. From the teenager's perspective, it's a wonder the teenager has survived into the teen years with such incapable, incompetent parents. "I don't need my parent's advice," thinks the teen. "I know more than they do so I'm going to do what I want. They don't know what it is to be me."

Once again, the Me stage is not bad. It's more of the natural progression toward creating a "oneness," an interdependent win–win relationship with the franchisor.

Tips for Managing the Me Stage

- ▶ Give credit where credit is due. Recognize the efforts of the franchisors and franchisees for getting the system and brand to where it is.
- ▶ Accept people as they are. The franchisor's staff was never as good as you made them out to be in the Glee Stage and they are probably not as bad as you're making them out to be now.
- ▶ Honor your written and verbal agreements. Respect the boundaries of the operating systems and integrity of the brand. Don't cross a line you'll come to regret later.
- ▶ Take time to be proud of your accomplishments, but don't sit on your laurels too long either.
- ▶ You're starting to win. Don't change the winning formula. Commit it to habit.
- ▶ Don't force your opinions down the franchisor's throat.

The Evolution of the Franchisee–
Franchisor Relationship

Franchisors generally recognize the "million-dollar ideas" come from the franchisees. Let your results speak for themselves and the franchisor and other franchisees will seek you out. You won't need a soapbox to stand on.

The Free Stage

As you can see, the relationship between the franchisee and franchisor shifted from dependence to independence. As franchisees become more competent and independent, their relationship usually grows strained for a time. The Free stage is characterized by more franchisee competence, and thus more strained relations. Franchisees in the Free Stage feel burdened by the "meaningless and frustrating systems and control" the "corporation" is "putting on them." Put another way, as the franchisee grows more confident and competent in their business, they pick at and further test the boundaries of the franchisor's system. They may deviate from the norms and change the winning formula of the business to their own detriment. The franchisor, once considered a trusted guide, may now be considered a storm trooper, who swoops down on them from their ivory tower to lay siege to the franchisee's business for the sole purpose of telling them what to do.

Franchisees in Nathan's Free stage, depending on their style, may get cynical and aggressive, combating with the franchisor's support team privately or publicly. Or they may fester and withdraw, choosing instead to gossip and create strained franchisee–franchisor relationships for other franchisees.

At the end of the movie *Braveheart*, Mel Gibson, portraying captured Scottish rebel William Wallace, is strapped down to a table and offered the opportunity to either repent and die a quick death, or to maintain his rebellious attitude toward his rulers and die a slow, painful death. When asked for his decision, Gibson yells, "Freeeedom!" And then the torturer does his business.

Some franchisees get stuck in this stage, and their relationship with the franchisor remains strained. Those who get stuck usually see one of three outcomes.

1. They get frustrated with the franchisor and sell. *"Freeeedom!"*
2. They frustrate the franchisor, and the franchisor either forces a sale or terminates the franchisee's agreement for material breaches in their franchise agreement (if such breaches exist) or forces the franchisee into compliance. *"Repent! Ordie a slow tortured death"* or
3. They learn to live together and stay out of each other's way, like two bad roommates sharing a college dorm room.

Franchisees who successfully navigate through the Free Stage unpredictably, almost miraculously, experience an epiphany ... a big "ah hah!" which dramatically alters the future of their franchisee–franchisor relationship. They finally grasp from the tops of their heads to the tips of their toes that both the franchisees and the franchisor need to be profitable to maximize the potential of their brand. These franchisees then start seeing it as their responsibility to help the franchisor maximize their revenue potential also, understanding full well that a large percentage of these incremental revenues will make it back to the franchisees in the way of better support, products and services, and system tools.

Tips for Managing the Free Stage

▶ Remember your commitments and honor your franchise agreement. No doubt at some time in your investigation of the franchisor, you agreed to conform with and master the franchisor's business system. You made a promise, so keep it and stop resisting. The franchisor is on your side (you just think they aren't). The franchisor is not trying to control you (you just think they are). Franchisors must protect both their investment and other franchisees' investments. Don't back them into a corner. Stay in problem solving and out of fighting. Remember the value of this relationship because it's what you paid for.

▶ Don't let open issues and unaddressed issues fester. Get closure. If you need to bring a third party in to be heard, do so.

The Evolution of the Franchisee–Franchisor Relationship

Don't fight, bring in a third party who will support you and stay in problem solving.

▶ Don't gossip and don't listen to gossip. Gossip is often defined as bringing your problems to someone who has no authority to resolve your issues. Gossip plants the seeds of ill will and destroys companies. Don't participate.

▶ Create win–win solutions. You know enough about both your business and the franchisor's business to recommend solutions where you both win. Get in their world. Franchisors are primarily concerned with four things: recruiting more franchisees, collecting more royalties, maintaining franchisee–franchisor relations, and building the brand. Show them how they can implement your suggestions to drive royalty collections to create results in one or more of these four areas. If they see your suggestion as all cost and no benefit, of course they will resist implementing your suggestions.

The See Stage

The franchisee gets it. They were blind to it, now they get it. The see if every franchisee within the franchisor's system pushed, pulled, fought with, and demanded things of the franchisor they way they do, the franchisor will die and most everyone will lose their investment. The franchisee sees the systemwide impact of their behavior and negative relationship. They see if they re-channeled their energy into creating positive relations with the franchisor and driving their own business, rather than in-fighting, resisting, and gossiping, everyone is better off. They get it that the franchisor isn't going anywhere. They understand their negative relationship with the franchisor can either be a short-term problem or a long-term problem and they get to say which.

They see they're part of a larger organic system, a bigger body consisting of the employees and owners of the franchisor, the franchisees, and the franchisees' suppliers. All are committed in their own way to build the brand and always were. As famed cartoonist Walt Kelly's creation Pogo once said, "We have met the enemy, and he is us!" The franchisee sees over time they slowly forgot how connected they were ... and still are. There is recognition the franchisor doesn't measure success the way the franchisee measures success. The relationship is no longer about one party winning and the other losing. The franchisee gets it. *Both parties need to win!* This invites mature, intelligent, commercially minded strategizing and problem solving, not petty, immature fighting, bickering, and gossiping.

The connectedness they experienced during the Glee stage starts to come back.

The relationship immediately begins to mature from an independent relationship to an *interdependent relationship*, which is all the franchisee and the franchisor wanted in the first place.

Tips for Managing the See Stage

▶ Mend fences with the franchisor's support staff. In the past, you probably tweaked some noses, caused some problems, and bruised some egos. Fess up. Take responsibility for your actions and take the initiative to repair relationships that need repairing. Just because you are ready to forgive and start over, don't assume others are. It takes two parties ready to move on to get to the next stage.

▶ Mend fences with existing franchisees. Chances are you enrolled others in your battles and gossiped with them about the franchisor. Perhaps you have trained other franchisees to relate to you as a trouble-maker or are partly responsible for other franchisees being mired in their Free stage. Fess up again. Invite franchisees to follow you into your new, mature See stage.

▶ Get involved. The franchise is one body with many members. Consider becoming an active, productive member of the larger body. In the past, perhaps you were a hemorrhoid, occasionally flaring up, grabbing some attention, and causing general irritation until someone gave you what you needed to go away. You could now become the belly button, serving no real purpose, passively coming along for the ride, and occasionally gathering lint. Or you can become the eyes, ears, hands, and feet of the organization: gathering data, testing new initiatives, and paying attention to the big picture for the benefit of all. You get to say which.

The We stage

The See stage opens the door to broader possibilities available only in the We stage. The door was always there, you needed look beyond your independent thinking to see it. This stage is characterized by mature, objective, global, problem-solving, strategic, interdependent thinking. The franchisor is no longer the enemy. The battle is for market share, not about who is right or wrong. The relationship is fully mended, assuming of course the franchisor is fully with the franchisee in the We stage. *Less competent franchisors get stuck in the Me stage also*, thinking the "ungrateful" franchisees are there to serve them. "It's our company," they think. "If they don't like it, they can get out!"

Nathan suggests that to create a franchise culture of We, a few things have to happen.

- ► Mature franchisees have to be winning, getting both an acceptable return on their investment and living the lifestyle they desired when they first joined the franchise system.
- ► The franchisor must also be on a winning track.
- ► Both the franchisees and franchisors must understand the other's viewpoint and respect it as if it were their own.
- ► Both the franchisor and franchisees must understand and respect each other's style and decision-making processes.

Franchisees and the franchisor must each be fully committed to the other's success. The franchisor must think, "When a franchisee fails, I fail." Conversely, franchisees must come from, "If my franchisor isn't winning, I am not winning."

Tips for Staying in We

Be an active, positive participant in networking with others in your system. Be a "We" advocate and evangelist. Most successful franchisees experience an obligation to give back to the whole. In the process, you will experience a greater sense of purpose, and with it, results.

Sit on committees or assist with mentoring new franchisees. You know what it takes to win and you experienced the four stages of the learning curve of a franchise and the six stages of the franchisee–franchisor relationship. You can help others navigate their stages.

Chances are by now you've become a thought leader in your chain. Use your influence and leadership for the benefit of the greater body.

From Glee to We

In the following diagram of Nathan's Franchise E-Factor you will note a natural progression from dependence, to independence, to eventual interdependence. Franchisors who have successfully created interdependent relationships with franchisees have a high probability of creating a lasting brand with significant value.

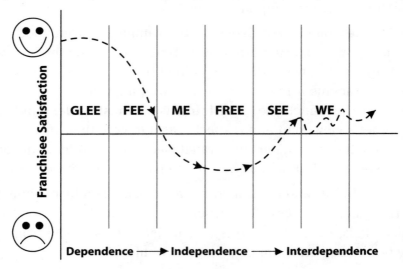

The Franchise E-Factor was developed and copyrighted by Greg Nathan

Figure 7-1. The Franchise E-Factor®

The Evolution of the Franchisee–Franchisor Relationship

Franchises who are mired in the "Me" or "Free" stage stand a high probability of imploding from in-fighting, with many people getting caught in the crossfire. Paraphrasing the Bible, Abe Lincoln famously said, "A house divided against itself cannot stand." When franchisors and franchisees forget they're on the same team, the unified brand disintegrates into a divided house. When conflicts arise, franchisees and franchisors invest time, energy, and money on guaranteed win–lose or lose–lose outcomes, which tarnish the brand, destroy the value of the investments, and severely damage the franchisee–franchisor relationship.

That isn't to say the franchisee–franchisor relationship isn't supposed to have its peaks and valleys. Like any relationship, of course it does. However, if the franchisee–franchisor relationship is currently in a valley, as long as it was built initially on a foundation of trust, respect, and commitment, the relationship will see a peak again.

If not, the franchisee–franchisor relationship has a tendency to keep spiraling downward. In these instances, there may a point where the relationship is so damaged, the parties have so much emotionally and financially invested in their opposing opinions, civil war breaks out. Nobody wins.

When you're investigating franchisors, pay particular attention to where franchisors and franchisees are in this relationship scale. If the franchisees and franchisor are at odds, don't immediately dismiss the opportunity. Dig deeper. As long as there is mutual trust and both parties continue to listen, they may just be in the valley leading to the next peak.

Back in the mid 1980s, the Subway franchisor and many franchisees were at odds. The Subway parent company had just made a sweeping decision, requiring all Subway franchisees to bake fresh bread every morning rather than having it delivered by bread suppliers. "More work!" cried out some franchisees. "Why break what isn't broken?" cried others. For a short time, their relationship soured. However, the decision was the right one and sales took off. Some customers called in saying, "I am not interested in ordering sandwiches; may I just buy your bread?" New stores also ramped up faster. Subway created a dynamic point of difference from other food chains. Customers became excited and new customers flocked into the stores. The delicious aroma of fresh-baked bread hung in the air while they anxiously waited to order their food.

Consider where Subway would be without fresh baked bread. Initially, not everyone was happy with this decision.

Success cures many ills.

Note: For more details on the Franchise E-Factor we would recommended *The Franchise E-Factor* and *Profitable Partnerships,* both by Greg Nathan and published by The Franchise Relationships Institute. Available from *www.franchiserelationships.com.*

Part Two

Investigating Franchises

8

Locating Franchise Opportunties

By completing Part One of this book, you have acquired a thorough understanding of what franchising is and isn't, and what it takes to win. If you haven't already dropped this book and run terrified, screaming into the night, it's time for you to explore the options available to you.

Franchising experts estimate there are currently over 2,000 franchise opportunities in the United States, representing more than 80 industries.

Additionally, in most years over 200 new companies a year start franchising. With so many franchise options available, you can once again ask yourself the question, "What do I want to be when I grow up?" If you like what you already do for a living, but it's just time to start doing it for yourself, you may find a franchise in a similar field or industry to the company you will be leaving.

If what you do no longer excites you, consider doing a

career "extreme makeover" by looking at franchises completely unrelated to your current career.

Whether you are looking to do something materially similar or radically different than you are doing now, be like a kid in a candy store and enjoy the shopping experience.

For people starting to look into franchising, franchise opportunity web portals are the first place most people go. There are many franchise-specific websites to choose from. Many franchisors advertise on more than one, so don't be surprised if you see the same franchise opportunities popping up again and again. Visit multiple sites. Each has its own twist, like articles and educational information, newsletters, search capabilities, or other unique features. The sites we recommend you explore (in no particular order) are:

Franchise Opportunity Websites

- ► *www.entrepreneur.com*
- ► *www.franchise.org* (the International Franchise Association website)
- ► *www.franchiseopportunities.com*
- ► *www.franchisesolutions.com*
- ► *www.franchisegator.com*
- ► *www.franchiseforsale.com*
- ► *www.franchise.com*
- ► *www.franchiseworks.com*

Franchisors advertising post brief descriptions of their history, their product or service, what makes them unique, who their target customer is, who their target franchisee is, and what their total investment is. While some of these websites offer links to the franchisor's home pages, you can easily find the home pages by typing the franchisor's name into an Internet search engine.

Depending on the franchise opportunity website you visit, you should find hundreds of franchise opportunities to comb through.

Important Tip: If you wish to request more information about a particular franchise opportunity or speak to a franchisor representative, go their website directly and fill in your contact information on the contact form. Franchise candidates who request information from many franchise portals often report being inundated by calls and e-mails from companies whose information they did not request, making the hunt for the right opportunity more frustrating than it needs to be.

Franchise Brokers

Because there are so many franchise opportunities available and people looking into franchising are so time starved, an interesting branch of business brokers has emerged known as "franchise brokers," "franchise referral agents," or "franchise coaches."

Franchise brokers are usually experienced businesspeople who specialize in working with people looking to start franchises. Most franchise brokers will know what franchises are available in particular markets along with the skills, aptitudes, and capitalization a franchise candidate needs to succeed. Like any normal bell curve distribution, the value of franchise brokers varies from broker to broker. Some offer their clients expert professional guidance and outstanding one-on-one career coaching. Others simply shove a few franchise brochures in their client's hands and say, "Call me if you're interested."

Most franchise brokers offer their services to their clients free of charge. If a client joins a particular franchisor the broker recommends, their commission is paid by the benefiting franchisor. Because you benefit from the experience of working with a strong professional franchise broker without incurring high upfront fees, we recommend you take advantage of their services.

Keep in mind, franchise brokers only work with a small selection of the many franchise opportunities that exist. Since franchise brokers have a wide enough inventory of franchisors who work with them and their clients are always free to investigate any franchise they wish to on their own, their clients seldom feel limited.

Also keep in mind that not all franchise brokers are created equal. Many are new to franchising and developed their skills and experience in industries outside of franchising. Franchise brokerage is a highly nuanced business that takes years to learn. Make sure you deal with someone who has earned their stripes, can add value to your search, and isn't learning their business with your time and money.

Since there are several hundred brokers across the United States and abroad, you most likely will find a broker who lives in or knows your area. Don't deal remotely if you don't have to. Speak to someone local. Because their compensation is tied to whether or not you purchase a franchise and not whether they protect your interests, it's best to look them in the eye and bring an extra dose of your humanity to the equation to help the broker walk the straight and narrow.

There are four major companies who have the most experience. They are (in no particular order):

- ▶ Franchoice (*www.franchoice.com*)
- ▶ The Entrepreneur's Source (*www.theEsource.com*)
- ▶ Frannet (*www.frannet.com*)
- ▶ Matchpoint (*www.matchpoint.com*)

Magazines

Entrepreneur magazine is the gold standard publication for people looking to start businesses. They often run articles that spotlight franchising. The January issue (often called The Franchise 500 Issue) rates the top 500 franchisors according to a proprietary rating scale.

Franchise Expos

The International Franchise Association holds annual franchise expos (called the International Franchise Expos or IFE), usually one in Washington, D.C., one in southern Florida, and another in California. These expos give you the opportunity to check out many franchise options and ask franchisor representatives questions. Go to *www.franchise.org* and check their events page for details.

Google and Other Search Engines

Once you have identified some companies and industries you are interested in, use search engines to locate other franchise players in that space.

After you have identified one or more franchisors you want to investigate, check out their online reputation by searching content, such as "tweets," Facebook, blogs, online publications, and consumer- and business-related websites. In addition search out what information is available online about the officers and leadership of the franchisor. Dig deep. There is far more information available today than in the past. After you are comfortable with the franchisor's, officers', and key managers' online reputations, proceed to the next chapter of this book. You will learn how to conduct a thorough, step-by-step franchise investigation to determine if you fit a particular franchisor's profile of a successful franchisee and the franchise opportunity you are investigating can produce your desired results with a high degree of probability.

9

Following a Six-Step Franchise Investigation Process

As you have been reading this book, you may have been struck by a paradox that affects franchising in a funny way. The more entrepreneurial and comfortable with risk a person is, the less likely they are to follow systems others create. Put another way, the people most likely to invest in a franchise are also by profile most likely to resist following the system they just bought into. While this is certainly not true in all cases, it's the rule rather than the exception.

While many high-risk-takers resist following systems, they are usually also strong producers who generate consistently great results. If you read through the history of their performance reviews you would see a consistent pattern of supervisor feedback that reads like "Steps on people's toes and routinely ignores internal rules and regulations. However, (s)he produces great results. Pain in the neck, but I wish I had 10 people like him or her."

Does this sound like you?

If so, as you investigate franchises, know this resistance-to-systems dynamic exists. Know the stronger your resistance the more you increase your financial risk. Even in the face of resisting systems, if you still found a way to produce consistently great results in the past, chances are you will probably produce great results in franchising. The best predictor of future results is past results. If you have produced for others, chances are you will continue producing for yourself. Your past job and career did not make you successful. You did the work necessary to win. Your company may have offered you the potential to win, but you brought winning into actuality. Winning isn't what you do; winner is who you are.

Conversely, if you have produced consistently poor results in the past, chances are you will produce consistently poor results in the future. Being in business for yourself is probably not going to change this dynamic. In the current economy you will need to step up your game. Mediocrity and minimal acceptable effort and performance simply won't cut it.

Remember, regardless of the franchise you investigate, every franchise has its own distinct KASH (knowledge, attitude, skills, habits) formula for success. You have your own personal KASH formula for success. The goal of your investigation process is to find a franchisor whose KASH success model closely matches your personal KASH model.

Also keep in mind, you probably won't find a perfect match, nor do you need to. You want to find a close match. The first several chapters of this book were designed to make you look inward, to help you determine your personal KASH model for success. Let's call this your "Starting KASH." Your franchise investigation process will answer the following questions.

1. What are my goals? (from chapter 4)
2. What is my Starting KASH? (from chapter 5)
3. What is the franchisor's KASH formula for success?

4. What KASH am I currently missing from this formula?
5. What training and support will the franchisor make available to fill in my KASH gaps?
6. What is the franchisor's track record for helping franchisees like me acquire the necessary KASH to win?
7. What is the probability I will achieve my goals with the franchisor's business model?

Regardless of how sexy the business appears, how cool the products or services are, how enjoyable the customers seem, how economically resilient the model looks, or how well you think you fit in ... if the franchise opportunity will not deliver your desired results with a high degree of probability, it is the wrong franchise for you.

The easiest way to compare franchise opportunities is to create a simple visual display that you can update as you gather information. We offer you a sample display later in this chapter.

In this chapter you learn how to research and compare opportunities against their ability to deliver your "must have" and "wish to have" goals from chapter 4. You may be a person who researches only one business at a time. Or you may be a person who compares two or more franchises at a time. Either way, the criteria you will use to compare and contrast businesses, regardless of whether they are in the same industry, is their ability to deliver your desired lifestyle.

Aside from evaluating the franchise as a viable business opportunity, it is equally important to evaluate the franchisor as a viable franchisor. Remember, a franchisor needs to be brilliant in following these key areas.

1. **Creating a unique product or service offering.** The products and services that franchisees offer their customers are unique to their company and can't easily be copied or replicated by competition. New and existing customers understand and see value in the offering and aren't likely to cut out their expenditures in cost-saving moves. Lastly, these

products or services offer franchisees a sustainable, long-term advantage over their competition and are not in danger of being obsolete, replaced, trumped, or outsourced in the foreseeable future.

2. **Sales and marketing.** The franchisor has a proven, intelligent system for communicating their value in a way that engages, calling them into action. The franchisor has a track record of building a brand that means something to the consumer in more than one market. The franchisor must have systems in place, which, if followed, are proven to help you generate new business and establish the same brand equity in your local market.

3. **Operations.** They have proven systems for managing employees, controlling costs, and profitably delivering products and services that add value to the customers.

4. **Financial controls.** They must have a deep understanding of how to measure and manage the business according key financial performance criteria so an acceptable percentage of the revenue generated by the business flows through to the bottom line.

5. **Recruiting high-quality franchisees.** The success of a franchisor is built on a foundation of successful franchisees. Skilled franchisors know how to identify and recruit franchisees that will succeed in their system and say "no" to everyone else.

6. **Training and developing franchisees into peak performers.** Peak-performing franchisors know what it takes to win and have their KASH model well identified. They know how to transfer their knowledge and develop franchisees' skills. They help franchisees acquire the mindset and habits of a master and hold franchisees accountable for consistently executing the high-priority activities that produce most of the results. They track franchisees' progress and offer consistent and valuable feedback on how to raise their game to

the next level. They value and embrace continual learning. Learning and advancement are strong fibers woven into the culture of the organization. They give franchisees the experience of being coached and supported, not managed and controlled.

7. **Creating positive franchisee–franchisor relationships.** Excellent franchisors have created a powerful, interdependent relationship with their franchisees. They work together to increase brand equity rather than fight to either control or resist being controlled by the other party.

A franchisor must be both a master at their own business and be a brilliant franchisor at the same time. When a franchisor is missing one or the other, this is a franchisor's recipe for future problems.

In this chapter we offer you a simple, six-step process for investigating a franchise. By following this process, you will complete an investigation of the franchise and a rigorous self examination as to whether you fit into a particular franchise system.

Although we are going to teach you a basic, six-step investigation process, be mindful that outstanding franchisors have their own franchisee investigation processes that may or may not mirror this one. If this is the case, defer to and follow the franchisor's investigation process, adopting the tools we offer you in this process. If they don't have a step-by-step investigation process, consider taking the franchisor through this process. Also keep in mind, a franchisor that doesn't have a clearly defined franchisee investigation process probably also doesn't have a clearly defined business model. Beware of these franchises!

In the previous chapter you learned where to go to explore different franchise opportunities. Once you have narrowed your options down to the two or three franchises you want to explore, use this systematic approach to narrow your choices to your best single fit.

Overview of the Six-Step Franchise Investigation Process

The six steps are as follows:

Step 1: Initial Interview
Step 2: Qualification
Step 3: Reviewing the FDD and Franchise Agreements
Step 4: Data Gathering and Analysis
Step 5: Visiting the Franchisor's Home Office
Step 6: The Yes/No Decision

Step 1: The Initial Interview

Step 1 is an initial interview and presentation of the franchise concept, most likely conducted by telephone and sometimes in person with a franchise sales representative. This interview is often 45–90 minutes of give and take of information. This is a "getting to know each other" step, where you help the franchise sales representative understand who you are, what makes you successful, and what you are looking to accomplish. The franchise sales representative in turn helps you understand who the franchisor is, what makes the franchise opportunity unique and who makes a successful franchisee. You both begin the process of determining whether your skills and aptitudes match the skills and aptitudes required to succeed within the franchise. It's designed to give you a quick gut read as to whether or not the franchisor's KASH model of success aligns with your personal KASH model and whetheryour objectives can be met with a high degree of probability.

Step 2: Qualification

Step 2 is either conducted by telephone or sometimes in person, usually depending on if the franchisor you are investigating has a local franchise sales representative in your area who can meet with you. The purpose of Step 1 was to give the franchisor a quick sketch of who you are, what your objectives and goals are, as well as giving you a general understanding of the franchisor and the business model. The purpose of Step 2 is to gather and offer more specific details. The overall objective of Step 2 is to determine if there is a fit from the franchisor's perspective. If you create an open and honest dialogue with the franchisor, they will probably see the potential fit before you do because they have an insider's perspective on what it takes to win. If, for whatever reason, you don't possess the necessary KASH or capital (from the franchisor's perspective), you want to find out now before you have invested significant time and money into the investigation process. If from the franchisor's perspective you do have the appropriate capital and KASH, you will still need to verify the details and performance levels of the other franchisees to see if there is a fit from your perspective.

Step 3: Reviewing the FDD and Franchise Agreements

During Step 3, you will conduct a business review of the terms and conditions of the FDD (Franchise Disclosure Document) and make sure you and the franchisor are in material agreement on all major points. The FDD is a document the FTC mandates each franchisor to offer franchise candidates. Some states may require additional disclosure information in the FDD.

There are two ways to look at a FDD, first is through the eyes of a businessperson. From a business perspective, does the disclosure make sense? Can you live with the terms and commitments of the agreement? Afterward, you can bring the FDD to an attorney who will review it from a legal perspective. At this stage you may not feel the need to bring in legal counsel as you are still gathering data. Once you have established the fit, then it will be time to conduct a legal review. At this stage, however, conducting a legal review may be premature and an unnecessary expense. However, it's time to become aware of what the business commitments look like and whether you are willing to honor those commitments. If for whatever reason there are commitments or obligations in the franchise agreement you can't live with, you will end the process here. If you can honor these commitments with integrity, you proceed to the next step.

Step 4: Franchisee Validation, Data Gathering, and Analysis

The purpose of Step 4 is to interview franchisees, gather data, compare the information you receive from franchisees with what you received from the franchisor, and determine whether you will produce your desired results with a high degree of probability. This is a period of intense data gathering and heavy analysis. Here is where you test the veracity of the franchisor's systems and determine whether the franchisor is a skilled franchisor and has a profitable business model positioned for the long haul. If the franchise appears to produce your desired lifestyle with a high degree of probability, it's time to invest in professional advice. You need to have a franchise attorney review your FDD and an accountant review your business plan.

Step 5: Visiting the Franchisor's Home Office

Never do business with people you have not met. Franchising at its best is a highly personal relationship. You are entrusting your dreams and capital into the care of the franchisor leadership. Decisions made on the executive level impact whether you are positioned to hit your personal objectives. Go to their corporate offices, meet the decision makers, shake their hands, look them dead in the eye, and ask tough questions. You have already evaluated the business model against its ability to produce your desired results. Now it's time evaluate your trust level of the franchisor's leadership and key management.

Step 6: The Yes/No Decision

It's time to make up your mind about whether you design a new life and career of your choosing or to go back to the way it was.

Now that you know the process in general, let's look at the steps individually.

Step 1: The Initial Interview

What does a successful Step One Initial Interview look like? At the end of the 45–90-minute conversation, this is what should have occurred.

► You offered the franchisor a basic understanding of your background, skills, aptitudes, and financial resources to determine if you fit the profile of a successful franchisee from the franchisor's perspective.

► You clearly stated and the franchisor clearly understood both your financial and "quality of life" goals. You received the franchisor's commitment to tell you if they feel your goals cannot be achieved with a high degree of probability.

► The franchisor clearly communicated to you the most important details about their business model to help you determine how your objectives can be met using their skills, systems, and training.

► You and the franchisor are both clear as to what the next action steps are and you have both agreed to take these steps.

The first indicator of whether you are dealing with a skilled franchisor is how they conduct this first conversation. They should know the questions they need to ask to begin qualifying you as a prospective franchisee. They should also know the type of information you will be looking for so you can qualify them. They should be prepared with both.

Prior to this meeting or telephone conversation, some franchisors will request you fill out a simple online questionnaire. If this is the case, skilled franchisors will prepare for this meeting by reading these questionnaires ahead of time. If you get a sense the franchise sales representative isn't prepared for your conversation, raise a red flag. Again, if they don't have a well-thought-out, well-organized, and well-executed franchisee recruitment process, it's reasonable to assume they don't have a well-thought-out, well-organized, and well-executed franchise business model either.

Part of being a skilled franchisor is to hire and manage one or more skilled franchisee recruiters. Being a skilled recruiter demands being a skilled interviewer. If a franchisor doesn't ask pertinent questions about your ability to succeed within their franchise system, raise the red flag.

On the flip side, answer openly and honestly. Begin to work in partnership with the recruiter to evaluate whether there is a match. Good franchisors won't try to hard sell you. They merely present their opportunity and let their results stand on their own merits. Good franchisors will be as concerned with the quality of the match as you are. Go into the meeting trusting this, unless you discover a reason not to. If, after the first conversation, you are left with the feeling you can't trust the feedback of the franchisor's recruiter, follow your instincts and move on to the next franchisor.

Questions you should expect to be asked are as follows:

Questions about your career:

- ► What is your work history?
- ► What do you currently do?
- ► What are your responsibilities?
- ► Why are you looking to start a business?
- ► What are you looking for a business to produce?
- ► What would you like to be earning in one, three, and five years?
- ► How does what you want to be earning compare to current your earnings history?
- ► How much cash each month does it take to run your household?
- ► What other financial objectives do you have (such as increase in net worth, etc.)?
- ► What does winning look like to you?

Questions about your family:

- ► Are you married? If yes, does your spouse support your starting a business?

► Do you have children? How many, what ages?

While some of these questions may be illegal or inappropriate to ask if you were applying for a job, this isn't the case with franchising. Starting a franchise will impact your personal relationships. Franchisors will want to know if you have communicated your intentions to others who will be impacted and whether or not you have their support. Franchisors don't face the same restrictions as employers as to what they can and can't ask you during an interview. Highly skilled franchisors will ask you highly personal questions.

Questions about your other career or franchise options:

► What other concepts have you looked at?

► What kept you from moving forward with these concepts?

► What other career options have you investigated? Why?

Franchise recruiters will want to know what stopped you from moving forward in the past because predictably the same issues may keep you from moving forward in the present. They know roughly 1 percent of the people who inquire about a franchise move forward. They want to know why you were among the 99 percent who didn't move forward when investigating other franchise systems and what makes you think you will be among the 1 percent who will be going forward with them. They will want to know who they are competing with. It's in your best interest to let them know who else you are looking at as it may help your negotiating position later.

Questions about your personal finances:
The franchise recruiter may ask questions such as:

► If I were to review your financial statement, what is the cash you have available to invest?

► Leaving out personal items such as furniture and cars, what would you ballpark your net worth be?

► If I were to pull your credit report, what would it say?

Although it may feel uncomfortable to discuss personal

finances with someone you don't know, it's in your best interest to do so. A skilled franchisor is going to ask you these questions upfront so they know if you have the necessary capital or the ability to raise it, as do you. Experts often cite the #1 reason for business failure is undercapitalization. If you are open and honest with the franchisor, you will know if you are undercapitalized in the first conversation. Not only do you need the necessary KASH (knowledge, attitude, skills, habits) you also need the necessary cash.

After you've answered the above questions, franchisors should offer you a good overview of their franchise model. Although neither of you will be able to tell with a high degree of certainty if the franchise is a match for you, you should be able to tell if you are a possible fit. If, after listening to and evaluating the information a franchisor provides, you get a sense you are not a possible fit, end the process and begin the investigation process with other franchises.

A franchisor should be able to offer you information or answer your questions about the following:

1. The mission of the franchisor.
2. The history of the franchisor: How did this franchise get started?
3. Number of units open and under development.
   - ▶ What markets are being targeted for development?
   - ▶ What are the development plans in your area?
   - ▶ Long-term growth objectives: How many units does the company eventually want and over what time frame?
   - ▶ Have any units failed? If so, how many, and why?
4. What is their concept?
   - ▶ What is their product or service?
   - ▶ What makes it unique?
   - ▶ What need does it fill in the marketplace?
   - ▶ How is it priced?
   - ▶ How many employees does it require?

- ▶ How is it promoted?
- ▶ What is the competition?
- ▶ How do they differentiate their products or service from what their competitors offer?

5. What is the industry?
   - ▶ Size and data.
   - ▶ Why is this industry attractive?
   - ▶ What does the future of the industry look like?

6. Who is the customer?
   - ▶ Demographics.
   - ▶ Buying behavior.
   - ▶ Why should they do business with your franchise?

7. How do you find customers?
   - ▶ Advertising strategies, marketing strategies, PR strategies, etc.

8. Where is the concept located?
   - ▶ What type of location is needed? Mall, strip center, office park?
   - ▶ Do I rent or buy?
   - ▶ Do I remodel or build?
   - ▶ How much space do I need?

9. What is the profile of a successful franchisee? What are the traits, characteristics, experience, strengths, background, education level, aptitudes, liquidity, and net worth of a successful franchisee?

10. What are the investment options?
    - ▶ Single unit, multi-unit, etc.
    - ▶ What is the investment level?
      - • How much cash is needed?
      - • How much can be financed?
      - • Where do I get financing?

11. What kind of support do franchisees receive? Such as ...
    - ▶ Location support.

- ▶ Assistance with financing.
- ▶ Assistance with construction.
- ▶ Initial and ongoing training.
- ▶ Marketing, graphic design, and advertising promotional support.
- ▶ Ongoing business coaching.
- ▶ Product research and development.

You should be able to offer and gather this information in 90 minutes or less.

Cut to the Chase: How Much Money Can I Make?

Most likely, this earnings information won't be made available to you in the first conversation. Franchising is regulated by the Federal Trade Commission, which has a process and structure for franchisors to follow to provide you with this information. As there is legal risk to providing earnings information, most franchisors elect not to. If a franchisor tells you, "It's illegal for me to give you this information," know this is an inaccurate statement. The truth is any franchisor can legally give you this information; they just have to present it in accordance with FTC guidelines. As a matter of fact, a recent study commissioned by the International Franchise Association Foundation showed about 25 percent of franchisors do provide some form of earnings information in their FDD. Franchisors who don't offer earnings statements to prospective franchisees don't do so for the following three reasons:

1. Historical franchisee or corporate unit financial performance doesn't make a compelling case for you to move forward (this could be because of poor performance or because they are a young franchise with a lot of franchisees still in start-up mode).
2. The data is difficult to obtain from their franchisees. Some franchisors don't require franchisees to report sales or operating expenses and don't have ways to collect this data.
3. They are afraid of getting sued.

Following a Six-Step
Franchise Investigation Process

If they choose to offer you this information, it will typically be presented in a document we referred to earlier as the FDD. At this point, franchisors may or may not offer you the FDD. Some will send it and direct you to the earnings statement within the FDD so you can better understand the predictable earning power of the franchise. Others will require you to complete an application and be approved for a franchise prior to receiving this information.

We briefly describe an FDD later in this chapter.

At the end of this first conversation, don't concern yourself with whether this is the right franchise for you, unless you are completely clear that it isn't.

After a successful first conversation, you will probably be left with one of four experiences.

First, "This is not for me." If this is the case, communicate this to the franchisor and move on. State your reasons and give the franchisor a chance to respond, making sure your decision is based on real data, not a misperception on your part. Many franchise candidates pass up great opportunities based on misperceptions.

The second is the cautious optimism ... a kind of "so far, so good" feeling. While the first conversation was successful, you aren't jumping to any conclusions right now. You are focused on what both you and the franchisor have determined are the next steps.

Third is an adrenaline rush. You may be left pumped up thinking, "When do I get started!" Cool your jets and take a step back. You only have the headlines, not the details. You don't know enough to determine if this is the right opportunity for you. Just as a person coming off a successful first date isn't wise to jump a plane to Vegas, grab the first Elvis impersonator they see for their witness, and get married, it isn't wise for you to mentally purchase a franchise after only one conversation. Create some distance between yourself and your emotions. While contagious enthusiasm is good thing, right now cautious optimism is a better thing.

Lastly, fear. This kind of fear is merely F.E.A.R, meaning False Emotions Appearing Real. What is there to be afraid of? You just had a conversation. You didn't make any commitments other than to possibly take one more step in the process. Nobody is trying to lift your wallet or steal your purse (not yet anyway). Give yourself permission to be afraid and then honor your commitment (if you made one) to take the next step in the process.

Congratulations. You just successfully completed Step 1. Only five more steps left to a "yes" or "no" decision.

Step 2: Qualification

At this point, many franchisors will ask you complete an application. Applications are often called such things as confidential questionnaires, qualification forms, approval forms, or a host of different names. However, they mostly request much of the same information, such as:

► Name, address, contact information
► Work history (or they will request you attach a résumé)
► Personal financial statement (summary)
► Earnings history
► Monthly expense budget (to see what it takes to run your household)
► Education history
► Goals and objectives
► Location/area preferences
► Strengths and weaknesses

An application may be filled out as a paper document, scanned, and e-mailed or faxed back or sometimes can be filled out securely online.

Additionally, some franchisors will ask behavior-based questions relevant to the running of their business, such as:

► What is your management style?
► How do you solve problems?
► How many people can you effectively manage?

Following a Six-Step
Franchise Investigation Process

- Are you a people person?
- How are you at managing our type of employees?
- How are you at servicing our type of customer?
- Picture yourself in our establishment. What do you think a typical franchisee's day is like? Would you enjoy a day like that?
- Are you looking to go home for dinner every night or do you will leave only after the job is done?
- Are your comfortable with risk?
- Do you see yourself as passionate about what we do?

It's in your best interest to be open and honest regarding this information. Skilled franchisors will evaluate you against their profile of a successful franchisee. Where puffery or inflating your credentials may help you get a job that pays more money, if you aren't feeding the franchisor factual information, your chance of surviving, if selected as a franchisee, has just been diminished. You want to know exactly which of your skills are and aren't relevant. You want to know exactly what you already have in place that can propel you forward and what you are missing. Shoot straight and be generous with information, and franchisors will generally respond in kind.

Please note you are not obligating yourself to purchase a franchise by filling out these forms. Also keep in mind the franchisor is not obliged to offer you one either. These forms are for information gathering only. Franchisors should use this information to help them determine from their perspective if you match their profile of a successful franchisee.

Some franchisors will ask you to divulge such things as social security numbers, banking account numbers, brokerage account numbers, and other detailed information. At this stage, they really don't need this information. While many franchisors request this information on their forms, generally they are OK if you leave this information blank for now. Typically, they aren't going to run credit reports or validate banking and brokerage account balances until they are ready to either invite you into their office or offer you a franchise. If they do ask you for this information, make note of it. They are jumping the gun and this may be a red flag regarding their skills or experience level as a franchisor or ability to relate to you as a franchisee.

At first, you may be afraid to provide such personal information. You may be thinking, "I'll provide it once I'm sure I'm going to buy the franchise." Remember, you are not entitled to own a franchise. A skilled franchisor is going make sure you are qualified. A franchisor can disqualify you for any reason they choose. Skilled franchisors are going to evaluate you with the same level of diligence you are going to evaluate them. If a franchisor finds you standoffish or closed minded, they may think, "This candidate is not a win–win person," and forgo offering you a franchise. Just because you have the money doesn't mean you are a shoo-in to be approved. Skilled franchisors are going to make sure you have sufficient starting KASH, and remember "A" stands for "Attitude," and attitudes don't often change. If they don't find you to be a win–win, problem-solving person, the competent franchisors are going to walk away from you.

You may also be afraid to provide this information because you don't know whom you are talking to and what they will do with the information you provide. You may think somehow your financial statement is going to be splashed all over cyberspace or the franchisor is going to sign you up to receive SPAM from online retailers. Perhaps there are a few exceptions, but usually the only people who will see your information at this point are the people who would need to see it, such as the franchise salesperson and others evaluating you as a candidate. At the end of the process (usually after step 4), if you express your intentions to be considered, many franchisors have formal or informal committees consisting of the department heads of franchise operations, franchise sales, and executive leadership such as the CEO and COO, who will verify your financial statement and run a credit report and criminal background check. However, this occurs generally much later in the process.

Following a Six-Step
Franchise Investigation Process

Step 2 is almost all about you. A skilled franchisor is going to prepare for this meeting by reviewing your qualifications and comparing your background, skills, attributes, and capitalization against their profile for a successful franchisee. They will identify what you are missing, bring it to your attention, and ask you questions to determine if you are willing to do what it takes.

For instance, they may ask, "I see you don't have direct sales experience. In this business you need to spend at least 10 hours a week networking for leads and cold-calling customers. The responsibility falls back to the owner. Is this something you are willing to do? Is this a skill you are willing to master?"

Franchisors will go into this meeting trying to determine with a high degree of accuracy if you are a match from their perspective. They will dig deep into your background, trying to understand how your skills will predictably transfer into your new business. They will ask financial questions to determine whether you can access the capital necessary to sustain your franchise operation until it's profitable while, at the same time, meeting your family obligations.

They will also give you an opportunity to ask them questions to fill in your information gaps. This stage is a simple give and take of information, with you mostly on the "give" side of the equation. This isn't a bad thing. If the franchisor you are working with possesses both skills and integrity, they will spot a potential match before you do. At the end of the conversation, don't be afraid to ask questions like, "Mr./Ms. Franchisor, . . .

▶ What do you see as my transferable skills? How do these skills relate to your business?
▶ How do I compare against the profile of a successful franchisee? What do I have? What am I missing? How will you support me in these areas?
▶ Knowing what you know now, where might I predictably struggle?
▶ How do you see me achieving my goals with your franchise?
▶ What concerns do you have?

- ► If you had to make a decision on me now, would you approve me as a franchisee? Why or why not?
- ► Given my existing skills and experience, what role do you see me playing in this business?
- ► Assuming I want to hire around my weaknesses, whom would I need to hire? What skills would they possess? What role would they play in my business?
- ► Am I a culture fit for your franchise?
- ► No matter what, what can I always count on the franchisor for?
- ► What do you count on the franchisees for?

At the end of the second meeting, although a franchisor may not offer you official approval for a franchise, any skilled franchisor representative who isn't supremely confident you will be approved when the time comes, will either end your investigation process or stall it in order to communicate what you are missing and give you the opportunity to provide it. For instance, you may be missing basic computer skills, which may disqualify you as a franchisee. A skilled, high-integrity franchisor may ask you to take some computer classes and invite you back into the process once you offer some proof of completion (such as a certificate).

At this point, you will generally have gone through two interviews, first on overall qualifications and second on your financial qualifications. Therefore, you should have the experience of being thoroughly interviewed, screened, heard, and understood. You should have the experience of having to earn the franchise the same way you would have to earn an attractive job offer. If you aren't getting the experience of having to earn the franchise, beware. Some franchisors are so eager to grow, they may offer franchises to people whom they wouldn't hire to run the same business.

In addition, the franchise representative should present themselves as a facilitator of the process, a buyer representative of sorts. If the franchise representative is occurring to you as "selling something" rather than "helping me discover if we are a fit," you simply should not completely trust their feedback from this point forward. In the first conversation they may occur to you as a salesperson because that's what you may be expecting to see. By the end of the second conversation they should be presenting themselves as something else. If this isn't occurring, then most likely they are trying to sell you something, so buyer beware. This doesn't mean they are lying to you, but it does mean you need to validate everything they tell you with the franchisees in the field to make sure you aren't getting the fairy-tale, sugar-coated version of what the franchise opportunity is and what it takes to win.

If you are having the experience of having to earn a franchise, this still doesn't mean you are working with a reputable franchisor. Do a quick gut check and you will find yourself having one of two experiences.

1. You will have an experience the franchisor is making a genuine effort to get to know you. You will feel like they are listening for what you want your life to look like, and if they can't produce your desired results, you would expect them to tell you, or

2. You will experience "being sleazed." You will have heard from the franchisor, "Not everyone will be awarded a franchise," or "You better keep the process moving forward because we have other candidates looking at the same area." In sales, they call this "doing a take-away." The franchisor representative is merely testing you to see if you are a viable buyer or if you are wasting their time.

At the end of the second meeting, make an evaluation as to whether you want to take the next step in the process. Don't concern yourself with having to someday write the franchisor a big check. That day isn't today. Skilled franchisors are not going to put any pressure on you at this point to make a decision. Some franchise sales representatives may ask you questions such as, "If you had to make a decision right now, what would it be?" Answer however you choose to answer. If you get the experience the franchisor representative is looking at you like a commission check rather than a person, make note of it. Or they may simply be trying to find what issues you have so they can help you gather the information you need.

If the franchise recruiter seems overly anxious, it could mean they are simply happy to have you in their pipeline. Only about 10 percent of people who request information about a franchise actually take the step to complete an application. Although filling out applications generally takes less than an hour and obligates you to nothing, franchisors recognize it's a big emotional step for you to take. You have moved one step closer to designing your life and career. They pay attention to people like you. In the eyes of the franchisor, you have elevated yourself from the 99 percent who don't do anything to the 10 percent who have taken at least one bold step of committed action and have the potential of being the 1 percent who join a system and take control of their lives and careers.

Step 3: Reviewing the FDD and Franchise Agreements

Generally after one or two conversations, whether these conversations take place over the phone or face-to-face, the franchisor will typically send you their Franchise Disclosure Document, or FDD as it's most commonly known. While the FDD is the document that defines the legal relationship between the franchisor and franchisees, the relationship between franchisees and solid and reputable franchisors extends far beyond the confines of a legal relationship and develops deeply committed personal relationships. These relationships transcend their obligations outlined in the FDD and franchise agreements. When franchisees and franchisors (or their respective attorneys) pull out the franchise agreement as a means to define their relationship, it's because the relationship has been damaged and the trust has been violated.

Although it may not be described in these words in the FDD, the roles and responsibilities of the franchisor are:

▶ To do whatever it takes (within reason) to give you the tools necessary to win, and

▶ To maintain the integrity of the brand.

The roles and responsibilities of franchisees are equally simple.

▶ To master the franchisor's business model,

▶ To deliver their products and services to your customers to the best of your ability, consistent with the spirit and intent of the franchisor, and

▶ To maintain the integrity of the brand.

Franchisees' profitability and contentment are the lifeblood of any franchise organization. If the majority of franchisees aren't happy and profitable, the franchise system eventually collapses like a house of cards. There's no other way to build a sustainable and profitable franchise system other than by building on the successes of many happy and profitable franchisees.

However, no franchisor is going to expressly state in a franchise agreement it's their responsibility to help make you happy and profitable. They are going to place the burden of responsibility squarely on your shoulders, absolving themselves of any legal responsibility if you lose. Even in the best franchise systems, for a host of reasons, not every franchisee wins. In our litigious society, the franchisor must protect both their investment and the investments of other franchisees. They do this by promising you little in the way of tools and support. That way if your business tanks, your relationship sours, and you take them to court, as long as they delivered on the minimal commitments they were obligated to perform under the franchise agreement, they win.

Franchise agreements are written for the express purpose of making sure that if taken to court, the franchisor wins and you lose. While at first this may seem unfair, consider the franchisor has an obligation to protect the investments all previous franchisees, partners, employees, and shareholders of the franchisor make in the franchise system, which requires such an imbalance.

The other franchisees and other stakeholders of the franchisor want to survive so they must design a franchise agreement that ensures that no one franchisee can take down the entire system. Franchise agreements are written to reflect the litigious times we live in. Simply because a franchisor promises you little doesn't mean they deliver you little. Competent franchisors regularly and routinely offer franchisees assistance and services beyond what's required under the franchise agreement.

The simple truth is if you go into the legal departments of most skilled franchisors, you can tell the file cabinets that hold the franchise agreements. They have the most dust on them because those cabinets are seldom opened and those agreements seldom read. Why? Because they know their survival is completely dependent on whether you and the other franchisees win. They are willing to do whatever it takes (within reason and budget constraints), regardless of what their agreement says or does not say.

We aren't saying, "Don't read your agreement." You have to be aware of what your agreement does and doesn't say. We are saying the only time to concern yourself with what your agreement says is when your committed personal relationship has failed.

In this section we are only going to touch on what to look for within the FDD. There are many fine articles available to you on the Internet and in publications.

All FDDs follow the same format, mandated by federal and state regulators. They all consist of 23 items, plus any exhibits and appendices the franchisor includes. We briefly describe what those 23 items are and what to look for as you conduct a business review. We recommend you hire a franchise attorney to do a thorough legal review. You will find a comprehensive list of franchise attorneys on the International Franchise Association website, www.franchise.org. Click on the tab for "Suppliers" and you will find a section for attorneys.

Many attorneys will tell you they know something about franchising and are perfectly capable of reviewing a FDD. However, franchising is a highly nuanced business, and unless an attorney specializes in franchising, (s)he won't know the ins and outs of franchising and what franchisors will and won't do. It has been our experience that franchise candidates who hire attorneys outside of franchising receive pages and pages of copious legal notes, high legal bills because the attorneys don't already know what to look for, and in the end, don't get the expert advice they paid for.

Item 1: The Franchisor, Its Predecessors, and Affiliates

This gives you a brief history of the franchisor, how it came to be, and what business they are in.

What to Look Out For. In the book *Outliers*, author Malcolm Gladwell asserts it takes a minimum of 10,000 hours of doing something to master it. Assuming someone works a business for 40–50 hours a week, it would take four or five years to master it. Therefore, if a franchisor has less than five years operating their own business model, they may be operating from theory rather than real world experience, which increases your risk. They may be testing and developing their franchise model with your money. However, if you or the key executives have substantial experience in a similar businesses, your risk may be lessened.

Item 2: Corporate Officers and Business Experience

This section offers you background on the decision makers.

What to Look Out For

► Do the officers have franchise experience? Have they grown other franchise chains before? If so, how successful are these past chains currently? Did these executives move onto another challenge after giving the chain stability or jump ship after they ran aground? Franchising is often described as a closed society. Many franchise professionals bounce around from company to company because companies look for experienced franchise executives. Keep in mind "experience" doesn't always mean "competent."

▶ Since many franchisors are family run, many family members are named officers, not because of merit, but because of their last name. Are they qualified?

Item 3: Litigation

Pay attention to this section. Franchisors need to disclose in this section which people (identified in Item 2) have pending civil, criminal, or other actions alleging violations of franchising, antitrust, securities law, and unfair or deceptive trade practices. They have to disclose a long history of such activity. Be mindful we live in a highly litigious society, so some legal disputes are normal and acceptable. A poll of franchise attorneys and experts taken by Franchise Performance Group once showed 50 percent of those polled thought it was acceptable if a franchisor has 1 percent or fewer of their franchisees engaged in some form of litigation. For instance, if a franchisor has 100 active franchisees and has one case of litigation (past or pending), this is normal. Another group of franchise attorneys and experts stated that you should look more at the nature and severity of the litigation rather than the percentage. Either way, litigation is an indicator of a breakdown in the franchisee–franchisor relationship. Even if the franchisor is winning these cases, take caution. Remember, the agreement is designed so they win. Read theses cases of litigation and see what the franchisees are alleging.

Item 4: Bankruptcy

Affiliates, predecessors, partners, and officers must disclose personal bankruptcies and bankruptcies of companies that they owned or were officers in or if the company declared bankruptcy shortly after their tenure as an officer. While bankruptcies are more common and less stigmatized now than in the past, still pay attention because someone who is supposed to be getting paid isn't. While the people declaring bankruptcy may have followed the proper legal processes to discharge their payment obligations to pay their creditors, you have to make a determination as to whether they have discharged their moral obligation to honor their commitments. Why is this important? Franchisors typically promise you little in their written franchise agreement. The success of a franchisee–franchisor relationship transcends any legal obligations that exist. It's built on a foundation of morality, integrity, ethics, and trust. Bankruptcy is a legal maneuver to avoid previous personal and corporate commitments and obligations. What's legal isn't always moral. If they successfully used the legal system to cancel their commitments to others in the past, it's highly possible they may do the same to you in the future.

Even if no moral issue exists, bankruptcy means business failure. Again, the past, left unchecked, has a way of repeating itself. Find out what the officers or people involved learned from their bankruptcy. Unless they have taken steps to put measures in place to prohibit this from ever happening again, take caution. If you hear excuses that are outside their control like, "The economy went south," or "Competition was too fierce," listen, but don't always buy the line. Perhaps there were plenty of companies in their industry doing business in the exact same economy with the same competitive pressures that didn't declare bankruptcy.

Regardless of whether the cause is integrity or skills, bankruptcy is a warning signal.

Item 5: Initial Franchise Fee

This section is to include all the fees and payments to the franchisor to open the business. If the franchise fee is not uniform, such as in larger or smaller territory fees, the franchisor needs to disclose how these fees are determined. Most franchisors charge $25,000–40,000 for franchise fees for single-unit territories (that may or may not provide a protected territory). Many franchisors will discount franchise fees (typically 20–30 percent) if franchisees invest in three units (or territories) or more upfront.

Beware of franchisors that take a large franchise fees (over $50,000) upfront. Franchisors who do this understand they are priced higher than what most franchisors charge. If they provide a higher level of support than most franchisors, this can actually be a bonus. Sometimes franchisors will charge a higher franchise fee if their business model produces exceptionally high financial returns, feeling as long as franchisees are producing strong financial results also, a higher fee may be justified.

However, some franchisors may charge more because they simply want to gauge franchise candidates and make their money by taking big fees upfront. Beware of these. After they get what they want and siphon your cash, they may be less concerned with your success over the long haul than other franchisors.

Item 6: Other Fees

Franchisors must disclose all recurring fees or payments that franchisees pay the franchisor and affiliates. They must also disclose how they compute those fees.

Those fees are typically:

1. **Royalties.** Royalties are the lifeblood of any franchise organization. Royalty rates fluctuate depending on the size, nature of the business, level of ongoing support, and financial returns. Most franchisors in the service, retail, and food sectors charge 4–8 percent. However, there are currently over 80 industries represented in franchising and different industries have different norms. Research the competitive concepts in the space to determine the norms.

2. **Local advertising.** Many franchisors will stipulate a minimum level of advertising expenditure per year. Some will direct which advertising vehicles you must use, such as direct mail, print, or SEO.

3. **National (or regional) ad fund.** Since the majority of franchisors in the United States have fewer than 100 units and, depending on the type of business, it can take 600 units or more to have the critical mass necessary to be able to afford national advertising and serve the customers it will reach, some national ad funds may not be able to effectively market the brand. Find out if some of these funds are used to offset

the salaries and expenses of their marketing department (salaries and expenses that should be covered by your royalty contributions). If the franchise you are looking to join has the necessary critical mass within the United States or within a region to benefit from mass media (radio and television advertising), these funds can offer franchisees substantial value. Where no such critical mass exists, these funds may offer little value beyond ego gratification to the franchisees and could be considered a second royalty. How much a franchisor charges and where these funds are allocated speaks volumes about the competency and integrity levels of the franchisor. Skilled, high-integrity franchisors will want you to spend your ad dollars where they are best spent to drive brand awareness and customer trial, regardless if it's on the local, regional, or national level. If they can create leverage by co-oping the advertising expenditures of their franchisees on a regional or national level to create substantial buying power, it's in everyone's best interest they do so. And responsible franchisors will. Look closely at how this money is collected and where this money is spent.

4. **Transfer fees.** Franchisors will charge you a nominal fee (generally less than the franchise fee) to train and develop the purchaser of your business. This is of great benefit to franchisees because once they sell their business, the franchisor will help with the training, development, and transition of new ownership. The seller is then free to focus on what's next. Since the transfer fee is often a fraction of the franchise fee, the new owner receives most of the same training and support of new franchisees, but paying a fraction of the cost.

5. **Renewal fees.** At the end of the term of your franchise agreement, franchisors charge a nominal fee to renew the agreement for another term. A typical franchise has a 10-year agreement and a 10-year renewal option. Renewal fees are the same or less than the cost of a new franchise.

Item 7: The Initial Investment

Your total investment is broken down into categories such as franchise fee, equipment, leasehold improvements, inventory, grand opening advertising, pre-opening expenses (such as travel and lodging for training), and working capital. You get to see where your money goes. You also get to see when the cash gets dispersed. In a typical franchise (aside from the franchise fee and some proprietary products), most of this money goes to outside vendors and contractors and these expenditures don't represent a profit center to the franchisor.

Most skilled and high integrity franchisors will do whatever it takes to help keep your front-end investment as low as possible so as not to deplete your cash and to increase your chances for survival.

The one cost franchisors have a tendency to underestimate is the working capital. Working capital is the cash you need to inject into the business to cover operating costs until the revenues generated can cover all your costs and you reach your break-even point. The FTC only requires franchisors to disclose three months of working capital. Since many business don't break even until after six to 12 months (some even longer) this number can be misleading. Make sure you know how long it takes to break even so you possess enough working capital.

Item 8: Restrictions on Sources of Products and Services

Franchisors must disclose your obligations to purchase products and services from the franchisor, affiliates, or approved suppliers.

It's reasonable for a franchisor to mandate whom a franchisee purchases from to maintain consistency and quality. However, talk to other franchisees to make sure these products are reasonably priced with reasonable terms and can't be purchased elsewhere for a lower price. Some franchisors will generate revenue from your purchases in the form of rebates from the supplier. Since money is often tight and many franchisors feel like they need the revenue, they often negotiate an attractive national price and then keep a percentage of the savings for themselves. While not entirely bad, negotiating best prices is a service skilled franchisors offer franchisees as part of the value of their royalties. These franchisors will often pass the entire cost savings along to the franchisees. A rebate may be justified in lieu of lower royalties. However, there are chains that gouge franchisees by forcing them to buy products at higher cost than they could negotiate on their own. This is a violation of the spirit of franchising. Many of these franchisors are now being called out by their franchisees on social media, blogs, and other searchable content.

There are franchise companies, like Chem-Dry carpet cleaners, who charge very little royalties and depend on profits from franchisees' direct purchases or rebates from other suppliers for their revenues.

If you take a step back you can see the different ways unskilled or low-integrity franchisors can put their hand in your pocket without your knowing exactly how much is being taken. Those ways include:

- ▶ Royalties
- ▶ National ad funds
- ▶ Rebates from your purchases from their approved vendors that could go to you

High-integrity and highly skilled franchisors will fully disclose and want you to know what your investment is now and in the future without hidden or hard-to-calculate fees or surcharges. They will take their money in royalty payments or in other disclosed ways. For those high-integrity franchisors that sell proprietary products and services, they will take reasonable markups and offer you reasonable terms. They will disclose what those markups are.

Item 9: Franchisee's Obligations

You will receive a detailed list of everything you will be held responsible for including (but not limited to) such things as:

- ► Purchases
- ► Initial and ongoing training
- ► Compliance standards
- ► Restrictions
- ► Warranties
- ► Quotas or minimum performance levels
- ► Fees
- ► Insurance
- ► Advertising minimums
- ► Staffing requirements
- ► Submitting to inspections and audits
- ► Recordkeeping
- ► Dispute resolution

Since this is a legal document, this section can be dense. It can also appear threatening. Don't be spooked by the language. The franchisors are protecting both their interests and the interests of the other franchisees. They make sure their agreements have plenty of teeth in case they are forced to protect the brand. You want to do business with a franchisor that has a solid reputation with its franchisees for win–win problem solving. When a problem or disagreement occurs, they don't go into their file cabinet, pull out your agreement, and force you into unwilling compliance. They listen to your issues, clearly state their issues, and craft solutions where both parties can get the most of what they each want. When you start interviewing franchisees in Step 4 of this six-step process, you learn how to identify these franchisors.

Item 10: Financing

Franchisors who offer franchisees direct financing disclose the terms and conditions here. However, most franchisors will direct you to outside lenders and leasing companies and don't finance franchisees themselves.

Item 11: Franchisor's Obligations

The franchisor must disclose the services they will perform prior to your business opening such as:

- ► Training (location, duration, and subject matter)
- ► Site selection assistance/lease negotiation
- ► Construction assistance and design assistance
- ► Advertising
- ► Permitting
- ► Software support

Item 12: Territory

If the franchisor offers protected territories or territory restrictions, how they determine territory descriptions and what those restrictions are will be spelled out here. Your actual territory description will appear in your franchise agreement.

We hear sad stories in the media about struggling franchisees from prominent fast-food chains who feel they are too close together and competing for the same customers. This is why having a protected territory is such an important issue. Ideally, franchisors and franchisees would like to do business in a wide enough area so as not to butt heads with each other. However, the area at the same time needs to be small enough to prevent the competition from staking a claim and camping out at your borders. Franchisees often come from the place, "Sure, I want to grow the chain, but not in my back yard." They feel threatened by another franchisee coming into their geographic area, even in a noncontiguous trade area, thinking, "This new franchisee will restrict my ability to grow in the future." Franchisors on the other hand want to keep the territories small in an effort to gain critical mass, dominant the market, and outpace their competition. Because of this dynamic, franchises many times won't achieve the same critical mass another, dominate, nonfranchise chain such as Starbucks has achieved. That is why Starbucks chose company-owned stores. Threats from franchisee litigation would have doomed the "Starbucks on every corner" strategy. When negotiating a territory, trust and open communication become critical. Do business with a franchisor that will offer you territory protection or be convinced you will succeed without one.

Some franchisors reserve the right to open company outlets within your territory, operating under the same brand name or perhaps under a different brand name. Their thinking is if you aren't upholding the standards of the brand, then they can open up in your territory and protect their interests. However, this also gives them the legal right to steal your brand equity if you are a top performer. Few franchisors would ever consider doing this, but may still reserve the right. Franchisors that have other protections under their franchise agreement typically don't need this right to protect their brand. If you can't negotiate this out of your franchise agreement, think carefully about proceeding further.

Item 13: Trademarks

Franchisors must disclose which trademarks, service marks, names, logos, and symbols they use to identify the franchise business. They must disclose if these are registered with the United States Patent and Trademark Office, the corresponding dates of registration, and proper identification numbers. If franchisees won't have such protection, the franchisor must disclose this lack of protection.

If a franchisor can't protect its trademarks, then it's entirely possible you can build your brand and have a competitor coming into the same market and advertise to your customers, using your name, logo, or slogans. Any franchisor that can't protect its brand is not a franchisor you want to sink your money into.

Item 14: Patents, Copyrights, and Proprietary Information

If a franchisor owns patents or copyrights, they must be disclosed here. Franchisors will often make general references to their proprietary business systems and trade secrets in this section. If a franchisor doesn't own patents or copyrights, depending on the industry, it might be okay. For instance, a residential cleaning franchise such as Molly Maids may use the same vacuum cleaners as other competitors, but the power of their franchise system doesn't depend on the proprietary technology of their vacuums. Their genius is in how they find, manage, and retain good help, satisfy existing customers, and market for new customers. Other chains, like Lawn Doctor, a large national lawn service business, have proprietary equipment and chemicals that give them a competitive advantage in the marketplace and add value to their system.

Item 15: Obligation to Participate in the Actual Operation of the Franchise Business

If a franchisor is going to require you to work full time in the business, it will be disclosed here. Many franchisors require you to work full time in the business, putting forth your best efforts in the early stages so your business makes it and your investment is protected. Other franchisors, such as Sport Clips or Great Clips, two national hair care franchises, want you to keep your job or other business interests so you can plow all your cash flow back into their business to accelerate your growth.

Item 16: Restrictions on What a Franchisee May Sell

Franchisors must describe your obligations to sell only goods and services they approve. They must also disclose any restrictions they will impose on the customers you can sell to.

Item 17: Renewal, Termination, Transfer, and Dispute Resolution

Franchisors will present a table that will identify the following:

► The length of term of the franchise.
► Renewal or extension terms.
► Requirements for a franchisee to renew or extend.
► How a franchisee can terminate their agreement. Many franchisors don't give franchisees the right to terminate their agreement. They expect them to sell the franchise to a new owner in order to protect their royalty stream. This is normal and acceptable. This also prevents a successful franchisee from suddenly taking down the franchisor's brand and putting up their own brand and forgoing royalty payments.

- ▶ How the franchisor can terminate their agreement without cause. Pay particular attention to this section. Most franchisors don't reserve any right to terminate your agreement without cause. It's not normal nor is it generally acceptable for a franchisor to reserve this right.

- ▶ How the franchisor can terminate the agreement with cause. For instance, a franchisee may be selling unauthorized, inferior products to their customers. A franchisor may default them as a result. As long as the products are removed from the store within an agreed time frame, the franchisee will be marked back in compliance. If they refuse, they run the risk of having their agreement terminated.

- ▶ "Noncurable" franchisee defaults, meaning a franchisee has no opportunity to correct a problem and it's grounds for immediate termination of their franchise agreement. For instance, a franchisee may be convicted of a felony, which may allow a franchisor to immediately terminate the franchise agreement. As long as a guilty verdict is reached, a franchisor may reserve the right to protect their brand and move swiftly by terminating the agreement without further hearing. This is normal and reasonable.

- ▶ Franchisee's obligations upon nonrenewal or termination. If a franchisee elects not to continue in their business or is terminated, they may have certain obligations, such as taking signs down, turning in their confidential operations manual and proprietary marketing materials, and paying outstanding balances.

- ▶ Assignment of contract by franchisor. Franchisors will typically reserve the right to sell their own business and assign their obligations to the acquiring party. This is normal and acceptable.

- ▶ How to transfer your business. Franchisors will discuss acceptable methods of selling your business to a third party. They will typically reserve the right to approve whom you are selling to and require the new buyer to go through their training programs. Most franchisors will charge you a transfer fee to cover their expenses to train and support the new owner. Some franchisors reserve a first right of refusal to purchase your business. In other words, you may receive an offer from someone who wishes to purchase your business for $100,000 cash. A franchisor may reserve a window of opportunity to purchase your business for the same $100,000 cash.

► What will occur if you die or become disabled and incapable of running the business. Franchisors will typically give your heirs or estate six months or so to sell the business to a new owner.

► Noncompete clauses during the term of the franchise agreement and after the agreement expires, is terminated, or you sell your franchise.

► Modification of your agreement. This agreement details the steps you and the franchisor must take if you both agree to modify your franchise agreement in any way.

► Dispute resolution. Some franchisors will restrict how you resolve disputes. For instance, many franchisors require you waive trial by jury and resolve your conflicts by binding arbitration or mediation. Some franchisors even require that you present your case first to a panel of fellow franchisees and key employees of the franchisor. In case of legal action, many franchisors will require you to resolve your dispute in the state they are located in and under the jurisdiction of their state laws. Usually this means travel expenses and additional attorney fees on your part, raising your motivation to try to resolve these issues outside of costly court battles. This is normal and typical.

Item 18: Public Figures

Franchisors need to disclose any financial arrangements they have with public figures in the use of their franchise name or symbols. Franchisors using public figures in this capacity run a high risk. For instance, at one time Kenny Roger's Roasters was a popular and high-growth quick service restaurant chain in the 90s. Then Kenny Rogers got caught up in a highly publicized scandal that tarnished his image and that of the franchise brand. We recommend you carefully consider the risks of doing business with any franchisors that are attached to high-profile people, such as sports figures, politicians, or celebrities.

Item 19: Earnings Statements

If a franchisor makes an earnings claim, they will be in this section. Many franchisors fear the legal risk and simply don't do it. However, more and more franchisors are honoring the requests of franchise candidates who want this information. Over time we predict most franchisors will get over their fear of being sued and disclose this information.

Item 20: List of Outlets

Here you will find an updated owners list, giving you the street addresses of the franchise locations, as well as the franchisees' names and phone numbers for you to contact.

Additionally, franchisors must disclose the names of franchisees who, over the last three years, sold their franchise, had their franchise terminated, weren't renewed, were bought out by the franchisor, or failed.

If a franchisor has a high failure rate, listen to the reasons why. If you hear them put the responsibility on the franchisees by making comments like, "Well, if the franchisees would have followed the system, they wouldn't have failed," keep probing. Isn't the franchisor responsible for bringing the franchisees into the system? Isn't the franchisor responsible for training and developing franchisees on their systems and holding them accountable for executing their business strategy? Doesn't the franchisor share equally in the responsibility of franchisees' failure? Ask follow-up questions like, "What is it about your recruiting methods that you are bringing in the wrong people?" and "What is it about your operating system that so many franchisees are refusing to or unable to execute it properly?" If you see franchisors absolving themselves of responsibility for their franchisees' poor performance, then chances are, if you struggle, they won't know how to help you either. Inexperienced or unsophisticated franchisors look at franchisees' failures as just that … franchisees' failures. They look at franchisees' victories as the system working. They take ownership of the victories and absolve themselves of responsibility for their losses. Consider eliminating them from consideration.

Top quality, responsible franchisors see the franchise network as one body consisting of the franchisor, franchisees, and perhaps even suppliers. If one member suffers, then the body suffers. If one member wins, the body rejoices. Franchisee victories are their victories and franchisee failures are their failures also.

As it relates to franchisees selling their franchises, it's normal and predictable for a mature franchisor (10 years as a franchisor or more) to have upward of 15 percent of their franchises for sale. Many franchisees keep their business roughly seven to 10 years. As you call franchisees, if you get a sense more that more than 15 percent of franchisees are selling, this may indicate a problem. Something may not be working within the system and disgruntled franchisees want out.

Item 21: Financial Statements

Franchisors must disclose audited financial statements in accordance with generally accepted accounting principles, and balance sheets. If you don't know how to read a financial statement, bring this section to an accountant for review. Pay particular attention to items such as:

- **Cash on hand.** The lower the cash balance, the more temptation a franchisor has to sell you a franchise and build their cash reserves.
- **Long-term debt.** Make sure the franchisor isn't so heavily financed they can't reinvest back into their system.
- **Cash flow.** Make sure the franchisor is cash flow positive, or in the case of a new franchisor, is on track to become cash flow positive shortly.

▶ **Balance Sheet.** Make sure the franchisor has assets in the company and has something at stake. Some franchisors show statements with fewer assets or net worth than the investment level they require franchisees to make. This is upside down. Franchisors should have as much or more at stake than franchisees.

Item 22: Contracts

Franchisors will provide copies of all documents you are required to sign in this section, including the franchise agreements, lease or financing agreements, etc. The terms of the franchise agreement should accurately reflect what is stated in the FDD.

Item 23: Receipt

This is a document you sign that states you acknowledge receiving the FDD. Signing this document obligates you to nothing.

Read your FDD, keeping these points in mind. Highlight anything in the FDD that appears off, that you are uncomfortable with, or that you simply cannot agree to. Make an appointment to review these with the franchise recruiter. After you review your issues with the franchisor, you will be usually be left with one of three experiences.

1. I'm OK.
2. I'm not OK, but it's OK I'm not OK.
3. I'm not OK, and not OK I'm not OK.

If you aren't okay, the process ends here. Trust your "not okay-ness" as an indicator the franchise isn't a match for you. If you are one who has looked at five or more opportunities and have come to the same place each time, take a look at the reasons why. If you see consistent patterns across the different franchise opportunities, perhaps franchising is not for you or perhaps you are looking in the wrong sector. Remember, franchising operates in more than 80 industries.

For everyone who is okay, it's time to start calling and, if possible, visiting franchisees to hear what they have to say.

Step 4: Franchisee Validation, Data Gathering, and Analysis

There is an old franchise joke that goes something like this.

> What are five words no franchisee has ever heard?
> What is on your mind?
> Why? Franchisees say what's on their mind before anyone asks!

Getting a franchisee to open up is typically easy. You will find them generally open and honest as it relates to answering all types of questions, including financial information, like "How long does it take this business to break even?"

You also must remember that where they are in the lifecycle of their business colors the feedback they may give you. You have to read between the lines. For instance, if you are interviewing a franchisee deeply mired in The Grind and ask, "Knowing what you know now, would you make the same decision again?" you will have a stronger likelihood of hearing "no," than at other times during the learning curve. It's the same as asking a pregnant mother in the midst of severe labor contractions whether or she thinks having a baby was a good idea.

You may also get skewed feedback from franchisees in The Launch. Everything will seem just splendid, whether it is or isn't.

When you are contacting franchisees, remember they have a business to run and time is their most precious resource. They are gifting you time the same way others donate money to charity. Respect their time by being prepared with questions. Don't take more than 15 or 20 minutes with any one franchisee. Franchisees have scores of candidates calling them all the time. Also, request an appointment. Just because you reach them by telephone or they are there when you stop in, doesn't mean it's a good time to speak. Find out when is the best time and remember to be flexible. Some franchisees may want to speak with you early before work begins and others at night when work is over. Regardless of the franchise they are in, they will only have certain hours in which to generate revenue and may not want to be interviewed during these hours. Respect their time by not wasting it schmoozing. They know this stage in your investigation because they have been through it. Prepare your questions in advance, stick to your outline, and ask the questions you prepared, then hang up the phone or leave their place of business. Be quick and efficient, but get your questions answered.

Lastly, remember what you are interviewing for. "People don't buy drills; they buy holes." You don't want the franchise, you want the results. The purpose of every interview is to gather data to make a final determination as to whether or not your "must have" and "wish to have" results will occur with this business with a high degree of probability.

When you start your interview, start by getting some open-ended background information.

- ▶ What did you do before you invested in your franchise?
- ▶ What were your reasons for joining this franchise?
- ▶ How long have you been in business?
  - • Franchisees with less than four months of experience are probably in The Launch. Unless they came into the franchise from a competitor or similar business, most of what they know about the business is simply theory. They haven't experienced all of what it takes to become successful. Additionally, most franchisees in The Launch are happy with the relationship with the franchisor. Asking a franchisee in The Launch, "How do you like working with the franchisor?" is like asking a newlywed on their honeymoon, "How do you like being married to your spouse?" They can, however, offer you terrific information on the quality of the franchisor's training programs and guidance in getting a new business open.
    - – Ask, "Did the franchisors training program adequately prepare you to launch your business? If not, what was missing?"

- "Did the franchisor adequately direct you during the pre-opening process, helping you stay organized and knowing what to do and when? If not, what was missing?"
- "Did the franchisor's grand opening strategy work? If not, what was missing? What would you do differently?"

• Consider franchisees who have been open four months to two years may be in some version of The Grind. While it's reasonable to assume they may be negative about the choice they made because of underestimating the level of effort involved or other issues, you can still gather insights into the skill level of the franchisor. Remember, franchisees in The Grind need high levels of franchisor interaction, plenty of coaching, training, and consulting. They should be in constant contact with the franchisor.

- Ask, "How often are you in contact with the franchisor?"
- "What support are you getting to help you get your business to the next level?"
- "What more could the franchisor be doing to help you win?"

Two of the best indicators of the competency level of any franchisor are:

▶ Franchisees' satisfaction with profitability, and
▶ Franchisees' satisfaction with the franchisee–franchisor relationship.

We look at these separately.

Determining Franchisees' Profitability

Even if a franchisee is relatively new in the business and may not be generating positive cash flow, you can ask them financial questions and they should know the averages and norms. They should know both what a high volume and low volume franchise looks like. Remember, when asking financial questions it isn't important to ascertain how well each franchisee is doing financially. It is to determine how well you will do financially. Franchisees are less guarded and more apt to want to answer questions about the franchise system's norms and regional or national financial averages than about what the results they are specifically generating. You can always ask if their financial results are meeting their expectations.

Since most franchisees finance and operate their businesses differently, their financial statements may have wide variations. Some will more aggressively write off expenses such as autos, trips, and medical insurance. Some will carry more debt than others. Some franchisees will pay themselves a salary, others will take no salary and pay themselves dividends. Some employ a manager and others are owner operated. Your goal is to ask questions that will give you consistent information. We recommend you get to what many franchisors call "total owner benefit." In other words, assuming franchisees take their entire benefit in one lump sum cash distribution at the end of the year, before debt, depreciation, amortization, and paying the owner's salary and benefits and aggressively writing off personal expenses, how much money would there be left over for them to take home? Ask franchisees:

► What can a typical franchisee expect to make in gross sales and Owner Benefit in Years 1, 2, and 3 (before debt, depreciation, amortization, and before paying the owner a salary and benefits)?
   Year 1: Gross sales _____ Owner Benefit _____
   Year 2: Gross sales _____ Owner Benefit _____
   Year 3: Gross sales _____ Owner Benefit _____

► What would a high-volume franchisee make?
   Year 1: Gross sales _____ Owner Benefit _____
   Year 2: Gross sales _____ Owner Benefit _____
   Year 3: Gross sales _____ Owner Benefit _____

► What would a low-volume franchisee make?
   Year 1: Gross _____ Owner Benefit _____
   Year 2: Gross _____ Owner Benefit _____
   Year 3: Gross _____ Owner Benefit _____

Following a Six-Step
Franchise Investigation Process

The three largest expense line items in any small business are: cost of sales, cost of labor, and total occupancy costs (for those franchises that require an office or storefront). "Total occupancy" is a common real estate term used that includes the cost of rent and the renter's pro-rated share of insurance, common area maintenance, and taxes on the building. Depending on the franchise opportunity, cost of sales, labor, and occupancy added up together represent 65 to 80 percent of the franchisees' entire cost of doing business. Make sure you receive consistent information regarding these cost areas as they represent the lion's share of the franchisees' expenses.

Ask the franchisees for typical operating cost information such as:

- As a percentage of sales, what should my cost of sales be?
- As a percentage of sales, what should my cost of labor be?
- As a percentage of sales, what should my total occupancy cost be?

Keep in mind, if you are investigating a business that required a retail storefront or office, your rent will probably be a predictable fixed amount each month, not a percentage of your sales. However, by asking franchisees, "As a percentage of sales, what should my total occupancy cost be?" you will hear what you can effectively budget for rent payment. As you look into local rental rates, you will know if the average sales volume will cost justify what you will be required to pay in rent.

Some franchisors will assist your information gathering by providing you simple, blank financial statements that you should use as a template to help you gather accurate financial data. Others will publish this data in Item 19 of their FDD. Possibly afraid of future potential lawsuits, others offer no assistance whatsoever.

For those who need assistance gathering the elements of what goes into a business plan, there are many resources available to you. You can go to your local office of the SBA, SBDC (Small Business Development Center), or SCORE (Service Corps of

Retired Executives). You can find your local office by visiting their websites.

- ► www.sba.gov
- ► www.score.org

There are software packages you can purchase, like Business Plan Pro, that will walk you step-by-step through how to write a business plan. For those who need additional hand-holding, you can get the assistance of a CPA to help you analyze the data you gather.

Ask the franchisor to help you determine the KASH model of success (described in chapter 6).

- ► What does it take to succeed?
- ► What skills do I need to develop to win?
- ► What activities do I need to be doing every day to produce outstanding results?
- ► What are the most common mistakes new franchisees make in this business?
- ► What advice would you give a new franchisee starting out?
- ► Where will I waste time if I'm not careful?

Determining Franchisees' Satisfaction Level

In chapter 8, we discussed how the franchisee–franchisor relationship evolves over time, from new franchisees' total dependence on the franchisor during the Glee Stage, to the franchisees' testing the boundaries of the relationship and asserting independence in the Me and Free Stages, to eventually a win–win interdependent relationship characterized by the We Stage, where each party is committed to the other's success.

Unskilled franchisors never make it to the We Stage. Some get frozen either trying to control franchisees or to avoid being controlled by them. Others go too far in the other direction by not enforcing standards or ensuring quality and letting the franchisees do whatever they want.

Questions to Evaluate the Franchisee–Franchisor Relationship

▶ How would you describe your relationship with the franchisor?

▶ No matter what happens, what can you always count on the franchisor for?

▶ How has the franchisor's ongoing support made a difference in your business?

▶ What value are you receiving for your royalties? Is the advice and support you are receiving and the value of the brand worth the money you are investing in royalties?

▶ Knowing what you know now, would you make the same investment again?

Grading the Franchisor as a Franchisor

A peak-performing franchisor needs to show a high level of competency in four key areas.

1. Recruiting top-quality franchise candidates
2. Training, consulting, and coaching franchisees from The Launch into Winning or The Zone
3. Building powerful franchisee–franchisor relationships
4. Marketing and building the brand

Ask existing franchisees to grade the franchisor using a five-point rating scale in the following areas (1 being failure and 5 being excellent).

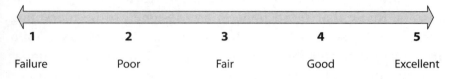

1	2	3	4	5
Failure	Poor	Fair	Good	Excellent

Ask, *"How would you rate the ... "*

▶ Franchisor's ability to recruit top-quality franchisees?

▶ Value of the franchisor's initial training program?

▶ Ability of the support and field staff to identify and help fix franchisees' problems?

- ▶ Value of ongoing training programs?
- ▶ Value of field visits to franchisees' locations?
- ▶ Value of national or regional meetings?
- ▶ Ability of support staff to help develop franchisees' skills in critical areas of their business?
- ▶ Franchisor's responsiveness to franchisees' issues and concerns?
- ▶ Franchisor's track record for keeping their word and making good on their promises and commitments to the franchisees?
- ▶ Quality of the relationship between the franchisees and the franchisor?
- ▶ Leadership ability of the CEO and senior management?
- ▶ CEO and senior management's vision of the future?
- ▶ Value of the products and services being offered to the franchisees' customers?
- ▶ Effectiveness of marketing and advertising programs?
- ▶ Total effectiveness of the franchisor's business model to produce outstanding results?

In any area in which a franchisor is rated from "failure" to "fair," ask one or two follow up questions:

1. What's missing?
2. What could they be doing differently?

There are two companies that measure franchise satisfaction: Fransurvey and Franchise Business Review. Ask franchisors if they have ever used these services and to forward you their results. Know that these reviews are designed to be marketing pieces for those franchisors that receive stellar reviews. So if a franchisor indicates they have hired one or both of these companies but the results are unavailable, draw your own conclusions.

How Many Franchisees Should I Call?

There isn't any magic number of franchisees you should call. We recommend you speak to a minimum of five to 10 franchisees (depending on the size of system, complexity of the operation, size of the investment, etc.) simply to be able to identify trends and patterns and to see some consistency of information. After interviewing eight to 10 franchisees, you should be hearing little new information, just confirmation of information you already have. Most franchisees will call four to eight franchisees before they make a decision as to whether they will visit the franchisor's home office and meet the officers and decision makers of the company.

Your decision-making style also will play a role in how many franchisees you feel you need to contact. Referring to chapter 4, if you are an Action Hero or Comedian, you possess higher risk tolerance than most, and make "gut-based," or instinctual decisions rather than data-based decisions. Since you typically err on the side of aggressiveness, play it safe and contact a few more than you think is necessary, just to flush out some information you may be missing before you decide if you will visit the franchisor's home office.

If you are a Faithful Sidekick or Private Eye, you make data-based decisions rather than emotional or instinctual decisions. You may want to contact most or all the franchisees. You err on the side of caution. Since you are more risk-averse than most entrepreneurs, you may have a tendency to try to search out and discover the "magic" missing piece of data that will complete the puzzle, guarantee your success, and alleviate your fears. This data, however, probably does not exist. Once you contact eight to 10 franchisees, the information you gather should be fairly consistent. You may feel like you don't have all the information you need to prepare for your visit to the franchisor's home office, but this doesn't mean you don't have all the information. Your fear could be F.E.A.R. (false experience appearing real). Two questions to continually ask yourself are:

► What information am I missing?
► If I had this information, how would it impact my investment decision?

Once you find yourself spending time gathering "nice to have" information that won't impact your decision, it's time to stop gathering data. You may be engaging in "analysis paralysis," meaning gathering information to avoid making a decision.

Garbage In/Garbage Out

Computer programmers have an express called GIGO, meaning "Garbage in, garbage out." The quality of the output is only as good as the input. It's the same thing with franchising. The quality of information you receive from franchisees will be in direct relationship to the quality of questions you ask. That's why this chapter frames some important questions for you. Remember, what you ask and what the franchisees hear may be two different things. Also remember, what they answer and what you hear may also be two different things. Take careful notes during and after your conversations.

For instance, a franchise candidate for a specialty retail franchise called a franchisee to inquire as to how they were doing. The franchisee being called was running a high volume store and had a quick start out of the blocks. The franchise candidate asked the franchisee, "What profits do you anticipate making at the end of the year?"

The franchisee thought quietly for a second, "Let's see," she thought. "After paying back my SBA loan, paying myself a salary, paying the expenses on my two cars, taking into account depreciation and amortization, I may not see a profit at the end of the year." Therefore the franchisee truthfully responded, "I don't expect to make any profits this year."

Now keep in mind, the object of a small business is not to make a profit because you get taxed on profits. The purpose is to generate cash flow and other financial benefits to the owner, such as equity build-up and write-offs, which are expenses that would otherwise have to be paid with after-tax dollars by those who have jobs instead of their own business. This includes such things as auto expenses and travel and entertainment (that's business related).

This particular franchisee was paying off the debt on her business (thus building equity), taking a salary, being aggressive with business expenses, but not showing a profit. She was, however, meeting her financial objectives and succeeding in business. This point was not clearly articulated and the prospective franchisee missed it entirely. As a matter of fact, the prospect hung up the phone thinking the franchisee was actually failing. The prospective franchisee missed out on a great franchise opportunity because he asked garbage questions and received garbage answers.

Therefore always check your understanding of what you heard. You might say, "Let me repeat what I just heard just to make sure I heard you correctly."

What if the franchise candidate used this technique and asked the franchisee, "If I heard you correctly, it sounds like your business is in trouble."

"Oh no," the franchisee would have responded. "What gave you that idea?"

Analyzing Your Data

Remember, you don't want a franchise, you want results. Franchise is a vehicle that produces results. Ultimately, your data should be organized to help you determine if your "must have" and much of your "wish to have" objectives can be achieved with an acceptable level of predictability. Ultimately, you want to determine if . . .

▶ The franchise business will produce your desired results,
▶ You are willing to do whatever it takes to acquire the KASH model of success,
▶ The franchisor will do what it takes to help you win,
▶ You have the necessary capital and you match the franchisor's profile of a successful franchisee,
▶ You are a culture fit for the organization, and
▶ The franchisees and franchisor work together to help each other win.

We recommend creating a spreadsheet or a visual display such as the following:

THE PROBABILITY A FRANCHISE WILL DELIVER MY DESIRED LIFESTYLE

1	**2**	**3**	**4**	**5**
No/Little	Low (25%)	Fair (50/50)	Good (75%)	Strong
(Under 25%)				(Over 75%)

My "must have" objectives and by when I'm committed to accomplishing this.	**Franchisor #1** What is the probability this will be achieved with this franchise?	**Franchisor #2** What is the probability this will be achieved with this franchise?
My "wish to have" objectives and by when I'm committed to accomplishing this.	What is the probability this will be achieved with this franchise?	What is the probability this will be achieved with this franchise?

If all of your "must have" and much of your "wish to have" objectives will be met with a high degree of probability, the franchise brand is either strong or building, the franchisees are winning, the franchisee–franchisor relationship is intact, and you appear to be a culture fit for the organization, make an appointment with the franchisor's representative to visit the franchisor's home office and meet and interview the officers and decision makers. Some franchisors have some form of Discovery Day that may be attended by other prospective franchisees. Discovery Days are tightly organized to persuade and inform. The chance to talk to and listen to the concerns and questions of other prospective franchisees can be invaluable.

If any of these are missing, end the process here, and perhaps start the process with another franchisor.

We offer you a worksheet at the end of this chapter that will help you crystallize your observations and reach a proper decision.

Why Should I Spend the Money to Visit the Franchisor?

As of now, chances are you have only had telephone conversations or possibly one or two face-to-face meetings with the franchise recruiter. The opinions of one person may not accurately describe the reality of the franchisor or the franchise opportunity. Additionally, the franchise sales representative's compensation is typically not tied to whether you succeed in business, but to whether you sign a franchise agreement. Therefore, franchise salespeople have a tendency to overlook information that may suggest future problems. Thus, it's imperative you travel to the home office, look the decision makers in the eye, and let them know who you are and what you are looking to accomplish. You are more likely to get straight feedback from the people who are held accountable for your success and whose problem you will be if you don't succeed. You will learn things from visiting the franchisor's office and looking people in the eye that you can't learn any other way. Visiting the franchisor's office will either validate the information or opinions you have about the franchise being a solid investment and career opportunity, or you may discover new information that isn't to your liking.

Step 5: Attending a Discovery Day or Visiting the Home Office

Many franchisors will set aside one or two days a month to host potential franchisees for the following reasons. While some may not have Discovery Day as part of their franchisee recruitment process, if you request to meet the decision makers, high-road franchisors understand what's at stake and will certainly oblige you.

High-Road Franchisors

Because both parties have so much at stake, the leadership teams of high-integrity and competent franchisors won't enter into a franchise agreement with anyone they haven't met. You risk your capital and they risk their corporate culture and the integrity of their brand. They will want to make sure you have an opportunity to thoroughly interview them and they will want the opportunity to thoroughly interview you. In the end you both want the same thing, to determine if you fit the profile of a successful franchisee and if your objectives can be met using their business model. Usually, at least half the day will be structured presentations to make sure you and others present receive consistent and accurate information about what it takes to win and what you can count on the franchisor for. The other half will be flexible; allowing you to ask whatever is on your mind. At the end of the day, you should have your questions answered and a realistic idea of what it takes to win and whether you fit in.

Anywhere from 50 to 80 percent of franchise candidates who attend a Discovery Day end up joining the franchise system they visit. For the remainder, due to the open dialogue, either the candidate or the franchisor spots something that leads them to believe there isn't a match.

Low-Road Franchisors

Regardless of what they say, the picture the low-road franchisor has of you is one of a deposit slip with thousands of dollars written on it. They know if they can get in front of you, this will give them their greatest opportunity to close you. Discovery Day is a code word for "Sales Close Day," meaning this is their big opportunity to reel you in. The day will be an eight-hour commercial about how great their opportunity is and how lucky you are if you are "chosen" to be part of it. Of course to be chosen, all you need to do is be able to fog a mirror, sign an agreement, and issue them a cashier's check.

Beware of franchisors that ask for a check during Discovery

Day. And beware of any franchisor that requests a fee up front to attend a Discovery Day.

Signs You Are Working With a High-Road or Low-Road Franchisor

Another thing you want to pay attention to is the franchisor's corporate culture, which may or may not reflect the franchisees' culture in the field. The franchisor's culture will fall into a range, anywhere from anarchy to dictatorships and everything in between. We spell these out for you.

Low-Road Franchisors	High-Road Franchisors
They appear slick, scripted, rehearsed, and fake.	They appear approachable and genuine. Whether or not they appear formal or informal is part of their culture, but you should be left trusting the feedback you receive.
After shaking hands, you notice your watch is no longer on your wrist.	They already own watches, paid for by the royalty collections generated by scores of successful franchisees.
After meeting them, you have the indescribable experience of being "sleazed" and needing to take a shower.	After meeting them, you have the experience they are telling it like it is in order to give you a realistic idea of the challenges ahead and how they will support you.
If after attending Discovery Day you decide not to join them, they try to make you feel stupid or like you did something wrong.	If you decide not to join them, they will probe into your reasons why. If your decision is based on inaccurate information, they will challenge you. If your decision is based on accurate information, they will support you.
They will apply high pressure sales tactics to force a "yes" decision.	They will hold you accountable for making a final "yes" or "no" decision, but they will not apply undue pressure.
You don't get the opportunity to ask the franchisor's decision makers hard questions. If you do, they tap dance around them or pretend your questions are not relevant.	You get ample opportunity to ask the franchisor's decision makers hard questions. They answer you truthfully.

Low-Road Franchisors	High-Road Franchisors
They try to prove how successful they are by wearing expensive suits and jewelry, expensive haircuts, and having expensive office furniture and an impressive conference room, which appears incongruent with what they appear to be able to afford after reviewing their financials in their UFOC.	They appear to have nothing to prove. They offer you an accurate picture of who they are, without pretense or bells and whistles. Their office furnishings and surroundings are consistent with their financial means.

Keep in mind franchisors are typically private companies. Presidents and CEOs are free to run their companies any way they they see fit and you aren't going to change them. Take famed basketball coach Bobby Knight for instance. Not every collegiate basketball player can play for such a volatile and sometimes demeaning coach like Bobby Knight. For others, Bobby Knight's style will bring out productivity. Just know whom you are doing business with and what you can expect from them moving forward. If you can't play for the coach, find another coach you can play for.

In this section we learn how to identify the different franchise cultures and what you can expect from each one.

The Four Franchisor Corporate Cultures

Do franchisees, employees, and leadership of the franchisor trust each other and work toward crafting mutually profitable campaigns, offers, and solutions? Do franchisees feel they are heard and understood? Does information routinely flow up and down the organization or just funnel down from on high? Would franchisees say they are informed about issues important to them? Would they say they feel like an integral part of a team or more like the low man on the totem pole?

The way franchisees would answer these questions speaks volumes about the culture of the franchise organization. And strong financial returns are not a substitute for strong franchisee–franchisor relationships. Enduring franchise brands offer franchisees both.

Following a Six-Step
Franchise Investigation Process

Franchisors with a strong, inclusive, collaborative, franchisee-friendly corporate culture attract more sophisticated and talented franchise candidates than more heavy-handed franchisors who resort to threats, punishment, and coercive command-and-control techniques to try to keep franchisees in line.

Dr. Jay Hall, PhD spent a lifetime studying the impact of corporate culture on individual performance. Dr. Hall has identified four prevailing corporate cultures, which FPG has licensed and modified to reflect what occurs in franchising. Each culture is marked by two distinguishing characteristics: the franchisor's level of concern for franchisees' results, and relationships.

Keep in mind that at any time any company can exhibit traits from any one of these cultures. However, over the long haul, franchise organizations tend to exhibit a dominant pattern of beliefs and behaviors. We look at these cultures in a progression starting with the least effective and moving toward the most effective.

The Bureaucracy

Bureaucracies are highly legalistic, highly layered companies where the lower you go in an organization, the less decision-making responsibility and authority an employee of the franchisor has. The organization seemingly exists to maintain the status quo, avoid accepting personal responsibility, and elude being held accountable for producing results. When a franchisee is faced with a unique challenge or makes a special request, the knee-jerk reaction throughout the layers of management is "no," coupled with "We don't do it that way." This occurs regardless of whether what the organization is currently doing actually works or remains in the franchisees' or customers' best interests. Change is met with stiff resistance and individual initiative is frowned on by management. Employees and franchisees are expected to follow the rules, do what's expected, and resist original thinking. Policies and procedures are set to control employees to ensure compliance, not to drive results.

Impact on Employees and Franchisees

Ponder the type of corporate employees and leadership that would survive in this franchise culture in the long term. Those franchisor employees who are dedicated, results-oriented, efficient, entrepreneurial, visionary, big-picture thinkers, or out to make their mark in the world would be ostracized and then quit or be fired. Only those who simply want to earn a steady paycheck while hiding out and avoiding personal responsibility would want to stick around for the long haul in this environment. Think about the type of person whose goal in life is to secure a good job with the Post Office or Motor Vehicle Department. Are you picturing a real go-getter and risk taker? Meaning no disrespect to those with loved ones working in either bureaucracy, we are saying they work there for reasons other than "I want to make my mark on the world."

Because bureaucracies value sameness and security over performance and efficiency, they remain a breeding ground for waste and underperformance.

Now think about the quality of the interactions among the bureaucratic franchisor support staff and the franchisees under their charge. Would these conversations and communications pertain more to tactics and strategies about how to drive franchisees' sales and results, or would the conversations tend more toward what franchisees must do to continually remain in compliance?

Recently, a somewhat bureaucratic retail chain forced its franchisees to adopt a management information system at a cost of tens of thousands of dollars per location to its franchisees. Franchisees who beta-tested the system reported that the system had bugs, routinely lost data, and was not ready for a national roll-out. Those in charge ignored the franchisees' warnings and forced franchisees at threat of default to adopt the new system. It was more important to the franchisor that all franchisees operate from one flawed standard system than several working systems. One year later, their newly adopted system still corrupts data and transaction information, making many reporting functions meaningless. Franchisees are livid over this, but powerless to do anything about it within the present bureaucratic structure of the company.

Impact on Results

Franchising is designed to make businesses more decentralized, flexible, and nimble by completely empowering those closest to the customer. As you can see, bureaucracies are designed to create the opposite effect. Therefore, bureaucratic franchisors have little staying power in today's competitive commercial marketplace because they kill off what we all know works. This is why most surviving bureaucracies exist in the public sector where people have no other alternative with regard to corporate cultures.

Benevolent Dictatorship

Benevolent Dictatorships are typically informal, folksy, low-stress companies where much attention is paid to making people feel good. "Feeling good," "being appreciated," and "loyalty to leadership" are more important than bottom-line results. This culture is commonly found in small, privately held franchisors where the founder or owner places friends and family in key management positions, not because they are the most qualified people for their jobs, but because they can be trusted to do the owner's bidding without pushback. Unless an employee possesses the right last name, marries into the family, or plays poker or golf with the owner, often there is little room for advancement. The owner isn't really out to build a powerhouse brand, but a little fiefdom where employees, friends, and franchisees are taken care of. If you were a franchise candidate attending a Discovery Day, at first glance this culture seems informal, unassuming, and perhaps attractive to a new entrepreneur. But the dysfunctional, undistinguished underlying belief of leadership that perpetuates the existing culture is "Employees and franchisees aren't capable of producing exceptional results on their own. They need to be 'taken care of,' as opposed to "Franchisees and employees are highly capable individuals who need the tools, resources, and freedom to win."

This attitude creates a top-down, paternalistic culture. While interpersonal relationships are held up as important to the organization, these relationships are skewed as they aren't marked by the typical characteristics of an adult relationship. These relationships more resemble the parent-dependent child relationship than a fruitful, problem-solving, win–win franchisee–franchisor relationship.

Impact on Employees and Franchisees

Because the founder or CEO has so little faith in the capabilities of managers, staff, and franchisees, power, money, and authority are concentrated at the top. The founder or CEO is the puppet master, pulling the strings and making employees and franchisees dance to a tune only he or she hears. As long as employees of the franchisor keep dancing and don't ask a lot of questions like "Why are we dancing? What is the song we are dancing to? What other dances could we be doing?" or heaven forbid, "Can we pick our own song and dance moves?" they will survive.

As in bureaucracies, information mostly flows downhill, instead of up and down the organization. The CEO or founder makes decisions from the ivory tower and leaves middle management the role of town squire to announce decisions to the franchisee citizens of the fiefdom.

Think of what happens to talented and upwardly mobile employees or talented franchisees of this kind of organization. The founder or CEO calls 100 percent of the shots. Those who want to see their own ideas implemented, wish to collaborate in the decision-making process, or are unwilling to consistently do the bidding of the benevolent dictator founder or CEO won't remain. They will find a culture that values performance and initiative. Think again of the type of leader or employee who would survive in such an environment ... and those who survive often stay forever. Where else other than the Department of Motor Vehicles can they find such a secure job where superiors have such low expectations of personal performance and results?

Now watch the vicious circle that forms. You start to see that group behavior is always designed to reward the existing group behavior. Carrying this observation forward, "The existing corporate culture is always designed to survive intact."

Impact on Results

Now think about the quality of training and ongoing support these surviving, low-skilled officers and employees can offer franchisees. Will it be enough for results and action-oriented franchisees to win or will they find it necessary to go outside the organization for tools and support? If these franchisees complain about either the quality of support or not being invited to participate in decisions impacting them, their comments aren't often heard in a commercial context. The franchisor will often respond with "Don't these unappreciative franchisees know how hard we work? Don't they realize we're just trying to help them?" In such a scenario intentions and appreciation are more important than performance and results.

A benevolent dictator CEO of one national franchisor doesn't give officers and department heads annual operating budgets. He makes the decisions on how his money is spent on a case-by-case basis. While he executes his own financial plan, he seldom shares what that is with others, keeping department heads guessing. In addition he regularly moves employees around to different departments without consulting department heads or the individuals being redeployed about what they want and need. The CEO believes he knows best and his employees and franchisees will understand over time. This is often a source of frustration for department heads who feel like they have the responsibility to drive results but very little authority to do what is needed.

Command and Control

Command and Control is probably the most common culture in franchising. Command and control companies have strong central authorities where most decisions are made. While power and authority may be more diffused than in the Benevolent Dictatorship culture, it's still consolidated at the top. While data routinely flows up from franchisees to the corporate office, decisions are more often than not handed down. While franchisors may have advisory committees consisting of franchisees, these committees aren't decision-making bodies. They exist to advise the decision makers who are free to accept all, some, or none of the advice. In addition, franchisor leadership isn't always transparent with information, disclosing only what they deem franchisees "need to know." While the franchisor leadership may verbalize such things as "franchisees are partners and stakeholders in the company," their attitudes and actions tell a different story.

From the get-go, it seems franchisors design themselves to be this way. For instance, almost every FDD and franchise agreement ever written perpetuates this culture. If you were to read any FDD right now, most likely you will see paragraph after paragraph about what franchisees must or must not do, along with corresponding punishments should franchisees fail to act accordingly. If you were to then read the franchisor's obligations, more than likely you will come across language such as "Although not required, the franchisor may from time to time at its own discretion choose to …"

Recently a franchise executive posted an article in a franchise group on LinkedIn where he proposed that in all practical terms the brand is community property and smart franchisors will enroll all stakeholders in building and adding value to the brand. This would include franchisees, employees of franchisees, employees of the franchisor, customers of the franchisees, and vendors.

For instance, mechanics prefer Snap-On Tools over their next competitor's tools to an amazing degree. If you were to ask any professional mechanic, "Who makes the best hand tool?" he or she would most likely say, "There's Snap-On and there's everyone else." To demonstrate the cult-like following of the brand, Snap-On's director of franchising collects funny photos people send them, such as men walking around NASCAR races with Snap-On hand wrenches tattooed on their shoulders, backs, and forearms.

This idea was mauled by other executives of other franchisors and franchise attorneys commenting on the forum, insisting it's legally the franchisor's brand and it's rented or licensed to franchisees.

From a legal standpoint, it's clearly the franchisor's brand. From a legal standpoint, it's the responsibility of the franchisor to protect the brand. From a marketing standpoint, franchisees of successful franchise brands successfully embed themselves into their respective communities and the psyche of their buyer. These brands create lives of their own, transcending both the franchisee and franchisor. Successful franchisees offer their brands up to their respective communities for customers to build relationships with on their own terms. In response, customers and stakeholders make it their responsibility to ensure the brand thrives in their communities.

The bottom line is franchisors can't command or control such brand excitement or loyalty. Nor should you want them to. This type of brand loyalty unfolds over time and takes on a life of its own. It's like the old cliché, "If you love something, let it go." But Command and Control franchise executives believe, "If you love something, keep it under lock and key and limit access to those with security clearance." If they could, some companies would force the customer to have that tattoo in the previous example removed for an unauthorized use of their logo.

Impact on Employees and Franchisees

Command and Control cultures are formed from several limiting and somewhat dysfunctional beliefs about the nature of people. Let's fast forward a bit and compare these beliefs against those leaders who operate from the "Achievement" culture mindset that we discuss next.

If you are a highly skilled, motivated, upwardly mobile franchise professional, in which of these two cultures would you rather work?

Command and Control Cultural Beliefs	Achievement Cultural Beliefs
Left to their own resources, people slack off. You need to stay on top of them if you want them to get the job done right.	Most franchisees and franchisor employees want to perform well and do the right thing. If they know what's expected of them and we provide the necessary resources, and eliminate red tape and bottlenecks, they will typically deliver what we need by the time we need it.
People's individual goals are less important than organizational goals. If you work here, leave your personal goals at the door.	High achievers want to achieve. It's my job as a leader to encourage and celebrate individual achievement and align an individual's personal goals with organizational goals. It's naïve to assume goal-oriented people are going to leave their goals at the door.
We franchise because we want to build our company using other people's money. Franchising is a necessary evil if you want to grow quickly and have limited access to other capital.	We franchise because our best chance of enduring success is to entrust our brand and trade secrets to skilled entrepreneurs who will typically execute better than those we would employ.
If you want franchisees or employees to perform, you must reward the behavior you want and punish the behavior you don't want.	While I can always dangle a carrot or use a stick to make a horse run, I choose a better way. I breed thoroughbreds and then open the pen and let them out. They will run because that is what thoroughbreds were born to do. It's their nature.
Mistakes are unacceptable and avoidable. You must create processes and systems to minimize and eliminate mistakes.	Mistakes are normal and natural. If people aren't making mistakes, they aren't trying hard enough. People learn as much or more from mistakes as they do from success. Demonizing mistakes destroys initiative. I want employees and franchisees to try hard, win big, and make some mistakes along the way. I just don't want them to repeat the same mistakes twice.

Command and Control Cultural Beliefs	Achievement Cultural Beliefs
This is our brand and we license it to the franchisees. We control the brand and they use it with our permission and approval.	Our brand belongs to the community and must have meaningful value to all stakeholders, such as customers, franchisees, employees of the franchisees, employees of the franchisor, and vendors. It's our brand and we all need to accept responsibility to add value to it in order to win.

If you were someone looking to invest in a franchise, which culture would be more attractive?

Impact on Results

The core values of a Command and Control culture are results, power, and control. Now here's the rub. Ask yourself, "Why do you want to start a business?" Is "I want more power and control" on your short list? So you can clearly see why in this culture, franchisee–franchisor conflict is inevitable. That's why companies with this dominant culture are so often sued by disgruntled franchisees, or routinely have franchisees banding together to create alliances to beef up their numbers to take a stand against the company. They end up fighting each other for control rather than the competition for market share.

In conversation with a Command and Control founder and CEO of a service franchisor, the executive team was discussing the needs and goals of the organization. He said he wanted to amass a $500,000 legal fund to protect the company from any future lawsuits from disgruntled franchisees. Several years later the same CEO was dragged into a class action lawsuit by a group of disgruntled franchisees. The case dragged on for two years and he spent that much and more. Think of how much time, money, and attention was diverted from growing both the franchisees' and franchisor's business. Think about what would have been possible for both sides had they been able to quickly settle and move on.

Recently a Command and Control board member of a food concept franchise walked into a new franchisee's recently opened place of business unannounced. It was a peak time and the new franchisee struggled to handle the customer volume. The board member became angry and bark out commands to the franchisee's employees, ordering them around. When the franchisee objected to what she believed to be inappropriate behavior, she was told, "We are the parent company and franchisees are like children. They have to do what we say." Later, she said, "I already have parents and don't need more. I wish someone told me I was going to be their child before they took my money." How motivated was the franchisee after that encounter? What is the predictable impact of this encounter on the franchisee–franchisor relationship?

Achievement

The Achievement culture creates the most fertile ground for cultivating outstanding long-term results by providing an inviting work environment that attracts and retains highly skilled and self-directed franchise candidates, executives, and employees.

Leaders see their jobs as facilitators. They routinely interact with the top-producing employees and franchisee thought-leaders, making sure they have what they need to win. They identify and eliminate potential bottlenecks or barriers to forward momentum. They are not egocentric. They give the necessary power, authority, and resources to those responsible for creating results. They are transparent with information. They are clear about the individual needs of employees and franchisees and work to align their individual goals with business objectives so everyone wins.

During these training events, one thought leader in franchising asks employees and executives of franchisors attending events, "How do you know when your franchisees are winning?" We often hear answers involving measuring operational key performance criteria, sales in particular. But when asked the follow-up question, "How do your franchisees measure success?" most franchisors are stumped. When pushed more and asked, "Do you know what your franchisees were looking to accomplish for themselves and their families when they invested in your franchise?" more often than not franchisors say, "no." The typical franchisor doesn't know if its franchisees are winning according to the franchisees' definition of winning.

Pita Pit, a quick-service food franchisor with operations in both the U.S. and Canada, is different. Pita Pit's support teams seek to understand who their franchisees are as individuals and what drives them. Their leadership works with their operations teams to show franchisees how by implementing their recommendations they can move closer to achieving their stated goals and objectives. The Pita Pit operations support team is trained to identify franchisees' communication styles and feed them information consistent with how these franchisees absorb and process information, minimizing communication breakdowns. Their support team is trained in adult learning principles, performing coaching techniques, and consulting best practices. As a result of the outstanding training, consulting, and coaching given by the Pita Pit support team, franchisees are holding their own in a brutally competitive QSR segment. And the company continues to add new franchisees.

Impact on Employees and Franchisees

Achievement cultures attract and retain top franchisor exectives and employees and franchisee talent. Leaders, employees, and franchisees thrive personally and professionally within the team-work-driven, results-oriented culture, unlocking the best of who they are and actualizing the most of what they can achieve. The franchisor and franchisees experience being valued and respected. Employees of the franchisor are rewarded consistent with their performance and promoted based on merit. Instead of consolidating power and authority at the top, the franchisor's leadership manages "bottom up" companies, dedicating time, money, and energy empowering franchisees to spend resources, make decisions, and ultimately produce outstanding results.

Franchisees and the franchisor enjoy rock-solid relationships. Both seem to understand that each needs to make a healthy return on their time and money and neither can perform at high levels unless all their companies are healthy and profitable. When faced with a problem, they engage in win–win problem solving rather than win–lose fighting.

What's the Lesson?

Achievement cultures attract and retain highly skilled and dedicated people. And these quality people are your best bet to build growing and enduring companies.

When comparing leadership styles of the most successful empire builders in history, Napoleon Bonaparte reportedly once said, "Alexander, Caesar, Charlemagne, and myself founded empires; but on what foundation did we rest the creations of our genius? Upon force. Jesus Christ founded an empire upon love; and at this hour millions of men would die for Him."

And of these empires Napoleon mentioned, only one endures.

How to Prepare for Discovery Day

- ▶ Get plenty of rest. This will be an exhausting day.
- ▶ Know whom you are going to meet and what they are responsible for.
- ▶ Know what you are going to ask each person. Come with a prepared list of questions.
- ▶ Be prepared to answer personal questions. Remember, interviewing for a franchise is not like interviewing for a job. Franchisors can ask you anything, so you may hear questions such as, Have you ever been fired? Have you ever been arrested? What does your spouse think about you wanting to buy this franchise? How much money will you need to borrow?

How to Successfully Participate in Discovery Day

▶ Be yourself. Show them exactly who you are and who you are not.

▶ Ask your questions. No question is left unasked.

▶ Pay attention to your surroundings. If you are the type of person who's distracted by taking notes, don't take notes. Instead, pay attention to every conversation and what's going on around you.

▶ Walk around. The franchisor may confine you to a conference room because they don't want you to see everything. Ask to be shown around the building. If not, walk around the building during a break time. Watch what the employees are doing. Pay attention to the looks on their faces. Are they organized or cluttered? Happy or frustrated? Concentrating or goofing off? Don't ask permission because you might hear "no." It's better to walk around, get chastised and apologize for it later than to ask permission and hear "no." And no sane, competent franchisor is going to disqualify a franchise candidate because they are curious about what is going on.

Post–Discovery Day Evaluation

▶ Organize your data.

▶ Consider not making any decisions for at least three days. Just hang out with the information you gathered.

Let yourself be afraid or excited, but don't be duped by your emotions. Being excited doesn't mean this is the right franchise for you nor does being afraid mean it is wrong. What does your data say?

Decision–Making Checklist

The Big Questions: If you answer any of these questions with a "no" end your investigation and communicate your decision to the franchisor.	Yes/No
Will the franchise opportunity produce my "must have" and "wish to have" objectives with a high degree of probability?	
Do I closely match the franchisor's profile of a successful franchisee?	
Are the other franchisees winning?	
Are the franchisees and franchisors committed to each other's success?	
Does the franchisor know how to give away the KASH formula of the business and accelerate franchisees from the Launch to Winning or the Zone within a reasonable time frame?	
Are the franchisor's advertising and marketing programs effective?	
Will the franchisor give me the proper direction I need to get started?	
Am I willing to accept complete responsibility for how my life and business turn out?	
If I invest in this franchise, will I enjoy going to work in the morning?	
Is this a "high-road" franchisor?	
Am I willing to accept complete responsibility for how my life and business turn out?	
If I invest in this franchise, will I enjoy going to work in the morning?	
Is this a "high-road" franchisor?	
Other Questions: If you answer any of these questions with a "no," do not immediately dismiss the opportunity. Ask "What's missing?", and "Can I live with out this?" or "How do I provide what's missing?"	**Yes/No**
Questions from Chapter 1	
Has the franchisor done a good job bringing in high-quality franchisees?	

Following a Six-Step
Franchise Investigation Process

Other Questions: If you answer any of these questions with a "no," do not immediately dismiss the opportunity. Ask "What's missing?" and "Can I live with out this?" or "How do I provide what's missing?" (continued)	Yes/No
Questions from Chapter 1	
Has the franchise sales representative treated me with honesty and integrity? Do I trust their feedback?	
Was the franchise recruiter making an effort to help me determine if I fit their profile of a successful franchisee?	
Will the franchisor do what it takes to help me win?	
Will I do what it takes to win?	
Questions from Chapter 2	
Knowing what they know now, would most of the franchisees make the same decision again?	
Am I willing to leave the path of 99% and take the path of the 1%?	
Am I willing to ignore the taunts of my inner critic and chase my dreams?	
Am I willing to do what it takes to make this business "the right business?"	
Am I willing to do what it takes to make this time "the right time" to start a business?	
Questions from Chapter 3	
Have I identified my primary behavior style (Action Hero, Comedian, Faithful Sidekick, or Private Eye)?	
Does my "value in business" match the profile of a successful franchisee?	
Does my "ideal franchise" match the franchise opportunity I'm considering investing in?	
Am I willing to work with the franchisor to guard against "what will kill me if I'm not careful?"	
Does the franchisor's support team have the skills, time, and knowledge to help me guard against "what will kill me if I'm not careful?"	

Questions from Chapter 4	Yes/No
Do I have S.M.A.R.T. goals?	
Do I trust that the franchisor's support people will take on my goals as their goals?	
Am I willing to chunk my goals down into a daily action plan and work this plan every day?	
Have I identified the high-priority activities that generate the most results?	
Am I willing to guard my time wisely and spend most of my time engaged in the high-priority activities that generate most of the results?	
Have I identified the activities that suck time and generate few results?	
Am I willing to not engage in these activities?	
Am I willing to go home every night with the experience of "it's not all finished" and "there's still something left to do"?	
Questions from Chapter 5	**Yes/No**
Am I confident I have clearly identified the franchisor's KASH model of success?	
Am I willing to not engage in these activities?	
Does the franchisor have a strong track record of imparting their KASH formula to the other franchisees?	
Am I willing to do what it takes to acquire the necessary KASH?	
Is the franchisor willing to do what it takes to impart the necessary KASH?	
Questions from Chapter 6	**Yes/No**
Do I fully understand what may occur in the Launch, the Grind, Winning, the Zone, and the Goodbye stages?	
Do I accept responsibility to do what it takes to move through the Grind and into Winning and the Zone?	
Does the franchisor have a track record of effectively supporting franchisees in the Grind, and helping them move forward into Winning?	

Following a Six-Step Franchise Investigation Process

Question from Chapter 7	Yes/No
Am I willing to do what it takes to maintain positive, interdependent relationships with the franchisor and other franchisees?	
Questions from Chapter 9	**Yes/No**
Do I understand and agree to the terms of the franchise agreement?	
Do I understand and accept the financial risk?	
Do I have the necessary capital to move forward?	
Do I have the necessary financing to move forward?	
Am I clear about what my territory is and do I believe the territory is viable?	
Will I allow the franchisor's leadership to lead me?	

Step 6: Making an Investment Decision

If you have diligently followed this or a franchisor's similar process, you have done an outstanding job of taking close look at what it takes to win as a franchisee. While you will experience intense emotions such as fear, anxiety, excitement, and possibly anger, this is normal and will be short lived. Upon making a decision, you will experience relief.

Thoroughly absorb and evaluate the information in your decision-making worksheet. Prepare to make a decision.

Many people at this stage of the decision-making process use emotions to corrupt their data. If you want to say "no," you will have a tendency to dismiss your research that validates the franchise opportunity and focus on the information that invalidates it. Regardless of the franchise opportunity, you can always find a reason to invalidate it and miss out on a tremendous opportunity in the process. Keep in mind, before they were well known, 99 percent of the people investigating McDonalds, Burger King, Dunkin' Donuts, and Wendy's found a reason to invalidate these opportunities also.

Back in the 80s, before Subway took off, franchise candidates used to dismiss the Subway opportunity by telling the franchisor representatives such things as "No one wants to eat in a bright yellow restaurant! Everyone will get headaches!" They also said, "Why did you name your chain 'Subway?' Have you ever ridden a New York City subway? There's graffiti, junk on the floor, gum on the chairs. No one will eat in a Subway!" So on one hand, you can say the critics are wrong because Subway has proven to be a dominant global brand. On the other hand, you can say these critics are right because most meals a family eats aren't being eaten at Subway. The point is you can make the data mean anything and this is exactly what you will do also. At this stage in your decision-making process, it's hard to take an objective look at your data.

To maintain objectivity you can do one of two things. First, you can pretend you are a business consultant. Your client just paid you to take a look their research and make a cold, hard recommendation based solely on their research. What would you recommend?

Second, you can actually go to a business consultant and ask them to make a cold, hard recommendation based on your data.

Either way, don't prolong the agony and don't give the franchisor the idea that you are a person who can't decide. You have the data. Now it's time to make up your mind.

Before you make your final decision, let's explore the four types of decisions you will make ... and you thought your choices were only limited to "yes" or "no"! It's a good thing you bought this book. You doubled your available choices! Whatever decision you do make, however, our goal is that your decision brings you peace.

The Two "No" Decisions

Your Research Says "Yes" But Your Emotions Say "No." You may discount and dismiss your high probability of winning because you lack confidence in your own abilities and are afraid of losing. Your inner critic is hurling loud, nasty accusations against you and, on some level, you believe he's right. Not wanting to make a fear-induced decision you will create normal and reasonable reasons to say "no." This decision is perfectly valid and will bring you peace as long as you are honest with yourself. Say to yourself, "I choose to say 'no,' not because there is anything wrong with the business or because the business is wrong for me. I choose to say 'no' because it's my choice and this is what I choose. I don't need to pretend or to make up a reason."

The Private Eye and Faithful Sidekick behavior styles (from chapter 4) are most prone to make this type of decision.

Your Research Says "No" and Your Emotions Say "No." You have done the work and your research clearly backs up a "no" decision. Perhaps you see that you have a low probability of achieving your "must have" and "wish to have" objectives. Maybe you are undercapitalized. Perhaps the concept isn't proven and the risk outweighs the reward. Maybe you aren't an organizational culture fit or you don't have confidence in the leadership. Whatever the reason, your reasons are valid. The responsible decision is "no."

Any behavior style is capable of making responsible, data-based decisions.

Your Research Says "No" but Your Emotions Say "Yes." This is a recipe for possible disaster because you bought into the hype without substance. You blinded yourself to possible warning signs because you really connected on a deep emotional level with this business. You are confident you can make it work, but you have perhaps ignored evidence that the system doesn't work or that you won't have all the tools necessary to win. This doesn't mean you will fail. It does mean, however, you have chosen a crooked path to success.

The Action Hero and Comedian are most prone to make this type of decision.

Your Research Says "Yes" and Your Emotions Say "Yes." You have done your homework, put your emotions in check, taken a cold, hard look at the data, and the data makes a compelling case for you to move forward. You match the profile of a successful franchisee and people like you are winning by your definition of winning. And of course you are pumped! While this franchise may not be the perfect business, you are going in with your eyes wide open because you have conducted a responsible investigation. You know what it takes to win and you have accepted the responsibility to do what it takes. You have contemplated the risks and determined that the reward outweighs the risk. You have considered your downside, and although losing won't be pretty, you are clear you will survive and rebuild.

Any behavior style is capable of making a responsible "Yes" decision.

Now you know what your four available options are, we offer you our last worksheet to help simplify your decision.

Final Decision Worksheet

Please read the following instructions carefully.

Instructions:

Check only one box.

I decide:

Yes ☐

No ☐

Communicate your decision to franchisor representative. Experience peace, freedom, and joy, and go create a great life and career.

Your process is now complete.

Congratulations.

Conclusion

When we wrote Street Smart Franchising, we had you in mind. We tried to anticipate every thought you would have, emotion you would experience, and action you would take as you investigate, start up, and run a franchise. We tried to help you uncover and dispel all your myths and misinformation about franchising, including ones you didn't even know you had. We intended to help you create a clean mental space where you could learn what it takes to win in franchising, regardless of what the economy is doing.

Since franchisors report that 99 percent of people who investigate their franchise don't move forward, we started with the premise that left to your own resources, most likely you won't move forward with a franchise either. It wasn't because you wouldn't win. Odds were you would throw in the towel before you even tried. By throwing in the towel, you might have passed on an outstanding opportunity presented to you by an outstanding franchisor, missing a chance to design a life and career of your choosing.

While an incredible number of throw-in-the-towel decisions are bad decisions, not all are. Neither are all "go forward" decisions good decisions. Our goal in writing this book was to help you discover and decide what to do with the towel, backed up by facts and information, without being emotionally hijacked by fear.

We wanted to help you be clear on how your skills, aptitudes, and character traits play out in business, so you can find a franchise that fits, one that builds on your strengths instead of exposing your weaknesses.

We wanted to dispel two prevailing misperceptions that exist. First, that all franchisors are created equal. Like any group, franchisors possess a range of talent and results. Some franchisors are brilliant and have it all figured out. Given the right franchisee with the right capital, success is almost guaranteed. Their customers are stark raving fans. Their marketing works. They know how to give away the success formula of their business to any potential franchisee seeking to learn their craft.

And while some franchisors may be good at running their own company operations, they may at the same time be completely incompetent in the business of franchising. Their systems and business methods are either missing or underdeveloped. Results are spotty. Their franchisees are left to their own resources to try to figure out how to win and in the end some do and some don't. Those who don't are faced with terrible consequences.

In the media, you may hear franchising described as either a distribution model or as a business opportunity. This is another myth we wanted to dispel. We wish to further the premise franchising is a business unto itself. For instance, a franchisor can have a brilliant retail or restaurant chain and at the same time be a lousy franchisor. We wished to raise your level of awareness about who is and isn't competent in the business of franchising. We wanted to show you how to pop open a franchisor's hood and take a critical and discerning look at their economic engine. We detailed every engine part, what function it has, and what happens to the engine if the part is missing or malfunctioning. Our goal wasn't to make you an educated franchise buyer, but a franchise connoisseur.

Lastly, the primary reason we wrote *Street Smart Franchising* was to bring purpose into our own lives by trying to make a difference in your life. We understand you are at a fork in the road. We know and appreciate the transformational impact of this decision on your life. We don't know which way you should go, but we believe that, armed with the right information, you will make the right choice for you and your family. We wish you much happiness journeying down whatever road you choose.

Index

A

Account numbers, 197–198
Achievement, behavior styles embracing, 42, 43
Achievement-focused cultures, 244–245, 246–248
Action Hero style, 42–48, 60–62
Actions, winning, 80
Advertising-driven franchises, 58
Advertising requirements in FDD, 208–209
Ambiguity, 54
Application forms, 196–198
Appointments, 88, 221–222
Arbitration, 217
Assets, 96, 220. *See also* Capital
Assignment-of-contract rights, 216
Attainability of goals, 70
Attention, 85
Attitude
    in Goodbye stage, 150–151, 152

in Grind stage, 129–135
in Launch stage, 120–121
role in success, 97, 98–99
in Winning stage, 143
in Zone stage, 147
Attorneys, 187, 204–205

B

Background checks, 9–10. *See also* Data gathering
Balance, emotional, 133–135
Balance sheets, 220
Bank account numbers, 197–198
Bankruptcies, 206–207
Behavior styles
    Action Hero, 42–48, 60–62
    Comedian, 48–52, 63
    conflicting, 59–62
    DISC theory, 37–39, 42
    Faithful Sidekick, 52–55, 60–62
    franchisor queries about, 196–197

Index

Behavior styles (*continued*)
  identifying in others, 62–63
  impact on franchising decision,
    229
  matching to franchising oppor-
    tunities, 38–42, 63, 96
  Private Eye, 55–59, 62
Ben and Jerry's, 12, 16–17
Benevolent dictatorships,
  239–241
Big Mac, 7
Binding arbitration, 217
Bluntness, 42, 46
Body analogy, 3–5
Boogey Man, 129, 134
Brands
  behavior styles embracing, 55
  contrasting views of, 242–243,
    245
  evaluating strength, 14, 184
Braveheart, 165
Brokerage account numbers,
  197–198
Brokers, 177–178
Bureaucratic corporate cultures,
  237–239
Business models
  communicating success
    requirements, 15
  evaluation by potential fran-
    chisee, 188, 192–194
  franchisors without, 8, 185,
    189, 257–258
  high-road franchisors, 10–13,
    21–22
Business planning resources,
  225–226
Business Plan Pro, 226
Business skills, 106, 114. *See also*
  Skills

Business stages
  Goodbye, 149–155
  Grind, 124–139
  Launch, 119–124
  overview, 109–111
  recognizing in current fran-
    chisees, 221, 222–223
  Winning, 139–145
  Zone, 145–149

C

Calling, franchising as, 3
Calls, planning, 89
Camping Test, 21
Capital
  FDD disclosures, 210, 219–220
  franchisor queries about, 96
  inadequate, 8–9, 192
Cash flow statements, 219
Cash on hand disclosures, 219
Celebrities in franchises, 217–218
Chain method, 6
Challenge as franchisee goal, 5–6
Change
  fears of, 24–25, 27–28
  to winning formulas, avoiding,
    141–142
Chem-Dry, 12, 211
Chief executive officers, 240, 241,
  245
Clock time, 74–75
Coaching
  elements of, 116–117
  in Grind stage, 138–139
  in sale of business, 155
  when to use, 118–119
  in Winning stage, 142, 144, 145,
    153–154
  in Zone stage, 149
Comedian behavior style, 48–52,
  63

Index

Command and control cultures, 241–246
Communication
  behavior styles and, 49, 60–62
  during franchisee training, 113
  as sales skill, 121–122
  skills self-assessment, 106
  winning conversations, 79–80
Communities of franchisees, 20–21
Community, giving back to, 6
Company outlets, 214
Compensation of franchise sales-people, 94–95
Competence
  conscious, 142–143
  as habit, 98
  training for, 123–124
Competitive advantage, 6–7, 100
Compliance, 38. *See also* Systems
Conferences, 124
Conflicts
  avoidant behavior, 49, 51, 54
  behavior leading to, 46
  corporate cultures breeding, 245
  from differing styles, 59–62
  in franchisee-franchisor relationship, 4, 164, 165, 166–168, 171, 217
Conscious competence, 142–143
Conscious incompetence, 129
Consensus building, 49
Consistency, 57
Consultants, predatory, 9–10
Consulting
  decreasing dependence on, 145, 148–149
  elements of, 115–116
  in sale of business, 155
  when to seek, 138
  when to use, 118–119

Contracts, listing in FDD, 220
Control
  behavior styles embracing, 45, 46–47
  behavior styles resisting, 45
  dictatorial cultures, 239–246
  as franchisee goal, 5
Conversations, winning, 79–80
Cooperation self-assessment, 104
Copyrights, 214
Corporate cultures
  achievement-focused, 244–245, 246–248
  benevolent dictatorships, 239–241
  bureaucratic, 237–239
  command and control, 241–246
  importance, 236–237
Corporate officers, 205–206
Cost containment, 51–52
Covey, Stephen, 66, 82
Creativity, 50, 51
Customer information, 193
Customer satisfaction, 100, 101

D
Daily planning, 88–89
Daily targets, 72, 136
Dale Carnegie, 80, 114
Data analysis, 231–233, 250–253
Data gathering, 188, 221–231
Deadlines for goal achievement, 70–71, 72
Death, awareness of, 76–77
Decision making
  about franchise investment, 250–256
  Action Hero style, 42–43, 44–45
  Comedian style, 50, 51
  corporate culture and, 237, 240, 241–242

Index

Deficit analysis (KASH model), 102–106
Deluca, Fred, 10
Desired futures, 33–35, 65–66
Detail orientation, 56, 57
Development approaches for franchisees, 17–20
Development representatives. *See* Sales representatives (franchisor)
Dictatorships, 239–246
Diplomacy, 54, 56
Disability, FDD stipulations, 217
Discounted franchise fees, 207
Discovery Days
    assessing corporate culture during, 239
    high- vs. low-road environments, 234–236
    importance of, 232
    preparation and participation in, 248–249
DISC theory, 37–39, 42
Dispute resolution procedures, 217
Distractions, planning for, 87–88
Distribution, franchising as, 1–2
Dominance, 37–38
"Do not disturb" signs, 89

E
Earnings potential, 194–195, 218
Economic changes, 14
Efficiency, 43
80/20 rule, 82–84
E-mail, 89
Emotional balance in Grind stage, 133–135
Emotional decision making, 253–255
Emotional support, 136–137

Employees
    developing, 142–143, 144
    fallacies about, 28, 29
Empowerment
    in achievement-focused cultures, 246–248
    from success, 139, 143, 163
Entrepreneur magazine, 178
Entrepreneurs
    behavior styles, 38
    satisfaction of being, 139–140
    self-assessment, 106
    strengths of, 7
The Entrepreneur's Source, 178
Errors, views of, 137, 244
Exclusive vendor relationships, 12
Expense estimates, 225
Expos, 178–179
Express Personnel, 11

F
Failure
    costs of, 100–102
    false experience of, 130
    fears of, 134
    franchisor experiences, 207, 218–219
Fair market value of business, 154
Faithful Sidekick style, 52–55, 60–62
False hopes, 132
Family support, 105
Fear of change, 24–25, 27–28
Fear of unknown, 54, 57, 196
Fee disclosures, 207–209
Fee stage, 161–163
Fighting, problem solving vs., 131–132. *See also* Conflicts
Final decision worksheet, 256
Financial controls, 184

Index

Financial data from current franchisees, 223–226
Financial goals, 6, 66–69
Financial statements, 219–220, 224, 225
Financing
  FDD disclosures, 210, 212
  by franchising, 7
  franchisor queries about, 96, 191–192
  inadequate, 8–9, 192
  main sources for franchisors, 11–12
  requirements for, 193
Five-Dollar Subs, 7
Five-point rating scale, 227
Five-year goal setting, 66–69
Flexibility goals, 5
Formulas, changing, 141–142
Franchise agreements
  elements of, 204–221
  honoring, 166
  importance of reviewing, 187–188
  limitations of, 202–204
Franchise brokers, 177–178
Franchise Business Review, 228
Franchise Disclosure Document
  earnings information in, 194–195
  elements of, 204–221
  importance of reviewing, 187–188
  limitations of, 202
Franchise E-Factor, 159, 170, 172
Franchisee-franchisor relationship
  asking current franchisees about, 188, 221–231
  corporate cultures, 236–248

evolution, 171–172
Fee stage, 161–163
franchisors' ability to build, 185
Free stage, 165–167
Glee stage, 159–161
legal obligations and beyond, 202–204
Me stage, 163–165
overview, 157–159
See stage, 167–169
We stage, 169–170
Franchisees
  common goals, 5–6, 23, 65–66
  costs of poor performance from, 100–102
  defined, 1
  definitions of success, 23–24
  developing, 17–20
  evaluating, 15, 16–17, 38–39, 63, 199–201
  goal setting principles, 66–73
  interviewing to gather data, 188, 221–231
  listed in FDD, 218–219
  obligations in FDD, 211–212
  peak-performing, 99–100, 111
  recruiting, 13–17, 91–96, 101
  strong communities of, 20–21
  training by, 144, 148
Franchise fees. See also Royalties
  dissatisfaction with, 161
  FDD disclosures, 207–209
  purpose, 111
  typical range, 11, 207
Franchise investigation process
  corporate culture analysis, 236–248
  data gathering and analysis, 188, 221–233

decision checklists, 250–253
final decisions, 253–256
home office visits, 188, 233–236
initial interviews, 189–196
overview, 186–188
qualification, 196–202
reviewing agreements, 202–221
Franchise model. *See* Business
models
Franchising
acceptance vs. rejection of,
24–28, 31–32
as business model, 10–13,
21–22, 258
conceptions of, 1–5
as extension of personal systems, 40
locating opportunities, 175–179
reasons for, 5–10
"right" businesses and times,
28–31
Franchisors. *See also* Franchise
investigation process
approaches to recruiting,
13–17
asking current franchisees
about, 188, 221–231
corporate cultures, 236–248
defined, 1
evaluating, 68–69, 183–185,
192–194, 250–253
FDD information about,
205–207, 219–220
finding, 175–179
help during Goodbye stage,
154–155
help during Grind stage,
138–139
help during Winning stage, 145
help during Zone stage, 148–149

high-road vs. low-road, 6–10
KASH distribution by, 112–119
obligations in FDD, 212–213
revenue sources, 11–12
Franchoice, 178
Frankl, Viktor, 158
Frannet, 178
Fransurvey, 228
Fraud, 9–10
Free stage, 165–167
Frustration with franchisors,
165–166. *See also* Grind stage
Future, envisioning and design-
ing, 32–35, 65–66

G

Garbage in, garbage out, 230–231
Gibson, Mel, 165
Giulianni, Lynn, 132
Giving back to community, 6
Gladwell, Malcolm, 205
Glee stage, 159–161
Goals
Action Hero focus, 43
answering questions about,
190
breaking down, 72–75
Comedian focus, 49
common to franchisees, 5–6,
23, 65–66
communicating to franchisor
reps, 189
required attributes, 69–71
three- and five-year, 66–69
weighing in franchising deci-
sion, 33–34
Golf, 124–125
Goodbye stage, 149–155
Google, 179
Gossip, 167
Grading franchisors, 227–228

Index

Grandma test, 21
Grand openings, 161
Great Clips, 215
Grind stage
  applying KASH model, 111,
    129–136
  basic features, 124–129
  current franchisees in, 221, 223
  success strategies, 136–139
Gross sales estimates, 224
Growth objectives, 7

H
Habits
  in Goodbye stage, 153–154
  in Grind stage, 136
  in Launch stage, 122–123
  role in success, 98, 99
  in Winning stage, 144
  in Zone stage, 148
Hall, Jay, 237
Harvard Business School, 69
Health self-assessment, 105
High-profile people in franchises,
  217–218
High-road franchisors
  advertising requirements, 209
  basic features, 6–7, 183–185
  franchisee development, 17–20
  home office visits with, 234,
    235–236
  identifying, 10–13, 14–17, 227
  product purchase agreements,
    210–211
Hobbies, 124–125
Home office visits, 188, 233–236
Hope, false, 132
Humility, 143

I
Ideas from franchisees, 7, 20

Impatience, 47
Implementation, 19–20, 44
Income goals, 6
Income potential, 194–195, 218
Independence, asserting, 164
Industry information, 193
Influence, 38, 49
Initial interviews, 186, 189–196
Initial investment disclosure, 210
Inner Critic, 27–28, 32
Instant messaging, 89
Interdependence, 168, 170
International Franchise
  Association, 178, 204
Interruptions, planning for, 87–88
Interviews
  with current franchisees, 188,
    221–231
  initial discussions with fran-
    chisors, 186, 189–196
  to qualify potential fran-
    chisees, 199–201
  skills for conducting, 121
Introversion, 52, 56
Involvement, 44

J
Job fit, 40–41
Jung, Carl, 37
Juran, Joseph, 82

K
KASH model of success
  applied to Goodbye stage,
    152–154
  applied to Grind stage, 129–136
  applied to Launch stage,
    119–123
  applied to Winning stage,
    142–144
  applied to Zone stage, 147–148

KASH model of success (*continued*)
  basic features, 96–100
  matching to franchising opportunities, 182–183
  obtaining others' assessment, 106–107
  self-assessment for, 102–106
  transmission to franchisees, 112–119
Kenny Rogers' Roasters, 217–218
Knight, Bobby, 236
Knowledge
  in Goodbye stage, 152
  in Grind stage, 129
  implementation vs., 19–20
  in Launch stage, 120
  Private Eye strengths, 56
  role in success, 97, 98
  skill building vs., 114–115
  in Winning stage, 142–143
  in Zone stage, 147
Kroc, Ray, 10

L

Launch stage
  applying KASH model, 111, 119–123
  current franchisees in, 221, 222
  success strategies, 123–124
Lawn Doctor, 215
Lawsuits, 101, 203, 206, 245
Leadership
  achievement-focused cultures, 246–248
  Action Hero approach, 44, 46
  dictatorial, 239–246
  Faithful Sidekick style, 53
  ineffective, 241
  self-assessment, 104
Legal reviews of franchise agreements, 187–188

Listening
  Action Hero weaknesses, 43, 45, 46
  multitasking vs., 85
  Private Eye strengths, 56
  as sales skill, 122
Lists of outlets, 218–219
Litigation section (FDD), 206
Local advertising requirements, 208
Long-term debt disclosures, 219
Low-road franchisors
  basic features, 8–10
  home office visits with, 234–236
  product purchase agreements, 211

M

Magazines, 178
Marketing systems, 184, 208–209
Marston, William Moulton, 37, 38
Mastery, 17–18
Matchpoint, 178
McCormack, Mark, 69
Measurability of goals, 69–70
Mental maps, 98
Mentoring, 144, 148
Merle Norman Cosmetics, 12
Me stage, 163–165
Mistakes, views of, 137, 244
Modeling skills, 114–115
Modification of franchise agreements, 217
Molly Maids, 214
Moral obligations, 207
Motivation self-assessment, 104
Multitasking
  behavior styles challenged by, 53–54, 57
  behavior styles embracing, 44
  fallacies about, 85

Index

Must-haves, 32, 71, 232

N

Nathan, Greg, 103, 159, 169, 170
National advertising funds, 208–209
Negotiation, 45
Networking, 169
"No" decisions on franchising, 254–255
Noncompete clauses, 217
Noncurable defaults, 216

O

Objective decision making, 254
Objectives. *See also* Goals
    Action Hero focus, 43
    answering questions about, 190
    comparing to franchise opportunities, 15, 189
    of franchisors, 192
Objectivity, 52, 53
Obligations to participate, 215
Occupancy costs, 225
Office hours, 88
One-body analogy, 3–5
Online questionnaires, 189
Operating costs, 225
Operational focus, 44
Operations, evaluating, 184
Opinions, sharing, 42–43, 45, 50
Opportunities for franchising, 175–179
Optimism, 49, 50–51, 132
Outliers (Gladwell), 205

P

Pain as progress, 126–127
Pareto principle, 82–84
Participation obligations, 215
Patents, 214
Peak-performing franchisees, 99–100, 111, 145–149

People orientation, 48
Perfectionism, 57–58
Performance/satisfaction curve, 110
Persistence, 53, 54, 57
Personal challenge, 5–6
Personal finances, answering questions about, 191–192, 197–198
Personal information on application forms, 196–198
Personality profiles, 96
Personality styles. *See* Behavior styles
Personal questions during interviews, 190–191, 248
Personal responsibility self-assessment, 105
Personal systems, 40
Pessimism, 132–133
Peters, Tom, 87
Pita Pit, 247
Planning, 87–89, 136
Poor performance, costs of, 100–102
Practice, 113, 136
Private Eye style, 55–59, 62
Problem solving
    Action Hero style, 44
    Comedian style, 48–49
    fighting vs., 131–132
    as sales skill, 121
Procedures
    assessing ability to comply with, 105
    behavior styles embracing, 52, 53
    behavior styles resisting, 45, 46, 50
Products and services
    evaluating strength, 183–184

Index

Products and services (*continued*)
restricted sources, 12, 210–211
Profitability, 203, 223–226, 230–231
Progress, 126–127, 129–130
Proprietary information, 214–215
Protected territories, 213–214
Public figures in franchises,
217–218

Q

Qualification of potential franchisees, 186–187, 196–202
Quality, 56, 58, 95–96. *See also*
High-road franchisors
Quality of life goals, 66–69
Questionnaires, 189, 196

R

Rating franchisors, 227–228
"Ready-fire-aim" approach, 47
Realistic timetables for goal
achievement, 70–71
Real time, 75–89
Rebates, 210–211
Receipt of FDD, 220
Recruiting. *See also* Franchise
investigation process
Discovery Days, 232, 234–236
evaluating quality of, 184
impact of franchisee failure,
101
measurement tools for, 38–39,
63
sales representatives for, 91–96
for top-quality franchisees,
13–17
Relationships, franchising as, 2,
157–159. *See also* Franchisee-franchisor relationship
Remedial training programs,
112–113

Renewal fees, 209
Renewal terms, 215
Rent costs, 225
Reputation, 9–10, 14
Restricted sales, 215
Results orientation, 42, 43, 98
Results/satisfaction curve, 110
Rewards of peak performance, 99
"Right" businesses and times,
28–31, 86–87
Risks
behavior styles avoiding, 52, 54
behavior styles embracing, 44,
47, 50
choosing to live with, 78
as excuses for rejecting franchising, 24–25, 27–28
fallacies about, 28–29
reducing by franchising, 7
from Winning stage, 148
Rita's Water Ice, 12
Rogers, Kenny, 217–218
Royalties
dissatisfaction with return on,
161–162
FDD disclosures, 208
maximizing, 12, 13
from peak performers, 99–100,
111
relative importance to franchisors, 11–12, 111

S

Sales of businesses, 149–150,
154–155
Sales representatives (franchisor)
Discovery Day pitches, 234,
235–236
initial interviews with, 186,
189–196
priorities and abilities, 91–96,
233

Index

qualification interviews with,
199–202
take-aways by, 201
Sales restrictions, disclosing in
FDD, 215
Sales skills, 49, 104, 121–122
Sales systems, 184
Sandler, David, 114
Sandler Sales Institute, 114
Satisfaction of current fran-
chisees, 226
Satisfaction/results curve, 110
Screening potential franchisees,
92, 93–96. *See also* Franchise
investigation process;
Recruiting
Search engines, 179
Security needs, 52, 54
See stage, 167–169
Self-assessments, 102–106
Self-management, 43–44
Services. *See* Products and serv-
ices
Skills. *See also* Training
business vs. technical, 114
in Goodbye stage, 152–153
in Grind stage, 135–136
in Launch stage, 121–122
modeling during training,
114–115
relation to behavior styles, 38,
60
role in success, 97–98
in Winning stage, 143–144
in Zone stage, 147
Small business resources,
225–226
S.M.A.R.T. goals, 69–73
Snap-On Tools, 242–243
Snipe hunts, 31

Social media, 9–10, 89
Social Security numbers, 197–198
Solitude, preference for, 57
Speaking skills, 122
Specialization, 58
Specificity of goals, 69
Sport Clips, 215
Stages. *See* Business stages
Starbucks, 213
Steadiness, 38
Structure, 51, 53, 56
Subway restaurants
early critics, 253–254
fresh bread conflict, 171–172
ideas from franchisees, 7
as successful business model,
10
Success. *See also* KASH model of
success
defining, 23–24
goal achievement principles,
71–75
goal setting principles, 66–73
job fit and, 40–41
KASH model features, 96–100
real-time truths, 75–89
requirements for, 193
Support, emotional, 136–137
Support from franchisors,
112–119
Survival thinking, 137
Systems
assessing potential deficits
with, 105
behavior styles embracing, 53,
56
behavior styles resisting, 45,
46, 50, 181–182
Systems orientation, 105,
181–182

Index

T

Take-aways, 201
T Bars, 24
Team development, 142–143, 144
Technical knockouts, 150
Technical skills, business skills
   vs., 114
Telephone calls, planning, 89
Tempers, 46
Termination rights, 215–217
Territories, 213–214
Thoughts, winning, 79, 80
Three-year goal setting, 66–69
Time, real vs. clock, 74–89
Time management, 74–75, 106, 123
Timetables, realistic, 70–71
Timing, fallacies about, 30–31,
   86–87
Toastmasters, 79
To-do lists, 81
Total occupancy costs, 225
Total owner benefit, 224
Trademarks, 214
Training
   asking current franchisees
      about, 222–223
   assessing ability to receive, 103
   behavior styles and, 40
   challenges for franchisors,
      18–19
   decreasing dependence on, 145
   elements of, 112–115
   evaluating quality of, 184–185
   by franchisees, 144, 148
   as ongoing process, 123–124,
      138
   in sale of business, 154
   when to use, 118–119
Transfer fees, 209, 217

Transfer-of-franchise terms,
   215–217
Trust, 2, 15, 160
Two Men and a Truck, 21

U

Unacceptable futures, 34
Unconscious competence, 18
Unconscious incompetence, 121
Undercapitalization, 8–9, 192
Urgency, 72

V

Vision, 43, 49, 66

W

Want-to-haves, 33, 71, 232
Wasted time, 82–84, 88
Wealth goals, 6
Websites
   franchise brokers, 178
   International Franchise
      Association, 204
   listing franchising opportuni-
      ties, 176–177
   small business resources, 226
We stage, 169–170
*What They Don't Teach You at
   Harvard Business School*
   (McCormack), 69
Winning stage
   applying KASH model, 142–144
   overview, 139–142
   risks in, 148
   success strategies, 144–145
Win-win solutions, 44, 167
Wish-to-haves, 71, 232
Working capital, 210
Work-life balance, 5
Wright, Steven, 128
Written goals, 69

Index

Y
"Yes" decisions on franchising,
   255–256

Z
Ziglar, Zig, 65
Zone stage, 145–149